The Help-Yourself City

# THE HELP-YOURSELF CITY

*Legitimacy and Inequality
in DIY Urbanism*

Gordon C.C. Douglas

OXFORD
UNIVERSITY PRESS

Oxford University Press is a department of the University of Oxford. It furthers
the University's objective of excellence in research, scholarship, and education
by publishing worldwide. Oxford is a registered trade mark of Oxford University
Press in the UK and certain other countries.

Published in the United States of America by Oxford University Press
198 Madison Avenue, New York, NY 10016, United States of America.

Library of Congress Cataloging-in-Publication Data
Names: Douglas, Gordon C. C., author.
Title: The help-yourself city : Legitimacy and Inequality in DIY Urbanism /
Gordon C.C. Douglas.
Description: New York, NY : Oxford University Press, [2018] |
Includes bibliographical references.
Identifiers: LCCN 2017013747| ISBN 9780190691325 (pbk.) |
ISBN 9780190691332 (hardcover) | ISBN 9780190691356 (updf) |
ISBN 9780190691363 (epub)
Subjects: LCSH: City planning—Citizen participation. | Community development.
Classification: LCC HT166 .D66424 2018 | DDC 307.1/216—dc23
LC record available at https://lccn.loc.gov/2017013747

Hardback printed by Bridgeport National Bindery, Inc., United States of America

To my parents, for making it all possible.

To Emily, for making it all infinitely better.

To Isla and Oolina, for making it all worth it.

# CONTENTS

# ACKNOWLEDGMENTS

Like all books, and especially works of ethnographic and interview-based social science, this book owes its very existence to an enormous number of people. It's hard to know where to start; it's almost tempting to try to construct a table of the sort that collects all my interviewees here. Indeed, every name in that list of interviewees would also appear in a new table of thanks! So, I'll start with them.

My sincere and heartfelt thanks go to the do-it-yourself urbanists and planning and design professionals with whom I spoke, and everyone else who participated in my research. From anonymous sign-makers to well-known (and in-demand) public figures, the individuals who took time out of their days to speak with me, despite concerns about the nature of their activities or their jobs, are very literally the heart and soul of this project. These pages are filled with their exciting and innovative ideas—some of which I have rather ignobly picked apart or used as less than admirable examples—and the study would have been inconceivable without them. If I am wary of the intentions or impacts of some interventions, the truth is I am filled with hope for their potential and for the dynamism that they represent. And I'm heartened to reflect on just how many of these inspiring people have become my friends.

Next, while I have been deeply privileged to spend so much of my life learning in formal educational settings, to equate learning, knowledge, even scholarship only with schooling is to undervalue the essential role of family and community in these things. I can say with certainty that I would not be where I am without the unflinching support of my parents, Kathy and Gordon Douglas. They have tirelessly nurtured my curiosity and encouraged my passions, academic and otherwise. They retired from ful-filling and inspirational careers just as I in many ways began my own (this coincidence is a fun side effect of having spent three decades in school), and it became only clearer to me how much I owe my parents for showing me how life ought to be lived, not to mention how to pass that on to a child. Academia can be an all-consuming occupation, yet my dad exemplifies balance across his passions as not only a committed scientist but also a loving father, voracious traveler, and ceaseless creator of beautiful things. My mom instilled in me creativity, imagination, and persistent inquisitiveness as foundational values and remains a wellspring of love and guidance to me and now to my children. My parents set me on my path and have emboldened me along it every step of the way. (They also chose to raise me in a richly intellectual, communitarian, and urban design-obsessed college town, which probably has something to do with this book too.)

If my parents set me on the path to my academic career, it is my friends who have actually kept me on it against doubts and obstacles, while helping keep everything in perspective. Over beers and long journeys, on balconies, rooftops, and bike rides, they encouraged and validated my pursuits and critiqued, prodded, debated, and improved my work. You guys. You are brilliant and passionate and if what I'm doing doesn't matter to you then it doesn't matter. Anyone who knows me knows how strongly I believe that scientific research, and especially social science, must speak to people beyond the academic paywall. My friends—in California, in New York, and in kick-ass towns and cities all over the map—are that critical audience; they keep me honest and ask the toughest questions, and I have tried to write this with them in mind.

The same goes for the rest of my family. My brother Alex and his wife, Abby, are models for living well, with conscience and without pretentiousness. My second set of parents, Jon and Susan Art, have done more for me than many people could hope for from their own parents and made Chicago home. Steve, Julia, Chris, and Hannah likewise welcomed me into a growing family without a moment's hesitation. Extended families around the United States and the United Kingdom have all taken me in, often at the dear cost of having to listen to a considerable volume of babble about urban inequality, the contradictions of hipster culture, and amateur architectural criticism. Each of these people sets a standard for love and generosity, and I am so grateful for their unconditional support.

Of course, as foundational as these informal role models are, after nearly three decades in the classroom you're going to have had some pretty important formal teachers too. I was fortunate to have the opportunity to learn from a series of exceptionally motivating, inspiring, and challenging individuals, all of whose impacts are felt in the pages of this book. David Andrus, Steven Lamy, and Geoffrey Cowan at the University of Southern California taught me not only to be a scholar but also to be a critical one. At the London School of Economics, I first met Saskia Sassen and Ed Soja, luminous thinkers who offered their generously sincere interest in my ideas and turned a half-interested student of globalization into an insatiable student of cities, space, and urban culture. This process continued back at USC Annenberg under the inspiring tutelage of Manuel Castells and Christopher Holmes Smith, who nurtured kernels of ideas that are now very present here.

By the time I arrived at the University of Chicago, I was primed to seek out and connect the dots between the thinking of geographer Michael Conzen on "reading the city as a cultural text" and the artist Theaster Gates on "intervention and public practice," and of course numerous influential sociologists. I had never even taken a sociology class before arriving at Chicago, but thoughtful teachers like Lis Clemens and Andreas Glaeser quickly inspired a love for the discipline. Terry Clark, Omar McRoberts, and Richard Taub shaped my love for urban sociology. These names read like a greatest hits list of the sort of research I hope to contribute to. I am incredibly fortunate to count them all not only as inspirations but also as mentors and friends. All influenced me greatly.

And then, there is the study itself that became this book. My sincerest thanks to my dissertation committee: Mario Luis Small, Andrew Abbott, and Kristen Schilt. Throughout my seven years under Mario's tutelage at Chicago, his always tough but highly generative questioning made me think and work harder than I ever had before. Andy draws out new connections and insights for the project every time we discuss it, while never ceasing to offer a graceful reminder that the life of the mind is a noble and joyful one. Kristen has provided ceaseless enthusiasm for my research and demonstrated a catholic approach to the study of culture and subculture that gave me courage to pursue my topic at UofC in the first place. This study is immeasurably stronger for all of their involvement and to them I am forever grateful.

The dissertation began its transformation into a book at New York University's Institute for Public Knowledge, where Eric Klinenberg generously supported my work while encouraging my engagement with new research as well. Eric also provided the best example of what it means to be a public sociologist—a serious scholar with a popular impact on issues of real importance to cities and communities. This also describes my friend Gianpaolo Baiocchi, a passionately committed activist scholar at NYU and always a ready ear on topics of both work and life, who also offered valuable comments on the manuscript.

My new colleagues at San José State University were likewise instrumental. Their sincere enthusiasm and astute local connections for my research have helped me to place it back in Northern California and in the world of academic planning. Their accommodation of my family and me in my first year after joining the department was incredibly supportive, and made it possible for me to finish the book. And I am thrilled to be in the company of so many others who share my feeling that academic pursuits are worth little if they do not connect to real life and at least try to improve it. I am thrilled to call SJSU home.

My sincere gratitude also to James Cook at Oxford University Press for his quick enthusiasm for this book and for maintaining that enthusiasm over time, despite having many more important things going on! He gave superb advice that made this a far better book, while allowing me to write the book I dreamed of writing. Believing in a first-time author's hopes for producing a (slightly) more accessible and relevant work of urban studies is something of a leap of faith, I suspect, and I owe him for taking it with gusto.

Innumerable others aided in the project in some way or another. In Los Angeles, the indomitable Serafina Costanza and Andy Rybicki provided, as ever, a welcoming home away from home on multiple occasions, sometimes for weeks at a time. John Pick lent a crucial bicycle; James Rojas, Steve Cancian, and Father David O'Connell—all interviewees—even drove me around, as did many friends. In Vancouver, Ryan and Naomi McCormick played host and found bikes. Sarah Clifford did the same in New Orleans, where Carey Clouse also put me up and spent hours driving me around the city. Ramona Corey, Shaun Slifer, and John Givens and Debra Lam all opened their homes to me multiple times in Pittsburgh, as did Dan Huebner and Bob Wiley in Baltimore, Oli and Davina Bird in London, and Justin and Becky Alarcon in Oakland. Christopher Art and the Isla Urbana project helped fund my time in Mexico City, where Jimena Veloz and Oscar Montiel showed me around the metropolis by bicycle and found me a couch to crash on. Wonderful people like these hosted me and sometimes my whole family time after time. I also want to thank Cathy Lang Ho, Anne Guiney, and everyone involved in Spontaneous Interventions for the opportunity to connect my research with the exhibition and all of its amazing participants.

Brian Cody, Jan Doering, Lizzy Kate Gray, Dan Huebner, Naomi McCormick, Abi Ocobock, Danielle Raudenbush, Michaela Soyer, Chris Takacs, and Alicia VandeVusse—all members at one point or another of the University of Chicago's finest diasporic international virtual writing group—provided invaluable feedback and camaraderie throughout the writing process. So too did members of the workshops on Social Theory and Evidence and City, Society and Space at the University of Chicago, the Politics and Protest Workshop at the City University of New York, and the NYLON Workshop at NYU. Special thanks in particular to Chad Borkenhagen, Daniel Aldana Cohen, Ugo Corte, Francesco Findeisen, David Grazian, Max Holleran, Brian Hracs, Liz Koslov, Jeffrey Parker, Michael Seman, and Richard Sennett for constructive input over the years. Siera Dissmore, Matt Wolfe, Sophie Ouahbi, Josh Jelly Schapiro, Garnette Cadogan, Sophie Gonick, Tom Sugrue, Ingrid Ellen, Becky Amato, Eric Banks, Gwynneth Malin, Simeon Hutner, Judith Helfand, Eyal Press, Lawrence Weschler, and many other colleagues at NYU all have my deep gratitude for insightful conversations about the project and support during the writing process. Many thanks also to Linnea Martin at the University of Chicago, and with her countless other incredibly knowledgeable and hard-working university staff members who help students and faculty immeasurably every single day for far too little credit.

More than anything, this entire endeavor was made possible by my partner, Emily Art. In addition to keeping us financially stable while I lived a life of travel, flâneurie, and academic dragon-chasing, Emily has been a rock of companionship, emotional support, and critical insight. She did all the hardest work in bringing our daughters Isla and Oolina into the world during the several years over which a dissertation was finished only to be wholly reengaged as a book, and has been a faithful hand-holder, whip-cracker, and cheerleader through it all. She also read every single chapter multiple times, clarified hundreds of thoughts and run-on sentences, and at one point copy-edited line-by-line. All this while working long hours to actually make life better for thousands of students and their teachers. The book has vastly improved as a result of her help, and our family's lives are vastly improved by her presence and love. And Isla and Oona, who went from mere thoughts to the singing, dancing, running, smiling reasons to live that they are today, were right by my side in our small apartment the whole way. Thanks, goons.

Some of the research and findings described in this book found the light of day in two academic journal articles. Much of Chapter 2, in particular, appeared in earlier form in my article "Do-It-Yourself Urban Design: The Social Practice of Informal 'Improvement' through Unauthorized Alteration" in *City & Community* (Douglas 2014). (Thanks go to Hilary Silver for her enthusiasm for the research!) Some of my writing about the presence of technical and scholarly knowledge in DIY urbanism (e.g., in Chapter 4) was first published in the *Journal of Urbanism* in a piece called "The Formalities of Informal Improvement: Technical and Scholarly Knowledge at Work in DIY Urban Design" (Douglas 2016). I also presented earlier versions of these results at annual meetings of the American Sociological Association, the Association of American Geographers, the Royal Geographical Society, the Urban Affairs Association, the Chicago Ethnography Conference, and the Exploring the Creative Economy Conference at Toronto's Martin Prosperity Institute.

I took most of the photos in the book, but any and all of the images by other photographers that are included here are used with their expressed permission, for which I am extremely grateful. Please see the image captions for photo credits throughout. (Also, more of my own photos of DIY urbanism can be found on my website.) The same goes for any errors contained herein: I certainly made most of them too.

# The Help-Yourself City

# 1
# Introduction

New York's Hell Gate Bridge is a monument to the sheer scale of urban infrastructure and regional planning. Spanning part of the East River between Queens and Wards Island, it was the world's longest steel-arch bridge when it opened in 1916 and the centerpiece of a 3.2-mile complex of viaducts that, in connecting the Pennsylvania Railroad through New York City to New England, provided uninterrupted rail service between Boston and Washington for the first time. It was more than two decades from conception to completion, a result of multiple design iterations and innovations by the engineer Gustav Lindenthal and several other giants of bridge-building. These men were supported by an engineering staff of 95 and, during construction, hundreds of workers every day. The final design involved calculations that had never been applied in practice, inspiring great interest and voluminous reporting on its achievements, producing what can rightly be described as scientific progress.[1] And the bridge itself was truly a marvel of engineering practice: heaped with redundancies of strength and capacity to anticipate heavy train traffic, yet so precisely designed that when its two independently constructed halves were brought together by hydraulic lifts, the connection required adjustments of a mere five-sixteenths of an inch. Nonetheless, by the late 1980s the Hell Gate Bridge had gained a reputation for dropping crumbling steel and concrete onto underlying homes. A hard-won repainting in 1992 was, with the exception of plentiful graffiti, the first in some 60 years. And, in 2009, a section of the railroad viaduct was leaking.

The leak, from a pipe under the viaduct crossing 33rd Street in Queens, was probably not the biggest of concerns for the indefatigable bridge itself (in fact, it has been noted that if humans suddenly disappeared from New York City, the Hell Gate could stand a thousand years without maintenance, twice outlasting any other East River bridge). But for passersby in the middle-class Astoria neighborhood, forced to circumnavigate the strangely colored and at times dangerously slippery effluence, it had been a daily obstacle for more than two decades. To some, in fact, the drainage oozing across the sidewalk amounted to what they called the Scum River—a "river" that two locals decided ought to have a bridge of its own.

Jason Eppink, an artist and self-described "rapid-prototyper" originally from the Houston suburbs, then 26, walked past the Astoria Scum River regularly on his way to the subway. A constellation of jurisdictional confusion and bureaucratic inertia—the railroad infrastructure is now the property of Amtrak—had left the problem unaddressed for years. But Jason and a visiting friend, the Toronto street artist Posterchild, thought they might be able to address it themselves. "We tossed the idea around for a month or two. There was an issue of materials and there was an issue of just getting started," Jason told me. "Then one day this neighbor was throwing away this old work bench. [ . . . ] We reconfigured it, enforced it, added some steps, and then we basically put it out there." They even added a plaque: "We did a little research, there's the Hell Gate Bridge and so we looked at, OK, how did they do this? The [Hell Gate's] plaque had how many feet the bridge spanned, so we were like, OK, our bridge spans seven feet. And we'll dedicate it to 'the comfort and safety of the pedestrian.'"

Over the next few weeks, people in this relatively quiet, immigrant-rich neighborhood began to use the new Astoria Scum River Bridge. Local news blogs caught on and wrote it up. Before long, the area's city council member got in touch. "Hi Jason," his office wrote, "Thanks for the bridge for residents." Within days Amtrak was working to fix the problem. The leaky pipe was fixed, the Astoria Scum River ceased to flow, and before long Jason's bridge was removed and dismantled.

The contrast between these two "bridges" could hardly be greater, despite their immediate physical connection. In addition to scale, the different processes by which each was planned and constructed (not to mention paid for) reflect the extremes of formal and informal urban infrastructure design. Yet the differences also highlight important points of comparison between the unauthorized and largely spontaneous act of creative local improvement that is the Scum River Bridge and the infrastructural mega-project that it sits literally in the shadow of.

A woman carries her groceries across the "Astoria Scum River Bridge," created by Jason Eppink and Posterchild in 2009. Photo by Jason Eppink.

This sort of unsanctioned but civic-minded effort at improving the local streetscape is not unique. In Los Angeles, one might find a group of friends painting a new bike lane along a road under cover of night. In Pittsburgh, a young man installing an official-looking sign to clarify traffic in a dangerous intersection. In New Orleans, a woman placing blank stickers on abandoned structures so neighborhood residents can write their own redevelopment ideas directly on them. In Chicago, a man converting old magazine racks into small community book exchange stations. What is happening here? What motivates some citizens to do local streetscape planning and design work themselves? How are such efforts perceived by communities and local authorities? What gives acceptability and legitimacy to some but not others? And what do the answers to these questions tell us about civic participation, creative transgression, and the persistence of inequality in the contemporary city?

Together, the examples from Queens, Pittsburgh, New Orleans, and elsewhere begin to define a group of practices that I call *do-it-yourself urban design*: unauthorized yet intentionally functional and civic-minded improvements to urban spaces, in forms inspired by official streetscape planning and design elements. In contrast to the widespread formalization and professionalization of urban planning practice in North America and Europe during the 19th and 20th centuries, the rising trend of do-it-yourself (DIY) urbanism over the last several decades indicates something of a shift toward, or indeed a revival of, informal constructive placemaking in these places. These are acts of creative transgression that can physically remake city streets in ways that individuals see as necessary. While countless forms of urban informality can be found in cities around the world, DIY urban design is a particular type. It stands apart from other more commonly recognized forms of unauthorized alteration or occupation of urban space in American or European cities (vandalism, street art, squatting, etc.) and calls for different analysis and understanding.

DIY urban design, and a variety of similar (creative, participatory, spontaneous, guerrilla, grassroots, etc.) placemaking activities, have seen a great rise in attention in blogs, magazines, exhibitions, and other popular fora since around 2010. They are frequently celebrated for their creativity, innovation, and authenticity. Indeed, they are hopeful signs of popular participation and sustainable urbanism, presenting innovative alternatives to the uneven priorities of cash-strapped local governments or profit-driven development interests. Yet these things, and their popularity, also pose real challenges for cities and communities that have not been given the attention they deserve. When we celebrate the innovative and beautiful and trendy in urbanism—as we certainly sometimes should—we risk forgetting about the just.

In this book, I turn a more sociological and at times critical lens on DIY urban design, its creators, and the contexts of their actions in particular communities and development environments. I extend this critique to some official "creative placemaking" trends as well, which I argue are closely connected. A persistent concern of mine throughout is the public and social benefit of DIY urbanism, both in terms of its direct impacts on neighborhoods and communities and its potential value as a form of active civic engagement. I explore the backgrounds, motivations, and self-perceptions of typical "do-it-yourselfers" and analyze the types of interventions they make, where they make them, and under what circumstances. I interpret these phenomena in the context of the sociostructural conditions of the late-modern city as well as the backgrounds and characteristics of their creators and the particular places where they act. I connect the findings to broader urban policy and planning trends and to sociological thinking about the significance of people's interactions with urban space and participation in civil society. I argue that, for all its promise, DIY urban design reveals the stark persistence of privilege and inequality in urban space and in civic participation, and demands that we think about urban placemaking (whether DIY or official) in terms not of legal formality, but of locally and culturally specific value, validity, and legitimacy.

Does DIY urban design offer hope for a more active, critical, and even transformative sort of participatory citizenship? Or does it perpetuate the very uneven patterns of local investment that it responds to? To what degree is a willingness to break the law to make a local improvement a factor of social privilege? Does the adoption of DIY tactics and aesthetics in official city planning signal a shift toward more populist and progressive planning policies, or the appropriation of a trendy tool for economic development? In answering these questions and others, the study of DIY urban design can help complicate our understanding of the relationship between everyday people and the urban planning and development process, and the challenging persistence of inequality therein, with consequences both exciting and troubling for communities and the aspiration to build more equitable cities.

## A DEEP DIVE INTO A SMALL TREND

This book is as much the study of a cultural trend (with an explicitly spatial nature) as it is the study of these physical practices themselves. It began simply with an earnest curiosity about a group of phenomena that seemed novel, poorly understood, and bursting with potential implications for both the immediate character of the urban environment and for understanding bigger issues at work in the contemporary city. DIY urban design is a small trend, but a trend that impacts directly the shared spaces and daily lives of countless people. It is a trend that has garnered considerable attention—most of it positive, even celebratory—with little concern for its potential downsides or its broader implications. And it is a trend that reflects back on the state of contemporary urban planning and development in which it occurs. I look to the traditions of urban ethnography and theoretically generative cultural analysis for assurance that the study of a particular group, subculture, or set of practices can open bright windows of insight into larger questions of social behavior, systems, and processes.

In fact, the study described in these pages began as a broad investigation into the meaning behind a much wider variety of unauthorized, place-based interventions in urban spaces, from the graffiti on a bathroom stall to the radical "occupation" of a public street. My early research on these things began turning up cases that did not fit my expectations, nor did they fit the existing interpretations offered in social science. People were making unauthorized alterations to their surroundings not as vandalism, not as artistic expression, not out of basic human need, and not as radical resistance to the system (or at least not primarily) but to improve them in functional and civic-minded ways. They were making the sorts of interventions that, in their minds, the city ought to be making, and they were doing so in forms and with functions more or less analogous to official streetscape planning and design elements. And, while they all have their historical antecedents, it seemed the practice had emerged as a trend in its contemporary form in just the last several decades.

Now, humans have forever been functionally improving their surroundings "informally" or "without permission," to the extent that in the deep past such distinctions are meaningless. We are among the planet's most powerful geomorphic agents.[2] And cities have been shaped by informal activities, including unsanctioned improvements, since their very beginnings. While ancient Rome had its planning regulations (restricting certain uses, prohibiting development in particular areas, even offering design guidelines), archaeological findings demonstrate that its architecture and streetscapes were overwhelmingly organic and informal products, from local services and sanitation (even public toilets) to multistory apartment buildings.[3] Some alterations, including graffiti, the posting of notices, and all manner of illegal structural modifications, have been with us ever since. In many cities in the developing world today, relatively substantial interventions such as paving streets, digging simple sewage systems, or posting large-scale signage—whether helpfully or just in one's own interest—are understood as normal. And then of course there is the prevalence of informal housing and informal economic activity the world over. Sleeping in urban open spaces, whether on a solitary piece of cardboard or in a tent or makeshift shelter in an encampment of hundreds, happens every day and night in even our most elite cities.

In the context of its time and place, however, the particular practice that I call DIY urban design is distinctive, perhaps even shocking. The cities of the United States and other advanced economies have become defined by more than two centuries of increased management and standardization, the professionalization of urban planning, and legal and normative controls over the use of urban space. Evolving over decades (as discussed in Chapter 4), this formalization of urban space hit a sort of apex in the 1950s with the triumph of professionally dispassionate scientific planning, in the company of the widespread social conservativism and faith in government (not to mention racism) that largely defined the era. Again, certain informalities always persisted, especially in underserved and predominantly low-income areas, from workaday alterations to make shared dwellings feel more like home and community murals projecting local identity to whole underground economies of getting by and making do. But urban placemaking became the domain of trained professionals. We simply do not think of the built environment itself—the streets, buildings, signs, and public spaces that make up the physical realities of our most human ecosystems—as open to casual reinterpretation and "improvement" by just anyone with the hankering to do so. It is today remarkable in American cities, and many others, that everyday citizens might put their own time, energy, and skills to work creating functional and civic-minded urban design contributions outside of any formal process.

I was, admittedly, rather taken with the idea. So apparently are many others, as the practice has only continued to gain visibility in recent years. My strategy was to dive in and start talking to everyone who could tell me about DIY urban design. I ultimately conducted 113 interviews, including 69 with do-it-yourself urban designers representing 80 projects in 17 cities in the United States, Canada, and beyond. (A list of all DIY projects in the study for which interviews were conducted is provided in Appendix 1.) Although relying on self-reported framings and justifications has its limitations, when combined with ethnography and other methods, a biographical approach makes for a deep level of cultural and personal immersion—extremely valuable in the study of a small and scarcely defined subcultural practice—and allows for a focus on the "how" and "why" of these people's activities, in addition to just the "who" and the "where."

I also learned about these projects and the contexts in which they were created through an intensive five-year immersion in the subculture of DIY urbanism, such as it is, including community ethnography and participant observation. I joined do-it-yourselfers on foot and bike as they built and installed their interventions; we talked through cultural, political, and legal questions over coffees and beers. Sometimes I simply spent time in the places they had tried to improve, whether with one of them playing tour guide or just by myself, getting a feel for the space and how the interventions were perceived and used. I took thousands of photographs of many hundreds of projects, including hundreds that I simply stumbled upon in every city I visited. And I conducted background research on the physical, social, and policy conditions that define the places where do-it-yourselfers choose to act. I ultimately came to do much the same in the world of professional planning and the broader context of popular urbanism growing among American urbanites in recent years. (A detailed discussion of my research design and methodology is provided in Appendix 2. Those interested in methodological questions and more of the "story behind the story" may want to give it a read.) In short, I have spent more than half a decade becoming a part of these worlds and, to some extent, both a booster and a critic of them.

A "little free library" community book exchange in Asheville, 2016. Photo by the author.

If my initial interest in DIY urbanism was one of wide-eyed curiosity, I soon began to see the complexity inherent to these practices, the tougher questions that needed to be asked, and some broader implications for how we think about urban space, social privilege, and the places we continue to create for ourselves in the contemporary city. A healthy skepticism has since informed what is a broadly critical stance. It does so, I hope, without minimizing the respect and optimism I do have for many of the projects described here nor my conviction that it is essential to better understand them.

The result then is a jointly ethnographic, geographic, and biographic study, informed by history, sociology, political economy, and planning and design scholarship. The findings have implications for major debates in social science and for urban policy, planning, and design. And they should also offer insights to everyday community members—perhaps even do-it-yourself urban designers themselves—working to protect and improve their neighborhoods. At its simplest, DIY urban design shows us how everyday problems are experienced by everyday people, and how these people sometimes respond. At its grandest, it has much to tell us about the complex and evolving conditions of inequality, privilege, local cultural identity, and the promise of civic participation, all in relation to urban space. Regardless, it calls us to approach the critical task of local urban improvement and community development more insightfully in the face of rapid, uneven growth and widening inequality.

## SEEING THE WORLD THROUGH DIY URBANISM

In addition to the general goal of turning a sociological eye on this little-studied yet increasingly visible practice, and thereby bringing to it some needed critique, my hope is to use the study of DIY urban design to advance our understanding of larger issues for contemporary urbanism, urban studies, and social theory. For starters, looking at DIY urbanism allows us to see how relatively intangible factors such as economic development pressures, design cultures, policy ideologies, and the machinations of capital are experienced and understood in physical space and everyday life. Urban space, as the philosopher and sociologist Henri Lefebvre powerfully observed in 1974, is both used and produced by capital. Studying the practices by which public spaces are actually created—through both DIY and official means, as I do here—shows us the human side of this production and its everyday meanings. It offers a look at the way everyday people experience and respond to conditions of uneven investment. And, by taking the bottom-up rather than the top-down as a starting point, this approach allows us to explore the ways that biography—from education and professional experiences to more immutable elements of social position such as race, gender, and class—influences people's perceptions of social and spatial problems in their communities and their relative willingness to transgress normative and legal boundaries to address them. Cultural context and social positionality matter a great deal in determining the kind of work people do, the things they create, and the lines they are permitted to cross.

Just as fundamentally, this focus on what are ultimately usually quite minor acts invites important discussion of design as everyday practice. Even as it has become an increasingly common and excitedly over-applied term, design, as a verb, a noun, and an industry, has also taken on an almost mystical elevated status. Although I found that DIY streetscape interventions are often created by well-educated individuals with skills relevant to the task, the phenomenon does nonetheless seem—or at least want—to democratize urban planning and public use design. In this sense, with the cultural elevation of design, DIY urbanism may be understood as a sort of rush of (certain) parishioners to the pulpit. This is significant, because designs—and by extension in this case our public spaces—are ultimately as reflective of those who produce them as those for whom they are produced.

The evolving interplay of DIY practices with official urban planning, where they fall on a spectrum of formality-informality, and how normalized or transgressive they are perceived to be, are for these reasons also of great interest. The uneven acceptance of certain DIY projects by authorities lays bare the links between aesthetics, class habitus, and capitalist development schemes. Mainstream creative placemaking trends and the growing embrace of so-called tactical urbanism in cities nationwide (described in detail in Chapter 6) must be viewed as the other side of the same coin—sanctioned efforts to open up and democratize planning while making it "lighter, quicker, and cheaper" to create new public spaces. And they too are nonetheless subject to the influence of underlying social inequality. This complicates binary notions of formality/informality in urbanism and invites critical analysis of even the most progressive planning.

Key to my analysis will thus be an evolving entanglement with the acceptableness—the *legitimacy*—of physical interventions in urban space, large and small, official and unofficial, on social, spatial, and cultural terms. On the one hand, competing notions of legitimacy and their uneven application to different actors or actions are a central part of the persistence of social inequality in urban space and civic participation. But thinking about legitimacy also invites us to empower local communities by recognizing their own important ability to confer it. This sort of locally contingent legitimacy is fuzzy and context-specific but is nonetheless essential to assessing the impacts of DIY urbanism (or any other projects shaping urban space).

Legitimacy—the social acceptance that is granted when an actor's behavior is deemed appropriate or valid in a particular context—is at play on almost every page of this book: from confident do-it-yourselfers making local improvements that they feel the city should thank them for, to longtime community members who are skeptical of seemingly innocuous improvement efforts, to the selective elevation of particular DIY projects by authorities. Although I don't always call it by name, whenever we talk about who has a right to alter their surroundings and how such an intervention is perceived, we are talking as much about legitimacy as formality or legality.

Urban places and public spaces are closely tied to identity, and it is no wonder that people are possessive and defensive of them. This is, at the root, exactly what motivates many do-it-yourselfers to try to improve their surroundings on their own! But changes to urban places and public spaces by others can for the same reasons be uncomfortable, shocking, and unwelcome, and questions of who has a right to intervene are central. So legitimacy here is a multifaceted but powerful concept because it cuts across other categories and draws our attention so crucially, as simple as it may sound, to what people actually deem acceptable. I work throughout the book to think about the legitimacy of DIY urban design interventions in different contexts and ultimately to operationalize the concept in pluralistic, democratic terms that might find application across the worlds of urban planning, development, and placemaking.

Finally, the phenomenon of DIY urban design shows us the possibilities and the limitations of participatory citizenship. If theories of democracy and citizenship have long been prominent in sociology and cultural studies, critical analyses of the actual practice of civic participation under the conditions of the contemporary American polis constitute a relatively new and evolving discourse. From the advocacy of Jane Addams and John Dewey to newer writing on themes as varying as social movement participation, community-based planning and participatory budgeting, or crowdsourcing and the promise of the so-called open city, we recognize that with every potential expansion of participation comes new questions of inclusivity, power, and legitimacy.[4]

DIY urbanism represents a potentially powerful populist alternative to the uneven priorities of city governments and development interests, a medium for direct participation in the design and use of community streets and spaces, perhaps even a transformative moment for democratizing our cities. Yet differences in who participates in informal urbanism, in how such actions are perceived, and in how they impact the places they aim to improve all showcase the persistence of social inequality in urban space and the ways in which participatory citizenship remains significantly limited. The challenge—and the task I hope to accomplish in this book—is to understand the latter so that we might realize the former.

These are the major conceptual concerns that guide this account. Certain other threads are recurring or even constant throughout: the dialogical relationship between DIY urban design and the consequences of market-driven planning; the use of technical and scholarly knowledge by many do-it-yourselfers; the possibility of overreaching, vigilantism, and antisocial impacts in DIY interventions; and the forms of socioeconomic inequality that are inherent to considering social relations in urban space. For the sake of organizational clarity, however, each chapter here focuses on a particular theme and engages a particular discourse in urban social science. I then connect these to each other and to overarching conceptual contributions in the conclusion. An advantage of this layout is that each chapter can take its time elaborating upon one element of the overall argument, with particular cases from the research used to illustrate it. A disadvantage is that each of the issues, which are always present, must wait its turn to be explored fully.

## A PLAN OF WHAT'S TO COME

This book is arranged into thematic chapters presented in an order that progresses analytically from initial definitions and examples to more critical interpretations and broader implications. The order of the chapters thus also aligns with my own analytical progression in carrying out the research and developing its principal findings and arguments. I hope this organization will carry the reader along from gaining an introductory familiarity with this intriguing phenomenon to a deeper understanding of the social and spatial conditions to which I argue it both responds and contributes, and its implications for how we think about participation, equity, and legitimacy in urban placemaking.

The next chapter, Chapter 2, steps back to define do-it-yourself urban design in detail. It does so first in contrast to the existing social science perspectives on what I call *unauthorized urban space interventions* more generally: unsanctioned place-based direct actions that challenge the normative uses of particular urban spaces. I argue that DIY urban design is distinct in its intentions and its form, a new type of unauthorized alteration that is increasingly visible in American cities and is attracting attention in design and planning circles as innovative and populist. I describe the process of inquiry and discovery at the outset of my research and initial observations that help to draw out and distinguish the new category of DIY urban design. Some additional findings about the actions themselves and the people who create them flesh out my definition and provoke many of the questions that guide the remainder of the book.

In Chapter 3, I focus on the political-economic conditions that define the contemporary American city socially and physically. I demonstrate that DIY urban designers are largely driven to act by problems in their neighborhoods and failings they perceive in mainstream, market-driven urban policy and planning, and I argue that understanding them in this context is essential for interpreting the phenomenon. While do-it-yourselfers respond to the problems they see in creative and sometimes inspiring ways, I begin here to show how their individualistic tactics in doing so can introduce problems of their own. I focus in particular on a trio of cases that concern bus stops that serve as a starting point from which to consider the lack of sidewalk seating in many cities, the privatization of street furniture for advertising revenue, and other inadequacies in local service provision. We see how potentially valuable DIY contributions can be in response to these things, but I argue also that in trying to correct the problems they see, do-it-yourselfers always impart their own personal and cultural values on urban space as well. At the extreme, I show how some alterations— exclusionary signage, parking spot saving, even a case of DIY bus stop *removal*—can be quite selfish and antisocial in impact. I thus interrogate the meanings of DIY urbanism in the context of urban policymaking in the "neoliberalized" city, arguing that even as these practices aim to counter the inequities of market-driven planning, they can also reinforce an individualistic, undemocratic logic in the shaping of our cities.

Chapters 4 and 5 connect to the broader context of DIY urban design from a different angle, that of social privilege and inequality. These things strongly shape who participates, where they do so, and how their efforts are perceived. In Chapter 4, I begin to challenge binary notions of formality and informality, both through a further discussion of the development of standardized urban planning and placemaking practices and by showing that many do-it-yourselfers also employ sophisticated knowledge of professional planning and scholarly urbanism in their interventions. Those with professional design training put these skills to use in their projects: sign-makers making signs, industrial designers creating chairs and benches. And where they lack such a background, DIY urban designers often seek information from official sources in order to strengthen and legitimate their interventions, from tools, techniques, and guidelines to justifications grounded in social science research. Although this may lead to better-designed and more effective improvements, it also gives the individuals a certain confidence in the quality of their actions and their right to make them.

This sort of hubris and elitism in the practice of DIY urban design is only heightened by the more fundamental demographic characteristics that also define its practitioners: most of the people I call do-it-yourselfers are white, educated, middle-class men and thus operate from a position of considerable privilege in public space and interactions with authority. People of color and people from low-income communities, however, are heavily disincentivized from participating in activities that skirt legal boundaries due to common societal prejudices and inequality in the eyes of the law. While of course members of these groups do still participate in informal, civic-minded placemaking, I find they tend to do so in very different ways. These contradictions and their implications are the subjects of Chapter 5. I argue that, although informal urbanisms of different sorts can be found in communities all over the world (and perhaps especially among under-served communities in some contexts) members of legally vulnerable groups in American cities are less likely to break the law to make a local streetscape improvement, even though their communities are more likely to be in need of investment. Meanwhile, interventions by privileged do-it-yourselfers and the cultural values they represent can provoke less than welcoming receptions in the communities they aim to improve.

The final empirical chapter, Chapter 6, extends the analysis to the world of official urban planning and placemaking, providing different perspectives on its relationship to DIY urbanism. First, through the voices of professional planners, I show how quick these planners are to note problems with DIY approaches and emphasize the importance of regulations, processes, and accountability for everything from basic functionality to social equity. Yet these same professionals express sympathy for do-it-yourselfers' frustrations and are often excited to adopt their tactics, harness their energy, and exploit their cultural value. I then describe how some DIY projects have found pathways to formal adoption and inspired popular "tactical urbanism" and "creative placemaking" approaches to public space design. Many such interventions can result in innovative public spaces with a variety of social, environmental, and economic benefits. But I also argue that the reproduction of an aesthetic experience selectively inspired by a hip grassroots trend and combined with "creative class" values can mark the resulting spaces themselves as elite and exclusionary. This can perpetuate unequal access and spatial privilege in the urban environment and potentially contribute to cultural and demographic displacement.

Finally, in my concluding chapter, I unite the study's findings and present their implications for the contemporary city, urban studies, and social theory. My aim is not to offer a summary but another substantive chapter in which the major conceptual and theoretical contributions of the book are fully explored. I confront the theme of a formality-informality binary in urbanism, which I argue my findings significantly complicate. I posit instead that the success or acceptability of an urban space intervention is better understood through the lens of legitimacy, and I demonstrate how some of the problems with DIY urbanism—and by extension many forms of urban placemaking—can be addressed through the operationalizing of this concept as a community-based metric of validity. I then consider what additional and perhaps more intangible value DIY urban design still has in its very informality—the inherent promise of unauthorized creative actions as sparks of popular participation and transformative potential that should be acknowledged by scholars, policymakers, and community members alike. In dialogue with research on participatory citizenship and its limitations, I use the study of DIY urbanism to consider how changing ideas of community, participation, and transgression imply a troubling acceptance of limited citizenship that celebrates individualism in the guise of populism and exploits authentic participation and creativity for legitimacy in economic development.

A detailed description of my research design and methodology is provided in Appendix 2. Those interested in a summary overview of the whole extent of the study, a discussion of my case and site selection rationales, and thoughts on the roles of personal narratives, the camera, and the bicycle as investigative tools in the conduct of ethnographic research may wish to read this before returning to the body of the book. In the chapters to come, I make selective use of particular cases from my interview data—rather than attempting to account for every distinct case at every point—in order to more fully explain particularly vivid examples and avoid overwhelming the reader with dozens of quick mentions. Again, a full accounting of the 80 DIY urban design projects connected to interviews conducted for the study, demonstrating the breadth of the individuals and projects considered and how they can be further typologized, is represented in Appendix 1. Also, the reader should note that while in many cases I refer to interviewees descriptively to protect their anonymity (they have, after all, often engaged in illegal activities), many individuals asked that their names be used in connection with their actions, and I have honored this request.

2

# Constructive Deviance

*What Is DIY Urban Design? And What Is It Not?*

It was in London in 2003 that I first encountered something that I would now (though certainly did not then) call "do-it-yourself urban design." I was walking, as I would most days, from my flat off Borough High Street along some improvised combination of the many winding lanes of Southwark, attempting to cut an efficient angle toward Blackfriar's Bridge, which would take me across the Thames to class at the London School of Economics. This time (and, it would turn out, on many occasions to come— it was a nice route) I wandered along Union Street and past a walled-off construction site at the corner with Redcross Way. Though the official signs were worn and covered in the occasional graffiti tag, one could make out that it was associated with rail infrastructure and, at least in part, the London Underground's then-recent Jubilee Line extension. Far more prominent, however, were a series of black and white posters pasted to the wall. Featuring a photo of a skull and crossbones, they declared, "This is the Crossbones Graveyard," and provided quotes about the history of the site and contact information for an organized effort to save it from further development.

My interest in London's vibrant street art scene was at that time already well piqued, and I regularly explored the city's backstreets photographing pieces. With their striking visuals and wheat-pasted installation, I took the Crossbones Graveyard posters to be in some way a part of that. It was also immediately clear that they were part of a local campaign of some sort. What really stands out in hindsight, however, is that the posters were

"This is the Crossbones Graveyard" posters installed on a Transport for London construction wall surrounding the historic burial ground in the London Borough of Southwark by Friends of Crossbones, 2003. Photo by the author.

informational signage too, telling passersby what lay behind the wooden wall, pronouncing its historical importance to the area, and offering a plea to honor and protect it, all in much the way an official local historical marker might (and, as it would happen, some years later ultimately would). I have since come to recognize informal signage as one of the more common ways that people act to make unauthorized contributions to the streetscape. I have documented many other such efforts to highlight, memorialize, and preserve the histories of past events in a place. These include simple markers and placards, the sadly ubiquitous ghost bikes and roadside memorials to the victims of America's unsafe streets, as well as a whole series of very official looking historical markers in Pittsburgh commemorating the events of the Great Pennsylvania Railroad Strike.

On a sunny day in 2008, while staying with friends in Los Angeles, I first visited a place called the LA Eco-Village. I had read that the Eco-Village's residents had been taking direct actions to make their neighborhood street safer, including blocking traffic altogether by holding the occasional dinner party in the middle of the street. I introduced myself to a man named Joe Linton who was gardening out front. Two years later, embarking upon the early pilot research for what was then a broader study of the ways that people challenge the proscribed uses or meanings of urban space (activities I refer to generally as unauthorized urban space interventions below),

I made Joe my first interview, and indeed returned to speak with him numerous times during my frequent stays in Los Angeles while conducting this research.

A soft-spoken white man in his 40s, an artist and urban environmental activist, Joe told me about the street closings there out front of the Eco-Village, in which residents would block traffic with wooden barricades and throw a party in the intersection, sometimes sitting around a table to share a meal right there in the road. He also told me about a number of other less theatrical interventions that he and his neighbors had made to slow traffic there, including permanent physical changes to the streetscape itself: they had painted their own crosswalks and a vibrant intersection mural and had even landscaped a small curb extension with plants and seating. Here I saw how everyday residents could physically alter the streets in very much the same way a city's department of transportation might; and indeed Joe is impeccably well-informed about urban planning and design.

Not long after that, in April of 2010, I attended a small conference and workshop at the City University of New York's Graduate Center in Manhattan, on the theme "Resisting Enclosure." I had been drawn to my research topic out of a long-standing interest in ideas that this provocative

A painted telephone pole, landscaped sidewalk extension or "bulb-out," crosswalks, and intersection mural created by residents of the Los Angeles Eco-Village in the street outside their home in 2009. Photo by the author, 2011.

title seemed to capture: efforts at reasserting communal or popular rights to public space and whether some such actions qualified as a sort of "resistance." Over two days, eminent critical spatial theorists spoke on the privatization and commodification of urban space and the radical, transformative potential in everyday acts of resistance to this—ideas I had been exploring in the writing of Henri Lefebvre and others, and in my own work at the time.

The panel that most excited me, however, was a handful of nonacademic practitioners speaking on the topic "Artistic Interruptions of Everyday Life." The personal examples of such "interruptions" that they shared varied considerably, from fairly straightforward public performance art to activities much more explicitly about challenging the uses of urban space and even making what they saw as valuable, civic-minded alterations to the streetscape. I wound up interviewing two of the participants; one in particular, an artist named Jordan Seiler who makes it his business to remove corporate advertisements from the sides of phone booths and other public places, ultimately became one of the more complicated examples I found of people who break the law in order to make what they consider needed improvements to the urban streetscape. I was beginning to feel out the subtle distinctions among the different ways in which people illegally alter their surroundings and the ways that cultural, political, practical, and personal explanations come into play to different degrees, and range in how provocative, artistic, or simply functional and official-looking the results can be.

And it was two years later still, now deep into the research for this book, that I interviewed a young man in Pittsburgh who shared with me one of the purest examples of what I had by then come to call do-it-yourself urban design. When the city altered the traffic pattern at a hillside intersection near his office there in 2010, he noticed that the change was confusing to some motorists and resulting in fender-benders. Seeing a need for better signage, he put his skills as an artist and illustrator to use, mocking up a design on his computer, using official fonts he had "picked up here and there," printing the design on a home vinyl plotter, and attaching it to an aluminum backing ("based on, you know, municipal criteria and things," he explained to me). The result, a shiny red and white sign reading "Cross Traffic Does Not Stop," he fixed to a pole below the stop sign at the intersection. Five years later it still stands as a seemingly valuable addition—as its creator observed, "there's a lot less plastic and glass in the street"— with the only indication of its origins the small lettering at the bottom that read "PGHDIYDPW": the Pittsburgh Do-it-Yourself Department of Public Works.

A homemade traffic sign (below an official one) installed on a street in Pittsburgh in 2010. Photo by the author, 2012.

## WHAT IS DIY URBAN DESIGN AND WHAT IS IT NOT?

I define *DIY urban design* interventions as unauthorized yet ostensibly functional and civic-minded physical alterations or additions to the urban built environment in forms analogous (however abstractly) to official planning and streetscape design elements. The definition is, admittedly, a slippery one. Intentionality matters; so does appearance. It is tempting to make a comparison to the old Potter Stewart "I know it when I see it" aphorism regarding hard-core pornography, although this is not quite right. I have defined DIY urban design precisely enough not only to know it when I see it but, I hope, for the critical reader to do the same. These are unsanctioned physical interventions into urban space that are, however artistic or political or even potentially problematic, intended as improvements of the sort that city planners or other officials might themselves create.

The purpose of this chapter is to expand upon this definition, in large part by distinguishing DIY urban design from other forms of unauthorized urban alteration that are more commonly recognized and discussed in social science research, and then by offering some further examples of actions that count and some others that I feel do not. Still, I do not claim that this unique category is a fully distinct one from all others. There can be considerable overlap in types of informal urbanism, in some cases almost coextensiveness, depending on other terms or definitions.

Walking and observing in the city, one can see all manner of unauthorized interventions and alternative uses in the built environment, from juvenile bathroom graffiti to organized political demonstrations. Social science—in anthropology, criminology, geography, sociology, and other disciplines—has offered interpretations and generated theory based on many of these now-classic examples. Depending on the particular subject and approach of the research, some informal urban space interventions are claimed to constitute radical strategies of political expression, even theoretically potent "resistance"; others are described as acts of artistic or personal self-expression; still others are understood as little more than vandalism or pointless juvenile acting out.

Although I began my research informed by these interpretations, I found that none of them provides a satisfactory lens for interpreting the work of the particular group of interventionists on whom I ultimately came to focus—those who, when confronted with something in their communities that they see as in need of fixing, improving, or enlivening, choose to do it themselves without asking permission. Civic-minded and intended toward the practical improvement of lived urban spaces through skillful, creative local actions, these increasingly visible yet often unattributed practices complicate common assumptions about urban space interventions. And they have received little attention from social scientists or urban policy and planning professionals.

In the next section, I examine the existing dominant perspectives in social science on what I call *unauthorized urban space interventions* in general: unsanctioned, place-based direct actions that challenge the usual or regulated uses of particular urban spaces. In doing so, I describe some examples that challenge them and draw out the new analytical category of DIY urban design, revealing how it is distinct from existing conceptualizations and better accounts for the real world phenomena observed. I then define and discuss the constituent terms of "DIY" and "informality." Next, a section focused on the "who, why, and where" of DIY urban design describes some basic demographics and other characteristics common to the do-it-yourselfers I spoke to and the would-be improvements they create. Analyzing and interpreting these initial findings raise questions that in many ways guide the rest of the book.

As I have noted, this study began as an investigation into the meaning behind a wide variety of unauthorized, place-based alterations and occupations of urban spaces and evolved in focus over several years (see Appendix 2 for more detail on the multiyear research process itself). At this broadest level, I was interested in many different phenomena, known by many names: graffiti, street art, happenings, big games, pervasive games, art interventions, culture jamming, space hijacking, place hacking, Park(ing) Day, Critical Mass, Reclaim the Streets, protestivals, artivism, craftivism, anarchitecture, yarn bombing, guerrilla knitting, guerrilla gardening, guerrilla theater . . . the list goes on. The motivations behind these practices are diverse, as are the scales of their intended and actual impacts. Yet all can be described as practices in which individuals or informal groups challenge expected, regulated uses of particular spaces through unauthorized direct action. I refer to them collectively here as forms of unauthorized urban space intervention,* a relatively satisfactory shorthand, although there are few widely accepted terms that encompass them all.

(Less transgressive actions, such as sanctioned community gardens and public art, or organized protests and demonstrations in urban space, are also worthy of attention, as is the simple act of putting pride into reimagining one's own property with decorative or functional additions. But I draw the line at actions undertaken illegally or without permission where it would normally be required. More transient or ephemeral unauthorized practices, such as sidewalk sleeping and squatting, or some skateboarding and cycling, constitute a gray area; they meet my definition as unauthorized urban interventions where they work to challenge the expected uses or meanings of the spaces they transgress, and some do involve temporary

---

* The word "intervention" here references its use in both the art and activism worlds, and an especially "activist" form of art in particular: initially the "art interventions" of the Dadaists and others (usually literally intervening in other pieces of art, audiences, and venues), but even more so its subsequent reinterpretation in so-called relational aesthetics (Bourriaud 2002 [1998]) and other site-specific practice as interjections into public space and everyday life (see Kwon 2002; Thompson & Sholette 2004; Klanten, Ehmann, & Hubner 2010). The term is used widely among practitioners of many of the different phenomena listed above, from street art to guerrilla theater, and exemplified in an exhibition on "the creative disruption of everyday life" called "The Interventionists: Art in the Social Sphere" (see Thompson & Sholette 2004). I use the phrase urban intervention to suggest actions directly impacting urban space itself without prejudging scope, temporality, or value, and making allusions to the art and activism contexts above without being beholden to either. Many of my own interviewees have also used—if not embraced—it as a general term.

physical alterations that go beyond bodily presence. Of course, not all urban interventions are DIY urban design.)

There are relatively few focused studies of unauthorized urban intervention practices in academic social science, let alone relevant analyses of their collected meaning. Among what has been written, however, three main perspectives or categories of interpretation can be identified, dependent largely on the particular subjects in question and the theoretical or disciplinary orientations of the scholars involved. The first perspective, with its grounding in mainstream urban sociology and criminology, considers a variety of practices as essentially just vandalism or trespassing and frequently implies that the acts have little deeper significance beyond serving as indicators of crime and disorder. Much criminological literature, and especially the well-known "broken windows" theory and its ilk, falls here, viewing illegal alteration from graffiti to tent cities as delinquency or simply a sign that "nobody cares."[1] The case of the Astoria Scum River Bridge and others described previously clearly complicate this perspective: they are just the opposite of situations in which nobody cares.

The second category of accounts is similar but more sympathetic to the practices in question, granting unique research value to some forms of unauthorized intervention as instances of concept art, personal expression and communication, or popular subculture. These approaches analyze the activities for artistic, textual, or sociopsychological meaning.[2] But as a result, they also consider their creators on these planes, making little accommodation for any intended physical or functional impact of the interventions themselves and assuming personal motivations that rarely include wider political, economic, and geographical factors. These perspectives would fail to appreciate, for example, why people engage in community-regarding and often selfless, anonymous improvements like the "cross traffic does not stop" sign in Pittsburgh, or the socioeconomic context of an unauthorized crosswalk, garden, or bench.

A final category—perhaps the most sympathetic to its subject—frames activities ranging from street art to street festivals in terms of radical activism and protest, sometimes with explicitly stated political goals and often inherent (if entirely theoretical) critical transformative potential. This perspective may actually be the most commonly advanced in the literature, at least about forms of urban intervention more elaborate than graffiti. It has been relatively clearly and objectively articulated by the cultural criminologist Jeff Ferrell (e.g., 1995, 2001), who is also one of the few scholars to explicitly connect various urban intervention practices to one another. Ferrell proposes that urban space has become increasingly regulated, policed, and commodified over the past several decades, and he views graffiti, busking, bicycle activism, and the other activities that he collects as "urban anarchy" as consciously reactive to these trends. Others present the alternative uses that "outlaw" bike messengers or skateboarders make of the urban environment as symbolic challenges to spatial regulation as well.[3] Some researchers in this camp, especially a number of contemporary "radical" or "activist" cultural geographers and art historians go so far as to suggest that the actions qualify as instances of outright "resistance" to authority, capitalism, or mainstream culture.[4]

This third perspective is harder to dismiss outright as inapplicable to DIY urban design activities, and I initially approached my own research on urban intervention from such a standpoint. Site-specific direct actions, such as the "Reclaim the Streets" demonstrations of the 1990s—where streets were illegally closed to traffic by raucous impromptu carnivals while jackhammers were used to replace asphalt with saplings—seemed to me empirical actualizations of the sort of popular resistance yearned for by Henri Lefebvre and other 20th-century theorists arguing for the transformative potential of "critical consciousness" in everyday urban space. This is an important but slippery proposition that I will return to from time to time throughout the book.

Indeed, even if essentialized somewhat here for comparison, none of the three existing perspectives I have just described is without empirical basis, nor are they mutually exclusive. To some degree the difference between the three perspectives has as much to do with case selection as interpretation. There is little doubt, for instance, that some graffiti *is* associated with neglect and "disorder," not to mention crime and violence.[5] And certainly a great deal of street art is as much about personal motivations like subverting the gallery scene or going "all city" with one's work as it is about any more ideological or whimsical effort to open the streets and buildings of the city for use as the people's canvas. Greg Snyder found in his 2009 ethnography of the New York graffiti scene that the primary motivation for tagging among the artists he studied was essentially achieving some minor degree of subcultural fame. And finally, from graffiti writers to participants in alter-globalization "protestivals" and "occupations," there *is* evidence that many site-specific artists and activists do see their interventions in radical, revolutionary political terms that go well beyond the sites in question. In some instances, like Reclaim the Streets or the attention-grabbing, conversation-changing, place-based efforts of the 2011 Occupy movement, there is a case to be made for that vision.

Yet my initial research in Los Angeles, New York, and London also turned up cases that simply did not fit with existing perspectives. I interviewed a range of people whose actions did align—from noted graffiti artists to the principal organizer of Reclaim the Streets—but I also talked to guerrilla gardeners, unauthorized streetscapers, and fake sign makers whose work seemed different. As described in the anecdotes that opened this chapter, I began to see that an analytical emphasis on critical resistance was missing the subtler and often more local and individual motivations that some have for altering the built environment and failed to appreciate their more limited intended impacts of simple, functional improvement to the streetscape. In this sense, I was finding examples of intentional improvements more akin to the functional, workaday informalities so common in the cities of the global South or low-income neighborhoods the world over. But they differ from these too in that they are not created so much out of a fundamental human need as a desire to address more "first world problems." In dropping my early assumptions, I found that many such practices are better described, and thus distinguished, by a fourth logic—the logic of DIY urban design.

Analyzing and interrogating this phenomenon is the purpose of the rest of this chapter and of this whole book. In terms of the existing accounts on DIY urbanism and related subjects, however, several more items are worth discussion here. Some design-oriented websites, magazines, and the occasional book have recently focused on practices of informal architectural and streetscape improvement.[6] In 2012, the US pavilion at the Venice International Architecture Biennale even celebrated similar phenomena with the exhibition "Spontaneous Interventions: Design Actions for the Common Good."[7]

In social science, some emerging interest in these themes can be identified. A 2010 study by Luca Visconti and colleagues conceives of some forms of urban intervention this way, if not explicitly. They argue that forms of "place marking" range from "pure resistance and contestation" to "public place beautification" and note the diversity of forms of alterations. Though ultimately focused "solely on those street marking practices imbued with multiple ideologies of reclamation of public place," among six types of marking that the authors distinguish is "urban design"—"an aesthetic practice applied in favor of the beautification of public architecture and urban style," where the ideologies behind the actions are about the right to alter that space and the goal is "enchanting" the city for city dwellers.[8] More recently, a handful of social scientists from across numerous disciplines—including Donovan Finn, Kurt Iveson, Emily Talen, and others—have been publishing research on similar themes and developing a discourse of DIY urbanism explicitly.[9] Yet nomenclature and definitions are still varied.

I define DIY urban design as small-scale and unauthorized yet intentionally functional and civic-minded physical interventions aimed at "improving" the urban streetscape in forms analogous to or inspired by official efforts. Why use the term "DIY"? These three letters have a great deal of meaning in Western subculture and counterculture, rooted in 19th- and 20th-century Arts and Crafts and "back to the land" movements, and emerging alongside punk and hip hop ideologies and aesthetics in the 1970s. The term refers most simply to any creating, modifying, or repairing, done by oneself rather than by professionals, but through its subcultural associations it has come to represent an ethic of nonmainstream self-reliance in everything from home-brewing, self-publishing, and traditional craftsmanship to illegal parties and performances and radical spatial protests.

DIY has lately been experiencing a boom in popularity, especially in reference to the revived interest in "craft" and handmade production that do much to define the hip contemporary urbanism of Brooklyn, Portland, and the myriad gentrifying urban neighborhoods that we associate with cultural trendsetting and the creative class. The term is also already connected with many urban intervention practices, especially graffiti,[10] but also guerrilla gardening, street performance, and squatting. When placed in front of the words for the quite formal practice of "urban design," the term suggests just the unique, unlikely combination of methods and motivations embodied in the act of altering the built environment without permission in order to make functional, civic-minded improvements to it. (I should note too that "urban design" connotes a wide array of urban placemaking efforts and is commonly associated with broader, even regional-scale concerns such as the very layout of a city or district; what I am looking at here might in most cases be more precisely described as urban streetscape, landscape, and traffic design elements, and I sometimes use these terms too.) By 2013 or so, something approaching a common use and received understanding of the term "DIY urbanism" could be identified in academic urban studies, and I use this evocative but again overly vague term interchangeably with my own "DIY urban design."

The words "formal" and "informal" are also of central importance here. The dichotomy of the formal and informal is a regular topic of inquiry in social theory, economics, urban studies, and planning, among many other disciplines; conceptions vary widely and sometimes contentiously. Social scientists dating to Max Weber have confronted formality and informality in the study of organizations and organized social or economic action, wherein the contrast is between the official, routinized, or bureaucratic

and the bottom-up, creative, and ad hoc, even the disorganized or unauthorized. Scholars of urban policy, planning, and development are familiar
students of ideas such as hazy regulatory environments and informal housing and settlement. Fran Tonkiss, in her 2013 book *Cities by Design*, demonstrated the essential fundamentality of informality to the very nature
of the contemporary city—from everyday life to urban morphology and
infrastructure.

The term "informal urbanism" is most commonly used in reference to
the growth of slum settlements and all manner of accompanying social,
economic, and city-making processes. This is especially associated with the
rapidly growing cities of the global South, where it has also been suggested
that informality has become a sort of new normal for economic activity
and urban development alike.[11] In cities in the advanced economies of the
global North, although the informality of unregulated businesses, services, and support networks, casual or undocumented labor, and criminal
enterprise have received considerable attention, the functional alteration
of urban space through informal means has not.[12] The meaning and context of informality in the literature is also part of the confusion, with many
above-board and official planning efforts nonetheless sometimes described
as informal as well.[13] Even the popular provocations of "insurgent public
space" (Hou 2010), "tactical urbanism" (Lydon and Garcia 2015), or "spontaneous interventions" (Ho 2012), which have much in common—even
overlap—with the unauthorized DIY improvements of interest to me, feature many examples of officially sanctioned or government-driven planning, architecture, and streetscape design.

Certainly informality is relative. It may be thought of loosely as on a
spectrum, with the place of its components shifting across cultural contexts.[14] Tonkiss proposes that whether through socialization (as casual
human-powered networks) or privatization (handed over to business and
property owners), in many places basic service provision and infrastructure from trash pickup to transportation might be considered "informal."
In many American cities, for instance, local business improvement organizations are often the only parties responsible for things like street upkeep.
Many corporate enclaves and private gated communities exist under their
own laws and covenants, signage, and transportation networks (not to
mention private security forces).

In this book, although my subjects are unauthorized interventions that
often respond to civic concerns and even mimic official designs and functions, I use informality to mean an informality of practice and product
directly counterposed to that which is officially sanctioned or produced,
which I call "formal" (i.e., legally and normatively bestowed with the right

and duty to shape urban space). While we can grant a different and none-theless valid sense of informality to participatory planning processes or "pop-up" shops in vacant storefronts, DIY urban design interventions are wholly unauthorized efforts at urban streetscape improvement—informal in a sense that finds more resonance with informal housing in a slum set-tlement or a person selling pirated videos on the subway. Yes, like some casually informal activity within formal organizations, DIY urban design is bottom-up, creative, and generative; but also, more like the underground economy, it is outside of official policy and planning control and is of highly questionable legality.

In addition to methodological considerations (placing a clearer limit on the cases of concern to this research), drawing the line here helps high-light the more exceptional qualities of DIY urban design practices, and the do-it-yourselfers behind them, that I wish to bring attention to with this book. These include the observation that informal placemaking of the more extra-legal variety does occur in the cities of advanced economies in the global North, and that it does so in more unexpectedly civic-minded forms than vandalism, art, or protest. It also provides a powerful, if extreme, example of the extent to which popular urbanism and urban planning con-cerns have permeated the collective air in many such cities, and the degree to which highly technical, professional, academic, and indeed formalized elements pervade even these informal efforts at local improvement.

## Illustrations and Articulations

As I have described, DIY urban design is distinct from other forms of unau-thorized urban space intervention. While more active, functional, and goal-oriented than what might plausibly be dismissed as "just art" or "just crime," these actions are far more subtle, limited, and place-based than the tactics of a broader political activism or resistance. Yes, some do constitute vandalism; many have creative, artistic, and personal elements; and few could claim to be truly apolitical. Yet they largely lack elements of destruc-tion, self-promotion, or political communication and are distinguished far more centrally by their thoughtful, civic-minded intentions and their func-tional designs and implementation.

Consider the case of the Highland Park Book Booth, a public book depos-itory created out of a long-defunct payphone booth that has—apparently quite successfully—been fostering literary exchange near a bus stop in its Los Angeles neighborhood since 2010. "It had the phone pulled out of it. It'd been like that for as long as we can remember," its creator, Amy, a book

The Highland Park Book Booth, a public free book exchange created out of an abandoned payphone by Amy Inoue and Stu Rapeport in Highland Park, Los Angeles, in 2010. Photo by the author.

designer and gallery owner, told me over lunch at a nearby restaurant. "And so, after like two years of trying on all these ideas, and walking by this thing, I decided 'OK, book giveaway!'" She had a bunch of books lying around and knew plenty of friends, colleagues, and neighbors did too. She and her partner cleaned up the old payphone, added a shelf and a sign, and filled it with books. In her observations and mine over the years it gets plenty of use, with a frequent rotation of books of all sorts, in both English and Spanish.

The Book Booth is a positive response to urban disorder and neglect, not a symptom of it. Artistic merit notwithstanding, the design is simple and functional (the major additions other than books being a shelf, a small sign, and a bit of yarn decoration that someone added later as their own DIY-on-DIY improvement). While Amy is happy to acknowledge and discuss creating it, it has no signature on it and conveys no obvious message besides the value of books and the modestly provocative fact that someone decided to creatively appropriate a neglected bit of city infrastructure and turn it into something useful, cheerful, and unexpected.

Much the same can be said of the illegal bike lanes created by Toronto's clandestine "Urban Repair Squad," which attempt to create a safer environment for cyclists on busy streets. The same goes for a faux-civic sign (in English, Korean, and Spanish, with all the usual names and departmental contact information) installed one weekend to declare and invite public comments on a new city "park for the people" on a prominent corner of Wilshire Boulevard in Los Angeles that was actually slated for condo development. So too for the myriad unauthorized benches, planters, plants, signs, and other streetscaping installed at needy or neglected locations by community members in many cities. These are neither situations where nobody cares, nor instances of juvenile acting out, nor (primarily) artistic expression. Attempts to fit them into such categorizations obscure their potentially deeper sociological and geographical significance, especially in terms of motivation and intended impact.

It is also a stretch to equate these actions with organized protest or resistance. Some of the do-it-yourselfers I interviewed do see their projects as campaigns of sorts (a series of similar interventions in multiple locations, even multiple cities), but most create things only sporadically, focused on particular spaces or types of places; some had acted only once to fix a specific problem and expected never to do so again. Some do-it-yourselfers certainly connect their actions to political beliefs around which they are mobilized (environmentalism, for instance, or opinions on urban policy issues such as cycling or pedestrian infrastructure), but many others do not. Nick, the president of an Atlanta group that builds unsanctioned huts for the chronically homeless and others in need of shelter living illegally on public or private land, sees it as a matter of priorities: "We're much more oriented as a service organization, which means that the protest politics of it is not our game, because it doesn't help our clients."

Others simply dismiss the idea that their interventions have a larger political impact at all. "I have too much respect for activists and what they do to call myself one," one New York do-it-yourselfer told me. Most also expressed little interest in promoting themselves or their work. Some enjoy seeing their creation noticed, but others argue that the best DIY contributions are those that are simply ignored or assumed to be legitimate, thus lasting longer and better serving their functional purpose. As opposed to organized political efforts, these actions more prominently represent a simple willingness to reshape the built environment on one's own terms for some sort of ostensible public benefit.

Furthermore, if it is true that many of the individuals involved have little love for "the system," their projects are no more aimed at overthrowing it than they are at vandalism, self-expression, or self-promotion. While this was one place I found plenty of differences in opinion, many of my interviewees actually expressed a clear disinterest in stirring things up politically and were resistant to the idea of themselves as radicals. "There's no reason this couldn't be done legally and with city authorization," explained one member of a Los Angeles group sometimes called the "Department of DIY," responsible for illicitly painting bike lanes, softening square curbs, and other such alterations.

As discussed in greater detail in Chapter 4, a majority of the do-it-yourselfers I spoke with demonstrated considerable familiarity with urban policy and planning processes in their communities, and some DIY actions even work to realize existing city planning goals. Martin, a photographer and representative of Toronto's Urban Repair Squad, described one of their interventions, some of first bicycle shared-lane arrows in that city:

> Again it was supposed to be installed [i.e., was called for in the city bicycle plan], it was a very easy job, it was 800 meters worth. . . . And [the Urban Repair Squad] did it I think in two night sessions on both the north and south sides of the street in like three hours? It cost $80 instead of $25,000 or whatever it's supposed to cost, including the design which takes up a lot of money. And that stayed up for two years, nobody ever caught on. Eventually—it's really ironic— eventually two years later they actually got around to painting it. So you now have like the city stencils and the Urban Repair Squad stencils side by side.

In these ways, many do-it-yourselfers see themselves as aiding the city, their fellow community members, and in some cases even landholders and developers. Their actions may be embedded in a politics of localism and a frustration with the formal process, but they are subtle in impact and statement, first and foremost about making a positive, functional contribution.

This does not mean that DIY urban design (or any of the other categories of urban space interventions delineated above) is necessarily exclusive of the others, just that the other categories miss out on its most essential features. Consider a case of DIY urban design that has at once some elements of vandalism, artistic expression, and political protest: Jordan Seiler, a formally trained artist in New York City, who removes corporate advertisements from streets, payphones, and bus stops and replaces them with anonymous artwork or blank canvases, which he feels is more in the public spirit. We met at the "Resisting Enclosure" conference at CUNY, described above. Before long we were walking the streets of Manhattan, in broad daylight, looking for offending ads. Well-versed in civic codes and ordinances as well as critical geography theory, Jordan's actions are anything but random, and he devotes a great deal of his efforts to removing illegal advertising (such as promotional "wildposting" on walls, poles, and construction sites) that the city should technically be preventing. As Jordan said:

> It's really nice to see outdoor advertising kind of fold under pressure, but at the same time, I would say the project gets clouded in the resistance to advertising, but it's much more about . . . playing with the city, and understanding that if you have an opinion about how space is maybe improperly being used, you really have the right and the ability to go out and make some sort of alteration to that situation. . . . I mean 150 people going out and whacking house on illegal advertising in the city should be a positive!

One could well assert that Jordan's "Street Advertising Takeover" actions do "resist" the prevalence of outdoor advertising and the commodification of public space. Guerrilla bike lanes, street furniture, or aspirational parks also, in a sense, "resist" the likes of car-centric urban planning, uneven investment, and other perceived problems. If these are the views of the do-it-yourselfers (and they largely are), it seems fair to argue that such actions are perhaps in line with the sort of targeted but subtle "everyday resistance" to dominant power structures that the political scientist James C. Scott has described among peasants and other oppressed populations. But a focus on more theoretical implications for such actions as truly radical or systemically transformative, as is found in much of the literature, misses the driving motivation toward simply improving the city, ostensibly for everyone, where authorities should, but cannot or will not, do so themselves. Ted, a member of the Brooklyn-based "tactical urbanist" collective DoTank (noted, among other things, for "chair bombing" the streets of Brooklyn with Adirondack chairs and other furniture built from old shipping pallets), summarized the logic of DIY urban design well:

> It's guerrilla. It's sort of unauthorized, and it's somewhat illegal, and it gives us anonymity in there because of that, but then it's not politically charged, and it's not defacing. Right? It's sincerely meant for—it's functional. From the standpoint of maybe helping you, or maybe it even helps everyone, or more than just yourself.

And yet DIY urban design practices are not simply noteworthy for the novelty of their distinction from previous assumptions about the unauthorized alteration of urban space. Differences across projects and types of projects indicate a wide variety of ways that people create unauthorized improvements and offer several useful dimensions on which we can typologize them. Most obviously, there are physical differences in the projects themselves, from sidewalk benches and planters to signage and bike lanes. I came to think of the activities in terms of three broad subcategories of DIY urbanism: *spontaneous streetscaping*—painting traffic markings or installing elements such as signage, ramps, and seating on streets or sidewalks; *renegade renewal*—planting, greening, or functionally converting unused land, infrastructure, or building facades; and *aspirational urbanism*—public notices, chalk boards, or other informational installations by which community members communicate their own policy and development ideas in and upon public space.

Specific examples of spontaneous streetscaping include painting bike lanes and crosswalks without city approval, amending road signs to improve wayfinding or traffic safety, and building and placing public street furniture in areas that lack it. In terms of the sheer number of individual projects

Spontaneous Streetscaping (clockwise from top left): A homemade sign in Brooklyn clarifies the law, 2013; a DIY share-the-lane symbol (or "sharrow") spray-painted on a Seattle street, 2011; a sign declaring a bicycle-friendly street in Los Angeles, 2007; a DIY bench built around a tree in San Francisco, 2016. Photos by the author except bottom right by Ingrid Peterson.

Renegade Renewal (clockwise from top left): Some of Richard Reynolds's guerrilla gardening efforts in London traffic island in 2010; a signpost in Oakland becomes a community "message center," 2010; an out-of-service ATM converted into a flower planter in Brooklyn, 2015; gardeners plant potatoes in a farm atop an old railroad embankment in Queens, 2012. Photos by the author.

it includes, this first category is the biggest one as far as my data are concerned; street seating or signage alone could compete with the others in terms of numbers. I lump them together at this level as the most physically impacting (they are always physical additions to the street) and the most quintessentially functional and officially inspired DIY urban design activities. Renegade renewal includes tending neglected road medians or vacant lots to create gardens, adapting particular streetscape elements for new purposes, and aesthetic efforts like advertising removal. Examples of aspirational urbanism include public wish-lists on vacant walls enabling community planning input, official-looking maps and "coming soon" signs for hoped-for parks, transit improvements, or policy changes, and physical

Aspirational Urbanism (clockwise from top left): A sticker on a vacant New Orleans building from Candy Chang's "I Wish This Was" project, 2010 (photo by Candy Chang); people enjoy a temporary Park(ing) Day "park" in a Brooklyn parking space in 2012 (photo by the author); Graham Coreil-Allen, with his self-published guidebook in hand, in one of the underappreciated urban spaces that he works to draw attention to in Baltimore (photo by the author); a sign by the group Heavy Trash announces a new Los Angeles Metro line, 2000 (photo from Heavy Trash 2000).

events in public places "suggesting" an alternative use, such as temporarily converting parking spaces or freeway underpasses into park spaces.

Across all three categories I found projects with more or less official-looking styles, and those with more practical and user-oriented or more political or artistic attitudes behind them. Another important distinction to make is between those interventions that directly impact streets and mobility, civic regulations, and the functional uses of public spaces and other vital infrastructure—most everything that I call spontaneous streetscaping, and some others—and those that are more innocuous, at least so far as public safety and vital systems are concerned. And then there are differences in the preexisting conditions a project responds to as well, and every do-it-yourselfer has his or her own inspirations, contexts, and intentions. While I do not organize the overall analysis around these categories, they inform the ways I understand and position them in the ensuing discussion. (The table in Appendix 1 lists all projects in the study in terms of the three primary subcategories, style, attitude, and motivating condition, and how physically they intervene, whether through signage, physical infrastructure, aesthetic changes, or other methods.) As a lead-in to the remainder of the book, I now discuss in basic terms the who, why, and where of DIY urban design practices and their creators. This leads to the next question: to what ends?

## WHO, WHY, AND WHERE?

In terms of basic demographics, some common characteristics of the do-it-yourself urban designers I interviewed and observed are worth noting here. All of my respondents were in their late 20s through late 50s (with most in their early to mid-30s), they are primarily white (though Asians make up a sizable minority, followed by a smaller number of blacks and Latinos), and I spoke to about twice as many men as women. They come predominantly from middle-class backgrounds, and most have at least some post-secondary education, ranging from undergraduate and art school coursework to graduate and professional degrees; a handful of exceptions include community members involved in projects in under-privileged parts of Chicago, Los Angeles, New Orleans, New York, and Oakland.

Most do-it-yourselfers I met have stable day jobs of a wide variety, from things like professional art practice, writing, and small business ownership to careers in formal design and urban planning—sometimes with direct relevance to the DIY projects they create "after work." In other words, though there are exceptions, the vast majority of the individuals I interviewed qualify as members of what Richard Florida (2002) famously labeled the "creative class." On more subjective measures of appearance (and less subjective measures such as geography and socioeconomic status), some of them fit the stereotype of the young and relatively affluent neighborhood newcomers looking for and building the hip urban cultural scenes that Richard Lloyd (2006) has called "neo-bohemia." Others of course are more "normal" professional types, hard-working moms and dads, and longtime residents of diverse neighborhoods

Suffice it to say, even in these basic demographic terms, do-it-yourself urban designers differ significantly from common assumptions about people who make illegal alterations to urban space in other ways (street art, vandalism, squatting, protest). And very few of them actually have done a lot of DIY urban design or any other quasi-illegal things at all. Many are interested in graffiti and street art as a cultural phenomenon, for instance, but only a few I talked with had any experience with it. When a group of cyclists planned to place a series of "pass with care"/"*pase con cuidado*" road safety signs up around Los Angeles in 2010, they enlisted the help of some veteran street artists to make the wheat paste.

With regard to motivations and inspirations, all of my interviewees could clearly explain why they do what they do in an immediate sense. Whether ultimately colored by particular interests, politics, or even selfish priorities, their motivations always featured seeing what they viewed as a specific spatial "problem" affecting them and/or their communities, and a feeling that they could help fix it themselves. In many cases, they went further, saying that not only could they help, but essentially that they felt they had to help because the city could not be trusted or expected to.

In addition to resembling—sometimes quite intentionally replicating— official streetscape features, particular DIY urban design responses are often inspired by their creator's own skills, interests, and backgrounds. Do-it-yourselfers with professional design training put these formal skills to use in their projects: sign-makers making signs, industrial designers creating chairs and benches. The handful of people I spoke to with direct familiarity with formal planning processes through schooling, careers, or engagement in local politics tend to intervene in ways that are clearly informed by this knowledge. And where they lack a professional background, DIY urban designers often seek information from official sources in order to strengthen and legitimate their interventions.

In many cases, both the idea to intervene and the model for how to do so were also inspired by learning—usually via the internet—about something similar that others had created. The DIY bike lane painters I spoke to in Los Angeles and Mexico City, for instance, all said their actions were a response to their city's lack of such infrastructure, which, as cyclists, they experienced firsthand. Yet they also invariably reported that they were directly inspired to paint their own lanes by Toronto's Urban Repair Squad, who had begun doing so a few years earlier and posted descriptions and pictures online. Joe and his neighbors' efforts to slow traffic and foster community life around their intersection in LA likewise responded to a visible need with an inspired solution. In this case, Eco-Village residents learned directly from the Portland-based

Painted intersections. At left, one of Mark Lakeman's projects, in the Sunnyside neighborhood of Portland, Oregon, which began as a DIY effort in 1996 and resulted in a city-approved plaza in 2001. At right, a similar effort inspired by his work, right down to the colors, created by volunteers with the support of local businesses and the city's Department of Transportation in Baltimore's Hamilton area in 2011. Photos by the author.

architect and organizer Mark Lakeman and created crosswalks, murals, and other design elements in the style of the "intersection repair" projects that Lakeman has pioneered in Oregon. Similar traffic-calming and community-building efforts through DIY intersection redesigns can be seen in Baltimore, Seattle, and other cities—often now with quite official backing—and developing a shared aesthetic.

Beyond immediate fixes, however, many do-it-yourselfers I spoke to seemed less clear about their long-term objectives or wider impacts. The intended outcomes of these actions vary widely, from the simple and place-specific (improve this street, repurpose that phone booth, brighten up those vacant lots) to more ambiguously inspiring others to see and think differently about the urban landscape and perhaps take actions to improve it themselves. But while they differ in the scope of the impacts they imagine for their projects, without fail they expressed confidence that what they are doing is good, needed, and filling a void where the city (or property owner, or whoever should be responsible) has dropped the ball.

If stepping up where the city has slouched is a motivation, then, would DIY urban designers *prefer* the city to do it? My respondents were divided on this and seemed fairly internally conflicted as individuals too. Many of the people responsible for what I have described as "aspirational urbanism" projects are more or less by definition calling for something to be done formally. A project by the Los Angeles group Heavy Trash in 2000, "announcing" a new imagined subway line with eight "Future Station Location" signs along the 15-mile would-be route, explicitly intended to spur the city to action on mass transit, much like the faux-official park proposal described above. (And, while the hypothetical park did not end up displacing the very real condominium plans, it's worth noting that the Los Angeles County Metropolitan Transportation Authority actually is now extending the subway along a long-planned route almost identical to Heavy Trash's fake one.)

In New Orleans, a group of architects and designers called the Hypothetical Development Organization crafted a dozen fantastical but detailed urban development proposals for sites throughout the city. Candy Chang's "I wish this was . . ." sticker campaign there after Hurricane Katrina invited community members to propose their redevelopment ideas directly on vacant properties with stickers. Similarly, during the height of the foreclosure crisis in Phoenix, a woman named Stacey Champion installed a chalkboard on the side of an abandoned building downtown, inviting community members to write their ideas for improving the city. The actual proposals in these cases are development projects of a scale beyond the capacity of an individual DIY intervention, but they make a demand for real change by giving voice to community ideas or simply by acting as if the change is already coming.

A Phoenix resident writes his idea for sustainable urban development in the city on a community chalkboard, created by Stacey Champion in Phoenix's downtown Roosevelt Row neighborhood. Photo by the author, 2011.

Other do-it-yourselfers responsible for pop-up parks, bike infrastructure, and local streetscaping improvements said they would love for the city to be doing a better job, effectively so they would not have to. "I wish the city would just do it," explained a woman who helped craft some guerrilla "Bicycle Boulevard" signage for a popular cycling route in Los Angeles. "I like when the city actually helps you to do the thing, and it doesn't have to be all activist-y." A group of neighbors in East LA who converted a dangerous alleyway behind their homes into a pedestrian-friendly community space (complete with murals, lighting, a basketball hoop, and brightly-painted mobile planters to block traffic), debated whether to continue the effort in adjacent alleys or whether "we should do this much and then the city should fix it."

However, as another guerrilla lane-striper affiliated with the LA Department of DIY put it, "We have the paint, we have the stencil, why wait for the city to do it?" I found widespread frustration with the bureaucracy of planning processes and a common feeling that the city does not or would not get it right anyway, so it is better when "the people" do it. Joe recounted the experience that led to Eco-Village residents taking matters into their own hands:

> We actually pushed the city to fund a traffic-calming project in this neighborhood, and we helped write the application, we did community meetings out in the street to get people's input. In 2001 it was funded, and it wasn't built until like [2008], and it was, frankly, built really badly as far as I'm concerned—I mean there was no crosswalks, there's only two legs of the intersection that actually have handicapped access, like they left out one-third of a T-intersection? I mean, there's just all this stuff that the city just doesn't do, routinely, that's so obvious to me.

Going further, many of those I spoke with promoted the idea that the unauthorized aspect of the action is important in itself. Joe put it this way: "It appeals to me a lot to get a bunch of friends together and just do something, and do it in an open, creative way. Don't wait for anybody to give you permission." Several do-it-yourselfers told me they would like to see a more "open" city in general, in which everyone is inspired to step up and make needed improvements. A few do-it-yourselfers with more radical political orientations included language of revolutionary transformation in their broader motivations as well.

And for some, of course, doing it yourself is also more fun. One man, responsible for stenciling a series of bicycle share-the-lane symbols called "sharrows" on a long stretch of boulevard in Northeast Los Angeles, spoke to me at length about the serious need for better bicycle infrastructure, his frustration with politicians, and how much more effective DIY actions could be, before summarizing the more pleasurable motivation to act illegally as well:

> I can get $20 and a bunch of old paint and some friends and we like fuck shit up and it's going to be funny, it's going to be great. We're all going to feel that little buzz and nervousness in maybe we're going to get caught and arrested.

As with Joe, Jordan, and the various folks with professional day jobs who described the thrill of almost getting arrested while painting bike lanes, or the freedom they felt throwing seeds over a chain link fence to spread wildflowers in a vacant lot, there is a joyful element of release, excitement, and creative accomplishment in these acts. Ethnographer Jack Katz (2008) described a similar sentiment in the motivation of some juvenile lawbreakers seeking "sneaky thrills."

A series of thoughts from one do-it-yourselfer from Los Angeles summed up the motivations and inspirations that I heard in many of my interviews, as she explained how she and her partner (both professional industrial designers) started making DIY improvements like the SignChair, a folding seat that attaches to existing street signs:

> We were just kind of looking into ways that we could make the street more comfortable for pedestrians. [ . . . ] I mean for me it's not really about whether it's authorized or non-authorized. I think I was just raised to believe that whatever you do in your life you should be helping other people. [ . . . ] I think for us to expect and wait and hope for the city to do something like this is unrealistic. And it's fun for us to try to participate in making and shaping our own neighborhood!

So DIY urbanism is largely motivated by a desire to improve one's surroundings oneself, without waiting for permission, out of both civic responsibility and a sense of creative enjoyment. Yet across all of these motivations, justifications, and goals, the decision to make interventions like these also implies a sense of self-entitlement. It involves a value judgment of some neglect or deficiency or opportunity in a space that the do-it-yourselfer hopes to address, and an eagerness to make changes to the community based in large part on his or her own preferences. At a minimum, "we're not hurting anybody" is a pretty common sentiment among everyone I spoke with, and yet from Jordan's advertising removal to the installation of signage or street furniture, one person's improvement may well be another's inconvenience, vandalism, or unwelcome intrusion. At an extreme, what one of my respondents called his "DIY urban planning" effort involved removing a bus stop entirely from the street outside his Seattle home after the city ignored his pleas to place a trash can there.

Jordan has experienced firsthand the difference in opinion about his efforts to remove illegal advertising from New York City streets: "Bloomberg should be like 'Awesome! Thank God I didn't have to send the anti-vandal squad after these dudes, you guys took it upon yourselves!' Instead, nine people are arrested." Deborah, the woman behind a mass planting of flower seeds in Brooklyn, was surprised that her effort, conceived as a "gift" to her adopted community, was met with a critical tone among some long-time residents who questioned whether a neighborhood newcomer had any right to organize a beautification effort and connected her project to deeper concerns and resentments about gentrification.

These examples—and especially the last one—bring to light another fundamental component of DIY urban design contributions: the specific community contexts in which they occur. I documented projects in all types of places, from leafy streets in suburban Los Angeles County, to isolated vacant lots in New Orleans' Central City, to busy avenues in Midtown Manhattan. Some interventions were effectively citywide and nonspecific, such as Jordan's advertising removal or the Urban Repair Squad's posting of green "bikes allowed" stickers in every Toronto subway station. Many others are undertaken in quite particular locations to address quite particular problems—for instance, the Scum River Bridge with which the book opened, or the public park "announced" atop a site where condos were planned.

On balance, however, the most common factor in a project's location seems simply to be relative proximity to the home or workplace of its creator. These, in turn, are frequently in or near the sorts of rapidly changing urban neighborhoods where we might expect the young, creative types most often responsible for these acts to be living. The "Book Booth" described above, for instance, is just down the block from the gallery that Amy and her partner own, in the currently trendy (though also historically artsy) Los Angeles neighborhood of Highland Park. Richard Reynolds, a London advertising professional noted for jump-starting the "guerrilla gardening" movement in 2004, began outside his own apartment building in up-and-coming Elephant and Castle. And Brooklyn's Bedford-Stuyvesant neighborhood, where Deborah organized her unexpectedly controversial "seed bombing" effort, is a current poster child for gentrification in New York City.

In fact, DIY urban design is frequently found in newly hip and gentrifying neighborhoods rather than in the impoverished inner-city "ghettos" or derelict postindustrial districts one might think of as the more visible victims of neglect and disinvestment, where informal improvements should ostensibly be most needed. Among the exceptions, a group of connected projects in California offers an interesting counterpoint: a series of seats, planters, and general gathering spaces that the architect Steve Rasmussen Cancian has helped organize in parts of Oakland and Los Angeles are largely initiated, designed, and built by longtime residents with the explicit goal of improving the neighborhood while discouraging gentrification. (I return to Steve's community-engaged work at length in later chapters.)

Finally, it is apparent that DIY urban design, as a practice and cultural phenomenon, overlaps in complex and increasingly important ways with formal urban planning and economic development processes. On the one hand, this very often involves interventions aimed explicitly at providing streetscape elements that could, at least in principle, be the very things the city would install; most do-it-yourselfers view themselves as helping the city in this way. Professional design experience, technical skills, and knowledge of planning and academic urbanism influence many DIY projects from conceptualization to implementation. At the same time, however, I found a surprising amount of cross-pollination in the other direction as well, as the aesthetics and tactics of DIY urban design have become an inspiration for mainstream planning trends, with some problematic (and largely overlooked) implications for urban spaces.

• • •

These primary observations about DIY urban design provoke a number of further questions for social science and for the policy, planning, and design professions, many of which will be addressed in the chapters to come. Perhaps most important though, we can see how these actions can have at once daily and long-term implications for the communities in which they occur. From seemingly innocuous efforts to plant flowers in a vacant lot to the installation of immediately impactful signage and streetscape infrastructure, DIY urban design actions do not occur in a vacuum. By definition, they happen in public space or on someone else's property, potentially costing landowners or taxpayers money and impacting anyone in the surrounding area. Certainly the characteristics of many do-it-yourselfers I studied (often members of the "creative class"), their goals (making creative, functional improvements where they see an unmet need), and the places they act (urban areas experiencing conditions of uneven investment and development, in which they may not be longtime residents) portend possibilities of overreaching. So who benefits and who does not? Do DIY interventions present a cost to local governments and an implicit challenge to their legitimacy, or a "free lunch" of civic benefits and even economic development potential? Are they novel avenues of popular citizenship and democratic participation in planning and placemaking, or expressions of the priorities of a relatively privileged few? How might communities and authorities respond? These are questions to be addressed in the coming pages, and the answers, of course, are far from black and white.

This chapter has introduced DIY urban design as a new way of understanding the unauthorized alteration of the built environment—a subject that most scholars in sociology have viewed as either self-centered vandalism or self-expression, or politicized tactics of radical protest and critical resistance. In and of itself, the concept of DIY urban design offers a more complete understanding of unauthorized urban space intervention. I also described some preliminary observations about who do-it-yourself urban designers are, why they choose to act informally, and in what contexts. I then briefly discussed some of the important further implications that will be explored in the remainder of the study. The next chapter begins this deeper problematizing of DIY urban design by connecting the phenomenon to the urban policy contexts that I argue it both responds and contributes to.

3

# Individualizing Civic Responsibility

## DIY Urban Design in the Help-Yourself City

B uses are essential components of most mass transit systems (in many places they are the defining or only components), and, despite some obvious limitations in terms of speed and capacity, they can be marvelous ways to get around. Americans took a total of more than five billion bus trips in 2015.[1] For many transit-dependent people, whether in sprawling Phoenix, bustling Brooklyn, or Chicago's depopulated South Side, buses are lifelines of mobility and important sites of social interaction. Yet waiting for a bus can be a lonely, anxiety-producing, even dangerous part of urban life.* And it is rarely a comfortable one. Standing peering up a street or refreshing a smartphone app in the blazing sun or blowing snow hoping for a bus is frustrating enough, only made worse by the usual lack of shelter or place for anyone to sit.[2] But if a frustrated community member is likely powerless to make a city bus come any more frequently, she might be able to build a place to sit.

Perhaps it is no surprise that among the most common types of DIY urban design intervention is the installation of benches, chairs, and other pieces of street furniture for sitting in public places. Many cities lack for such seating in official form. Even at bus stops, where large numbers of

---

* A simple internet search for "killed while waiting for bus" reveals just how tragically common a circumstance this is for would-be bus patrons standing at the roadside, whether as targets of assault or victims of vehicular homicide. A search I performed in 2017 yielded 990 results.

A homemade bench installed at a bus stop in Oakland by Larry Davis and the group Hood Builders in 2012. Photo by the author.

people should be expected to gather and wait, often there is nothing more than a sign on a pole, casting a narrow shadow in the hot sun, providing no shelter from the rain or snow. Even in America's older, denser cities such as New York, rightly assumed to do better than the American average in accommodating their large numbers of pedestrians, sidewalk seating can be hard to find. What's more, the benches, bus stop shelters, and other such streetscape elements that do exist are often managed by private interests and designed with public use value as a secondary consideration to functions like security or advertising. Some are even designed to make them less inviting to people: so-called bum-proof benches, for instance, can be found in numerous iterations around the world, all expertly intended to make them uncomfortable for sleeping, skateboarding, or just sitting too long.[3] In some cases street furniture is avoided altogether, even removed, as a preferred alternative to enabling its use—and the use of the larger area—by unwanted interlopers, especially the adolescent, poor, or unhoused.

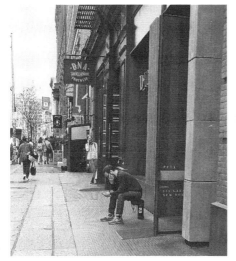

Street Seats. At left, a New York man grabs a seat on a fire department stand pipe in SoHo. At right, a similar stand pipe designed not to be sat upon. Photos by the author, 2016.

The sociologist and urban design thinker William H. Whyte (1980) thought that the fundamental quality of any urban space should be defined first and foremost by the presence of comfortable places for people to sit. The absence of street seating at bus stops reflects at once the retreat of cash-strapped city governments from traditional service provision and the real-location of these responsibilities to the private interests that have become increasingly common in American urban policy over the past half century. It also provides an example of the sort of everyday failings of public space and infrastructure to which DIY urban designers frequently respond.

This chapter focuses on the significance of mainstream urban planning and development policies—and common instances of their failings—as both physical and theoretical context for understanding DIY urbanism. I use an analysis of interventions focused on improving access and streetscape conditions for pedestrians, and especially those around bus stops, as a lens through which to consider the everyday impacts and perceptions of insensitive, uneven urban design.

## FAILURES OF LATE MODERN PLANNING

Although informal urbanism is as old as cities themselves, most of those unauthorized urban space interventions of interest here emerged in their contemporary forms within a short time of one another less than half a century ago. Site-specific "culture jamming" interventions, which prank popular culture or intentionally disrupt everyday life, were pioneered by the Situationists in the 1960s. Modern graffiti writing started in Philadelphia and New York around 1968 before going worldwide. "Guerrilla gardening" (as such) first appeared in 1974 in the company of squatting and other place-based protest on New York's Lower East Side and has flourished ever since, with the term reinvigorated in the early 2000s. The unauthorized installation of public seating and the repurposing of things like magazine racks builds on a number of urban experiments in the late 1960s and the rise of interventionist art in the 1970s; do-it-yourselfers also connect these activities to street art and "place hacking" trends that have been prominent since the 1990s. While people have doubtless been altering official signs for as long as they have existed, the earliest example I found of anyone posting a fake but official-looking sign "announcing" a hoped-for civic improvement is as recent as 2000. Most creators of DIY traffic signage, bike lanes, and crosswalks pointed to seminal examples from just the last 10 or 15 years.

One might speculate a number of explanations for this rise, or reinvigoration, of DIY urbanism. One thing that is clear is that it has coincided with a period of profound changes in American cities. These are changes that I believe provoke and even enable people to take local placemaking into their own hands. On the one hand, the early 1960s saw a powerful spark of social consciousness around urban design in the United States and Britain. Reacting to the modernist and autocentric planning of those years, influential planning scholars such as Kevin Lynch, public intellectuals like Lewis Mumford, and informed activists like Jane Jacobs brought their concerns into popular conversation and started a lively public debate. Jacobs's impassioned outsider approach has been credited with opening "a floodgate of community activism" around an issue that had, in the words of New York radio journalist Philip Quarles (2012), "previously been considered a subject only fit to be pronounced upon by disciples of Le Corbusier and the like." Yet despite a few notable successes by the activists, conditions on the ground largely worsened.

Piling on to the postwar sociospatial patterns that were already damaging many American cities (white flight, suburbanization, "urban renewal"), by the early 1970s the world had entered an era of profound global economic restructuring. Manufacturing industry collapsed in urban centers and the economy contracted under stagflation. What the urbanist Neil Brenner (2004) has termed "spatial Keynesianism" in the organization and management of urbanization gave way to a more desperate and market-driven form of governance and planning: local governments followed their national counterparts into what is often described as the neoliberal period.[4] The term is far from perfect—it is imprecise and ideologically loaded—nor does it capture all the urban conditions that define this era, some of which long predate the 1970s. Yet an appreciation of the spatial consequences of economic restructuring and market-driven policymaking is essential to understanding the state of American cities in the early 21st century because these processes have had especially visible impacts on urban space and society. Every stage of this late modern political-economic drama has played out in metropolitan areas, from the austerity and privatization imposed on New York City in the 1970s (and on Detroit in 2014) to the megadevelopments, municipal bankruptcies, gentrification, and vast inequality of investment in public infrastructure seen in cities throughout the United States today.

Put simply, with an increase in inter-urban competition for capital investment, economic growth and development became what the geographer and planning scholar Mark Purcell (2008: 2) describes bluntly as "the dominant imperative for urban policy and planning," with the niceties of social services and democratic decision making often taking a back seat. The result is what David Harvey, Neil Smith, and other Marxist urban theorists have called "uneven geographical development"—in everyday terms, a help-yourself city in which one locale sees an intense infusion of growth, infrastructure, commercialization, and other investment, while another sees neglect and abandonment by state and private actors alike. The exchange values of even the tiniest spaces become operationalized for development advertising or other productive purposes. Meanwhile, many long-segregated and underprivileged low-income and racial minority neighborhoods, which might once at least have been economically and demographically stable, have been gutted by lack of employment and investment. In time of course, these "abandoned" spaces may too find themselves ripe for "rediscovery" as new frontiers of financial investment (not to mention cultural exploitation), often becoming spaces of exclusive new growth at the expense, once again, of the underprivileged.[5]

Although ideologically neoliberalism features the retreat of the state in favor of an unregulated free market, the reality is quite concerted state facilitation of market dominance through policy. At the level of urban governance, policymakers have handed increasing responsibility to private interests even as they are still looked to by capital to provide the large-scale infrastructure and political order needed to facilitate commerce.[6] Where the state has yielded responsibility, the reins of authority have simply been decentralized to developers, advertising companies, wealthy homeowners associations, and other elites. In 1995, for instance, the *New York Times* could report that "the fastest growing residential communities in the nation are private and usually gated, governed by a thicket of covenants, codes and regulations."[7]

Appearing in tandem with this period of economic restructuring and deregulatory policy, DIY urban design interventions can be understood as in many ways reactions to *and* products of these structures and processes. It is at all extremes of uneven development—privatization, commodification, gentrification, disinvestment—and those in between that DIY urban designers seem often to find their calling. Guerrilla gardening, hypothetical development ideas, and spontaneous street improvements are direct responses to the neglect of some spaces, while advertising removal, aspirational policy proposals, and pro-pedestrian interventions react to the perceived hyper-commodification, enclosure, or insensitivity of others.

Of course, it is not just the spatial consequences of market-fundamentalist urban policy per se to which DIY urban design responds. Planning that favors exchange value over use value—economic development over public benefits—certainly predates the neoliberal era (it was no less prominent for much of the 19th century, for instance). So too does urban design that privileges the automobile over human scale, and the concerns of pedestrians and cyclists are central motivations behind many DIY improvements. Nor should the neglect of transit services, sidewalk amenities, or other basic socially attuned urban infrastructure be linked only to capitalist political-economies; many actually existing socialist societies have been famous for poor services, infrastructure, and urban investment as well.

In truth, many of the planning tropes and resulting spatial conditions that do-it-yourself urban designers react to are better characterized as legacies of a variety of ideologies, interests, and planning best-practices (not to mention simple oversights) that colluded to define 20th-century urban design. And in the early 21st century they have even begun to show some signs of shift: many cities now view select public goods, including cycling and pedestrian infrastructure, as more worthwhile than they did in the past—however unabashedly opportunistic and limited in scope this change may still be. Nonetheless, for the sake of interpreting the structural conditions shaping American urban policy and planning of the late 20th and early 21st centuries, and indeed the language used by many of the do-it-yourselfers I spoke to, terms like "neoliberalism" and "uneven development" can be potent and helpful shorthands. For the era in which these conditions are dominant—*this* era, dating from the 1970s but very much persistent in advanced forms today—I also use the less-loaded term "late modern." Whatever name we give it, I argue that DIY urban design acts in response to, yet is in many ways also a *part of*, these conditions of the help-yourself city.

In the rest of this chapter, I present cases illustrating the symptoms of what do-it-yourselfers view as failures or inadequacies of late modern urban policy and planning, including the privatization of service provision, the commodification of public spaces, and the general nonresponsiveness or impotence of local government. An overwhelming majority of all DIY urban design projects that I documented respond to what the makers see as neglect and spatial inequality or overdevelopment and privatization. And they reveal diverse informal local reactions to these conditions.[†] I focus on a trio of cases that concern bus stops and outdoor advertising.

## DON'T LET THE MARKET DRIVE THE BUS

The bus shelter is a kind of prism through which we can read the uneven modernization of everyday life and the changing priorities of society. It is no longer primarily a functional piece of architecture; it is a marketing opportunity.

Joe Moran (2005: 7)

In Los Angeles, as in many cities, amenities such as seating and shelter at public bus stops are provided through contracts with outdoor advertising firms.[8] Generally, the firm—the largest in the case of LA, actually being a partnership called CBS Decaux—has a contract with the city to place and maintain a certain number of benches, shelters, and other pieces of street furniture in exchange for the right to use them as platforms for advertisements. The city pays nothing for the infrastructure and, in addition, receives a share of revenues generated by the advertisements, an appealing arrangement for a cash-strapped transit agency. In Los Angeles, while each installation must be approved, there is no contractual stipulation of how they should be distributed in general; the responsibility for determining their particular locations is divided roughly among the Bureau of Street Services, fifteen local city council offices, and the advertising partnership.

---

† Other common focuses of DIY urban design include the perceived failure of local governments to provide public spaces, green spaces, and adequate bicycle infrastructure, all of which can likewise be understood as reactions to the same broad discontent with mainstream planning policy. All of these topics receive attention elsewhere in the book. In the table in Appendix 1, a column indicates the conditions that each project responds to.

Outdoor advertising firms have a clear interest in placing their ads in certain types of places: in CBS Decaux's own words, "the best locations," "main upscale neighborhoods," and near major entertainment venues and universities. Due to a combination of the city's cumbersome permitting process, slow-moving council offices, and the firm's prioritization of revenue-generating locations, relatively few shelters have received permits or been installed anywhere in Los Angeles, and the agreement with CBS Decaux has nearly collapsed. In areas where there is less advertising revenue to be made, there may be no seating or shelter at bus stops at all. In 2011, when a smaller firm with exclusive rights to manage some 6,000 bus stop benches was denied a new contract, it began removing "its" benches altogether.[9]

The absence of street furniture is especially notable throughout much of predominantly low-income and transit-dependent South Los Angeles. This includes an area around St. Michael's Catholic Church, about seven miles south of Downtown Los Angeles, where, in 2008, parishioners and other community members worked together to create their own series of wooden benches, chairs, and planters at major intersections and bus stops. The multisite project, aided by a local environmental group and under the guidance of the landscape architect Steve Cancian, aimed to build benches and planters in the style of Cancian's "urban living rooms" concept (first developed with another low-income community up north in Oakland) to respond to the lack of public seating.

When I met the Reverend Msgr. David O'Connell, pastor of St. Michael's, at his church, he spent a long time describing the various symptoms of crime, disinvestment, and civic buck-passing that he views as widespread there in the heart of what is colloquially still widely referred to as South Central. Arriving by bicycle on a warm spring afternoon, I observed wide avenues busy with buses and speeding cars and lined with discount stores and vacant lots. There were few mature trees or shelters of any kind on the sidewalk, despite the presence of more pedestrians than in many parts of Los Angeles. (In the summer, it is not uncommon to see people standing in the tiny slivers of shade provided by lampposts, shifting occasionally to stay in the sundial's shadow as they wait for a bus.) I also observed a temporary shelter made from a blanket tied between a small tree and a shopping card by a person camped out with his belongings.

Father David is a kindly Irishman with a white beard and an easy smile, now in his late-60s. Though originally from County Cork, and still in possession of its lilt, he has worked in LA's archdiocese since he was ordained there in 1979. As I walked the streets around the church with him, he told me it had long been a goal to "get some kind of improvements—small things you know, but to get some improvements in this neighborhood, so it has a lived-in feel." And so, as was the case with other informal "urban living rooms" I visited in East LA and Oakland, community members organized days on which dozens of people of all ages came together to build and paint new seats and planters for their neighborhood streets.

The results have not been perfect. In one location the benches proved problematic, attracting vandals and drunken loiterers, Father David said, and had to be removed. (Interestingly, this is a frequent concern faced by officially sanctioned street seating as well—loitering, vandalism, and other "misuse" are regularly given by transit authorities as reasons for removing benches.) But others became small symbols of community initiative and pride. Walking and cycling through the neighborhood, and even riding in Father David's car on a personal tour, I could see that even after half a decade, many of the installations were still in place and getting frequent use from people waiting for buses. "They make it a bit pleasanter, you know?" Father David said.

People waiting at a bus stop make use of two of the many benches and other sidewalk furniture installations built and placed around South Los Angeles by community members in 2010. Photo by the author, 2011.

The lack of street seating (like auto-oriented planning in general) is an issue throughout Southern California. Seven miles northwest, in a more middle class part of West Los Angeles, a local couple responded to the lack of seating in their neighborhood by designing several pieces of street furniture that integrate into the existing infrastructure. Being professional industrial designers and product developers, Ken Mori and Jenny Lang designed their "SignChair" to affix to standard perforated street sign posts; the "SignBench" screws in between the existing supports of something larger, like a freeway on-ramp sign.

Ken and Jenny's interventions came out of their mutual interest in doing projects together and taking responsibility for often-neglected pedestrian spaces in Los Angeles, recognizing what they view as a real need for seating that the authorities responsible are unlikely ever to rectify. As Ken put it:

> [The place where we built] SignBench is just down the street from us, we'd walked by it many times. And on weekends there's a little fruit cart vendor, and one time we bought some fruit and we wanted to just eat it right away, but had nowhere to sit. And so we thought, wouldn't it be great if there was just a bench right here so we could sit and enjoy it? So it kind of comes out of just a necessity of things.

The highly relative necessity of needing to sit and eat something "right away" notwithstanding, the fact of the matter is that there is actually more street seating in this part of West Los Angeles than near St. Michael's, despite South LA being more transit-dependent.[‡] That said, it is nonetheless true that there are still long stretches, including bus stops, without any seating along the eight-lane, usually high-speed thoroughfare on which the SignBench sits (which is not to mention the side streets, some of which are also fairly large and host bus lines but have even fewer benches).

Though theirs is a more economically comfortable part of the city than South LA, Ken and Jenny were attuned to numerous symptoms of civic disinterest in their streets, describing piles of trash, unkempt sidewalks, and their unanswered emails seeking fixes and improvements from authorities.

---

‡ Surveying one mile in each direction from the corner at which the SignBench was installed (effectively two miles of Venice Boulevard from the San Diego Freeway to Lincoln Boulevard) in the summer of 2012, I found a bus stop with at least one bench on average every quarter of a mile. My parallel survey of a two-mile stretch of Vermont Avenue, a comparably major street around St. Michael's Cathedral in South LA, found an average of fewer than one bench per half-mile in each direction. I did observe more informal seating in that area, from the "urban living rooms" described above to folding chairs, milk crates, and other improvised seating that people bring out to the front of businesses or wherever they are hanging out on the street.

The SignBench, designed by Ken Mori and Jenny Liang, attached to the perforated posts below a freeway sign on the West Side of Los Angeles, 2009. Photos by Ken Mori.

"Because the city [government] is not walking around on our corner, you know?" Jenny observed. "And even if they did know, and even if we could ask them, it took them three weeks to get the trash can! We're gonna be placing responsibility with the city?"

An Asian American woman in her 30s, Jenny has professional design training and considerable understanding of urban policy and planning at a systemic level. As she sees it, "The city keeps things in order more in some places than in others." Especially in terms of the pedestrian experience, she noted the differences between "the nice part of the city" (she referred here to the relatively affluent and famously progressive urban beach town of Santa Monica, where, she said, "it's awesome to be a pedestrian") and "poorer" places where "there's a lot of bus stops, a lot of people using it [. . . and] a lot of people walking" but "trash everywhere," few receptacles, and unmaintained pavement that looks like a "crummy mess." And, again, no place for people to sit.

This sort of explicit recognition of uneven investment and development across different parts of the city was quite common in my interviews with DIY urban designers. Another creator of DIY bus stop seating, a man named Larry in Oakland, compared his predominantly low-income neighborhood known as the Bottoms to other parts of the city:

If you go downtown you'll see all bus stops. If you go to [affluent] Rockridge, you'll see more bus stops than you will out here. [ . . . ] You don't want your kids sitting on the concrete—I know I don't want my kids sitting on the concrete—as dirty as this stuff is, but if you go downtown and look at the sidewalks there, the sidewalks are a lot cleaner because they actually have resources to clean them. But they won't bring any of that stuff down here.

Ken and Jenny, like dozens of other DIY urban designers I spoke to, perceived clear and simple needs in the physical environments of their communities. Conscious of the history and ongoing economic realities that make official remedies to these problems unlikely, they acted on their own to address them. Another community member even stepped up to address the crumbling pavement as well. Ken explained: "The sidewalk didn't get maintained, so somebody poured their own concrete. It looked totally like an amateur just poured concrete, like they wanted to make this thing not this crummy mess or a dirt patch, so they made their own little sidewalk for one little section."

Jenny went on to frame the overall situation quite explicitly in terms of urban governance influenced by market-based concerns:

There's not a big business reason to invest in the pedestrians in this neighborhood. I just think it would be a huge battle to do it. And kind of a small battle, considering like, seriously they're talking about defunding their school system and all these people got laid off. To be like, we want a chair so people can be more comfortable on the street—you know, it would be great if the city did it but I think for us to expect and wait and hope for the city to do something like this is unrealistic.

Several conclusions stand out from these examples of DIY street seating. First, even though theirs is a wealthier part of the city than South LA, Jenny knows it is unlikely to receive attention in terms of urban design for pedestrians. Planning in Los Angeles—and especially West LA—has long been oriented toward cars. Places like Santa Monica, which Jenny rightly pointed out for its pedestrian promenade and generally pleasant, walkable downtown streets, remain the exception and tend to be driven as often by commercial interests and private developers as by progressive planning policies.[10] Jenny also placed these local deficiencies in the context of the enormous economic challenges that the city faces in its ability to fund other public services, suggesting that seating may well be a comparatively low priority.

This raises a question of whether streetscape improvements in general should be thought of as needs or simply as amenities. Sociologically, we can already see how the answer is highly site-specific and context-dependent.

Where a larger number of people depend on public transportation and their numbers include the elderly or the disabled, street seating, especially at bus stops, seems as necessary as transit itself; in other circumstances it may be less so. This distinction, however relative, is important to our assessment of the potential physical and cultural impacts of DIY urban design interventions.

## THE OTHER SIDE OF THE COIN: COMMODIFICATION OF PUBLIC SPACE

As in Los Angeles, many parts of New York City also lack public street seating. Until the early 2010s, when a culture shift in the Department of Transportation led to some new efforts at public seating (see Chapter 6), nearly every bench in the city that was not in a park was either private property, a thinly disguised security fixture, or, again, part of a bus shelter run by an advertising company for the primary purpose of making money. Do-it-yourselfers in the city have responded to this with things like the "chair-bombing" effort by the Brooklyn-based collective DoTank mentioned in the previous chapter and similar projects by others throughout the city, creating seating that they say is simply for sitting. One person I spoke to even put chairs on subway platforms to provide more seating down there. At the same time, the actions of another New Yorker with whom we have become familiar address a different concern related to the privatization of bus stops and other infrastructure: the use of public streets for advertising.

Jordan Seiler began his personal campaign against outdoor advertising in 2000, when he first considered how much of the visible space of New York City streets is taken up by commercial messages. A white man in his early 30s, he has himself received summonses from the city for putting up illegal street art. Feeling that art like this is more in the public spirit and has "more right" to be there than paid advertisements, Jordan views the dominance of advertising as "in direct conflict with properties of public space" and a misuse of public property that limits people's ability to engage with their surroundings. He noted:

> It commoditizes and monopolizes outdoor advertising and media space, and by doing so competes with all the other sorts of non-authorized uses of public space—graffiti, street art, random scrawl, posters for your lost cat, band posters, all those things. [ . . . ] Wiping out all other forms of communication is what their M.O. is because, straight up you know, the only message should be

"*the* message" with advertising, and all other forms of communication should be squashed and immediately removed.

Sitting in a Brooklyn bar with me one night before we headed out to realize some of his advertising removal in the neighborhood, Jordan almost sounded sorry for the city when describing this state of affairs. He continued, noting "one of the more fucked up things" (and one of the more revealing) about this whole situation:

> The city sells it all for so cheap! You know, CBS Outdoor is a huge, *huge* advertising company, making millions of dollars off of just straight up platform advertising in the New York City subway system, and yet the MTA is under immense pressure to find money from anywhere, laying off station agents, ruining lives, all sorts of problems. And you would think that the city, interested in serving the people, would say, "Alright, you know CBS it's been a good run, but I think we can make more money on our own, and we're just gonna take this back." You know, but that's not how the model of how we run governments and how we run cities works. [ . . . ] CBS is making *oodles* of money, and our transit system is in like total disrepair, we're millions of dollars in debt. Why are we firing station agents, cutting services, and not going to the people who are making all the money off the services that the MTA could be offering themselves?! I mean, I don't know what it cost in the recent cuts to cut all that service back, the toll wages and stuff, but it was probably in the line of $30 million, $20 million, something like that. I guarantee you CBS is making way more than that *a month* off of the hundreds of thousands of advertisements they're associated with in the New York City public transportation system.[11]

It is also the case that, while the city has sold these advertising contracts to some companies, they are in Jordan's view failing to crack down on the illegal advertising that pervades the city as well. This includes everything from large billboards without permits to the nearly ubiquitous posters, bills, fliers, and stickers known as "wild posting" that promotional companies place on walls, fences, and other surfaces throughout the city. Viewing such advertising as urban blight, Jordan gathered a group of like-minded volunteers to take action for themselves: "We went out and painted them all white in about an hour and a half, took over 20,000 square feet of advertising in one fell swoop." He has even tried to get workers that he's caught in the act arrested, and their employers fined. Jordan is confident he is doing the right thing in painting over the ads, "really doing good and really doing the city's job for it." In this case, where the official word of law has failed, it is essentially unauthorized advertiser versus unauthorized

Jordan Seiler installs a piece of anonymous artwork in place of a corporate advertisement he has just removed from a subway station entrance in Queens in 2005. Photo by Adam Amengual.

do-it-yourselfer: vigilante versus vigilante—one driven by profit, the other by an ideal of an ad-free world, both with their own ideas about the appropriate uses of public space.

Jordan's (and others') advertising removal efforts differ in important ways from DIY projects like the placement of unauthorized street furniture that I saw in Los Angeles and from many other less controversial instances of informal urbanism in which there is ostensibly "no victim" (though as we saw, even one of the seating areas built by Father David's South LA parishioners had an unintended negative impact on the community and was removed by its creators). The word "vigilante" does seem to apply better here than in those other instances. Jordan's efforts are similar in both action and (perversely) in spirit to those of anti-graffiti vigilantes that have been documented in cities around the United States by the filmmaker Max Good[12]—even if Jordan feels graffiti is an important part of the urban fabric and that it's the advertising that is the vandalism in need of removal. Back in Los Angeles, for example, a man named Joe Connelly (who goes by the moniker "Graffiti Guerrilla") has since the early 1990s been buffing out graffiti in the mixed-income MidCity district near his home, and even tagging "AMB" (for "all my bitches") on other graffiti crews' work. Graffiti-removing vigilantes have also made headlines in New Orleans and the San Francisco Bay Area.

But from Ken and Jenny to Jordan and Joe, the ideological and motivational common ground is the premise that their unsanctioned actions are needed and warranted because the city should be providing a certain thing (infrastructure, service, aesthetic experience), but is not, and that this failing is a symptom of the very way that the city operates. Do-it-yourselfers tend to understand urban policy, planning, and development processes and assume that signs of urban neglect like vacant lots and defunct phone booths are likely to persist, with no one in particular to hold accountable. They expect the city to ignore the basic maintenance of infrastructure in poorer neighborhoods more than in wealthier ones. They know their Departments of Transportation, strapped for cash and seeking an expedient way to unload some of their maintenance costs, have sold advertising rights to the highest bidder at the expense of equitable social benefit. Jordan laid out for me what he sees as the bigger picture:

> The problem might not be advertising so much as the last 20 years of kind of neoliberal tactics of basically incorporating public authorities and private corporations, [ . . . ] the fact that companies now are providing cities with infrastructure for the exclusive rights to advertising, and therefore cities now have a vested interest in getting rid of all other forms of communication as a way to further monetize the spaces that they're offering these people [ . . . ]
>
> So you have a commodity here. And why would the city provide bus stops when they could sell those rights to somebody else and then they'll build the bus stops? And the problem associated with that is that the city has a responsibility to serve the public, where the advertising company that they've now sold that space to doesn't. And so, as citizens, we can argue with the city and say, well, if the city controls that bus stop then why are there not PSAs [public service announcements] there? And why are there not, you know, forums for artistic communication? And why are there not just general blank boards for all sorts of other like, really kind of small public communications? And the city would sort of have to listen to those things. But once they've sold it off, it's not their problem. [ . . . ] And in doing so they cloud the line between what is commercial and what is public.

Jordan's command of these policy issues, and of some academic literature as well, reflects the level of familiarity with professional and scholarly urbanism that I found common to many do-it-yourselfers, discussed in detail in Chapter 4. Whether or not one agrees with Jordan's politics or his tactics, the connections he makes between the problems he observes and broader urban structural and policy conditions are logical. And his concluding sentiment rings true: the line between public and private space is deeply blurred in the contemporary city.

The vigilante nature of Jordan's efforts also reveals how subjective the value of all DIY urbanism can be. Seating, especially at bus stops, is widely recognized as an important element of an urban street.[13] Yet Jordan's advertising removal and Joe Connelly's graffiti removal are also motivated by a personal aesthetic ideal, shaped by their own personalities and politics. In these cases, the "victims" are advertisers (sometimes illegal ones) or graffiti writers (always illegal, and some of whom in Joe's neighborhood are gang affiliated).§ But "vigilante" is a term that could be applied to *any* do-it-yourselfers who feel morally justified acting outside the formal process to right a perceived wrong.

DIY urban design interventions are, just like official improvements to the streetscape, Janus-faced in their impacts and justifications, able to impress and offend. One more example involving a bus stop takes us a step further into the murky waters of informal improvement efforts that, while no less a response to the perceived inadequacies of the formal system, can hurt as much as they help. This is the curious story of a Seattle resident who removed the bus stop from outside his home.

## GOING TOO FAR? BUS STOP REMOVAL AND OTHER CASES OF "ANTI-SOCIAL" DIY PLANNING

The problem, the Seattle man would explain, was not the bus stop itself but the garbage it attracted. There was no trash can at the stop, which was near his house. With its proximity to a grocery store and shopping center, a huge amount of rubbish piled up regularly on the sidewalk. "Like at first I would clean it up and put it in a garbage bag," explained the man, a white artist in his early 40s named Derek Erdman. "But after a while I got so mad at it that I would just put it in a pile at the bus stop, so that people would have to stand in the garbage." Then, after the city ignored his pleas to place a trash can at the location, he undertook what he called a "DIY urban planning" effort and removed the stop altogether: "I just went out there with a socket wrench one night. It was probably one or two in the morning. And I just unscrewed it—it was so easy to unscrew! And I just lifted it up and I put it in the bushes."

§ Of course, people have been known to remove other things from public spaces that they disagree with as well. In the summer of 2017, anti-racist activists brought down a Confederate war monument in North Carolina as part of a protest in Durham. The act, which at least one report described as a "do-it-yourself removal" of the statue, corresponded to official policies of removing racist symbols in some Southern cities, if not in the same manner that officials and others might prefer (see Astor 2017).

A "before and after" look at the Seattle bus stop removed by nearby resident Derek Erdman in 2012. Photos by Derek Erdman.

Derek's removal of a public bus stop was patently antisocial in impact; the bus soon began passing the block without stopping. Yet he still framed his actions as explicitly in response to the city's apparent failure to provide another basic public service, the trash can:

> We petitioned the city and the Department of Transportation for months to put a garbage can at that bus stop, because what happens is people get food, or they're waiting for the bus after a grocery store trip, and [ . . . ] they just leave the garbage in the bushes or on the ground there. [ . . . ] I mean it makes sense. [ . . . ] I sent a series of emails and made a series of calls. I was always told that someone would get back to me. [ . . . ] And they would never. They're never going to respond to me.

Derek admitted that removing the bus stop was a selfish choice, even if he felt it was a choice forced on him by the city's failure to respond to his requests. "I can see a lot of people, um, being like dismayed by what I did," he said. "Public transportation is pretty important, especially for a certain economic demographic." He said he never asked the city to remove the bus stop—"the bus stop is fine"—just to put in a trash can. Then again, he also feels justified:

> There's another [bus stop] closer to the grocery store, and there's another one like two blocks farther down the street, so it's not like I was putting anyone out terribly. [ . . . ] I mean, if the stops weren't so close, I would have felt bad. And

I guess I do feel a little bad. But not really. [ . . . ] I was punishing the people who littered there. And the other people were gonna have to face that punishment as well unfortunately.

When I asked Derek if he had ever considered putting in a trash can himself, rather than removing the sign, he told me that he had briefly toyed with the idea of installing a simple chicken-wire basket around the signpost, but then realized this would be futile, because the city would never come and pick it up—"it would just overflow." Feeling he had made his point in removing the stop (and removing several temporary fixes brought in by the city in the weeks thereafter as well), once authorities finally reinstalled the sign a couple of months later, he decided he would not remove it again.

Selfishly motivated interventions with potentially harmful impacts on the broader public such as Derek's are, like more civic-minded projects, at once as old as cities and products of contemporary conditions. Derek felt the city had let him down in failing to respond to his seemingly reasonable requests for a trash can, even as he realized he was doing harm by removing the bus stop sign. This is not unlike the decisions sometimes made by transit agencies or their contractors, sometimes at the behest of local merchants, to remove existing seating, shelters, or bus stops altogether to discourage unwanted uses:[14] something or someone at the stop has become a nuisance? Remove the stop. (And again, even Father David and his parishioners removed some of their DIY seating when it attracted an unwelcome element.) Nor did Derek feel especially bad about the inconvenience he knew he was causing, adopting something of a sink or swim attitude.

This self-described "DIY urban planning" project, then, demonstrates how easily one person's improvement can exacerbate the very conditions of neglect that other well-meaning do-it-yourselfers might attempt to resist. And it reminds us that all DIY urban design activities ultimately come down to particular individuals taking the responsibility for shaping the urban streetscape into their own hands and out of the hands of government. In this way, one might argue that they are in fact quintessentially neoliberal actions themselves.

Derek's bus stop removal is at least nuanced, framed as a response to the garbage situation and the city's failure to place a trash can there. There are more extreme examples of what we might call "anti-social" DIY planning interventions. I refer not to workaday vandalism (which has no functional intent or faux-civic form) but rather urban space alterations intentionally affecting the use and function of the streetscape that are motivated by selfish rather than social or civic concerns. For instance, it is common in some cities for anyone who has shoveled snow from a parking space to place an

A parking spot being saved on a street in Brooklyn, 2016. Photo by the author.

old chair, table, or other piece of refuse there when they move their cars in order to "save" the space for themselves.[15] I have observed the practice of "spot-saving" or "dibs" in parts of New York City and Pittsburgh even in summer months, and in parts of California where it never snows.

People have also been known to place trash cans over fire hydrants to disguise the illegality of a parking spot—again I witnessed people doing so in Brooklyn—and to physically remove or obscure Handicapped or No Parking signs for the same reason. In Los Angeles, a San Fernando Valley resident had neighbors and officials on their toes for weeks by repeatedly painting a red curb gray in order to create an extra parking space. (Officials, noting that cars parked in the spot dangerously obstructed visibility for drivers and pedestrians near an adjacent driveway, ultimately triumphed by adding No Parking signs around the spot. But for how long?)

In these cases, as much as the do-it-yourselfers responsible clearly disagree with existing planning and streetscape design in their community, rather than providing an intended social good, their interventions work against safety elements that have been responsibly installed by local authorities. While likely perpetrated by individuals of all socioeconomic statuses and political persuasions, these actions resonate both with the sorts of "above the law" attitudes that we associate with urban elites and with something of a libertarian or anti-government ideology. Indeed, perhaps the best example of just this sort of attitude comes from one of the most famously elite corners of Southern California. Although the state constitution requires coastal property owners to provide for public beach access, this has long been difficult to enforce and intentional violations are commonplace. Homeowners in Malibu have been known to close access ways or make them difficult to find, hiring security guards, and even, as one interviewee explained to me, "putting signage up saying 'private beach'!"[16]

Though brought into stark relief by these actions that many community members (and most do-it-yourselfers I interviewed) find objectionable, the truth is that all DIY urban design activities, by their very nature, have individualistic characteristics. The perceived failings or inadequacies of government are a primary motivation for all of these interventions, and many of my interviewees feel their improvements are more responsive, more efficient, and simply better than what the authorities are capable of. Yet while some interventions (those that are civic-minded and thus meet the full definition of DIY urban design) intend to effectively aid local government, or at least to briefly fill in for it to the benefit of the community, others (those I have referred to as selfish or anti-social) actively work against such interests. DIY urbanism thus responds *and contributes* to the extremes of the so-called neoliberal city: reacting to the inadequacies of government planning and the commodification of public space while at the same time claiming planning and development rights for the individual, in some cases rejecting policy and even privatizing public space. In highlighting ethically unambiguous offenders, anti-social DIY actions reveal just how similar all unauthorized changes to the built environment are to the insensitive planning conditions that many do-it-yourselfers attempt to rectify.

## HELPING OR HURTING?

Whether or not do-it-yourself improvers say so (and in some cases, like Jordan's above, they quite explicitly do), their actions are framed in response to symptoms attributable to the shortcomings of contemporary, market-driven urban planning and development. Yet we can see how they are also, in principle, not too different from the actions of a self-interested corporate contractor or private developer. In either case, a truly democratic planning process would seem to be a low priority.

Indeed, it is important to remember that—considerable evidence of uneven investment and insensitive development notwithstanding—democratic input and equitable community benefits are at least ideally fundamental considerations of official planning. As Purcell (2008: 174) has noted, "even as they operate under the dominant logic of privatization, [planners] retain an explicit and deep commitment to *public* solutions to urban problems."

This is something I found in my interviews with professional planners and designers, who often emphasized that talking to communities and mediating between pro-development politics and the true "highest and best use" was why they joined the field. And they too see these contradictions in DIY interventions. "I am highly supportive of these kinds of grassroots interventions," one New York City planner told me, "but many times they're not representative of the community as a whole." Surely no responsible planner would condone Derek's removal of the bus stop sign near his home (even if they would acknowledge, perhaps, that the city should have placed a trash can there). And we can see from the other examples of selfish alterations, like painting over a red curb, how unauthorized streetscape interventions can work directly against the designs of professional planners, public safety, or the best interests of the community. This underlying concern will continue to dog our understanding of DIY urbanism.

Can the opposite still also be true? Do DIY urban design activities that aim to aid overwhelmed and underfunded public agencies make a positive impact? The evidence suggests that yes, some of them do. Some have even received tacit approval from authorities. "If I could put a bench in every shaded area or something, I would, if I had the money," Ramon Arevalo, chief of Parks and Beaches for the City of Long Beach, California, told me. "We don't have it." But, he continued, "in certain different parks, I've seen people bring their own benches and put them in there. [ . . . ] If it's not unsafe, more power to them." I likewise heard stories of do-it-yourselfers running project ideas by city workers or officials in New York, Chicago, and Pittsburgh and being told to go ahead (but to stop bringing it up!).

This may explain why I found that some DIY benches and other street furniture remain in place for years even at well-trafficked locations like bus stops; they are more likely to be stolen as curiosities than removed by authorities with larger concerns. In contrast to the dangerous painting of a red curb gray, another LA do-it-yourselfer's painting of an unmarked curb red, to prevent cars from obstructing an adjoining bike and pedestrian route, has been untouched by the city. A Los Angeles Department of Transportation planner laid out the difference: in the former case, "it's a safety hazard there because it restricts the sight lines for this one driveway. And I think there's been a couple collisions there"; in the latter, "someone painting something red that wasn't there? I don't know that that would even register with us." The same official spoke supportively of a more prank-like parking intervention as well, in which someone in Hollywood had been stenciling the words "douche parking" on red curbs in that area, "because people in Hollywood always think they're special and they pull up in the red to park there." He said, "we would prioritize anything over painting that stencil red again. Unless someone complained about it or unless a councilman saw it, unless someone took offense at it and wanted us to paint over it red, how's that become a city priority?" Then again, when residents in nearby Beachwood Canyon began painting curbs red in order to discourage tourists from parking there while seeking a view of the Hollywood Sign, their guerrilla tactics became more of an issue.[17] And Joe, the "Graffiti Guerrilla," told me that although the city cannot publicly support him, numerous officials, including a member of the city council, have quietly praised his efforts and conceded that he is more efficient and effective at reducing graffiti in his area than they are.

These admissions from city officials are by no means the mainstream. I was told repeatedly that things like guerrilla bike lanes can essentially never be condoned by a litigation-wary city, and even simple DIY sidewalk seating was dismissed as a nuisance by most officials I interviewed. Nor do these opinions imply official government approval, much less any actual positive outcomes for everyday users. Yet they do suggest that planners recognize the limits of their effectiveness and, however uncomfortably, sometimes acknowledge that informal actors (whether moneyed interests or DIY interventionists) are part of the placemaking process in an era of limited resources and increasing redistribution of service provision and other responsibilities.

Most do-it-yourselfers aim to address what they view as systemic failures of policy, regulation, and economic ideology in their cities. They act without permission but in ways that—whether or not one appreciates the sentiment—intend to "help" the city. However, with the more vigilante do-it-yourselfers in mind—like Jordan, whose efforts respond as much to the civic wrongdoing of private actors as they do to the insufficient action of a hapless local government—how far can this go? We might wonder, to return to Derek in Seattle, if the city just remained entirely out of the picture, never installing a new bus stop after he removed it, then might some other do-it-yourselfer have come and put one in? A back-and-forth of DIY activities begins to seem like a fairly logical reality in the help-yourself city.**

• • •

** As discussed in detail in Chapter 5, such a back-and-forth ensued on one Brooklyn street in 2009 when several cyclists first attempted to repaint a popular bike lane through a predominantly Hasidic area (a bike lane that city officials had recently removed at the Jewish community's request), and the do-it-yourselfers were, in turn, stopped and detained by the neighborhood's informal security force. The vigilante versus vigilante conflict resulted in real arrests and a lingering tension between the Hasidim and the cycling community.

Not so long ago, the argument was being made that the era of unfettered free market capitalism had come to an end, at least ideologically and politically, with the global economic crisis and recession of 2008.[18] Yet if neoliberalism was momentarily out of fashion—and it is true that some of the ideology's most notable proponents and profiteers (Jeffrey Sachs, George Soros) have become vocally critical—less than 10 years later this perspective seems remarkably shortsighted. It has certainly not proven true in the on-the-ground reality of America's cities, where inequality, commodification, gentrification, and uneven development show no signs of relenting. A 2013 *New York Times* article, titled "A Private Boom amid Detroit's Public Blight," declared the city "the most extreme example of a city's dual fates, public and private, diverging."[19] Even the proletarian city bus has gone both neoliberal and DIY, with privately run services ranging from Brooklyn's quasi-informal dollar vans to the Bay Area's exclusive and much-maligned tech company buses.[20] If policies in certain cities at the leading edge of American planning innovation offer hope of more equitable and sustainable priorities entering the mainstream, we must note that even these progressive local governments are still unabashedly pro-development.

Regardless, the issue is more complex than the term "neoliberalism" can convey. It is not always as easy to identify who is responsible for the social ills of an out-of-balance planning process as the do-it-yourselfers quoted above seem to suggest. The emphasis on planning for cars in Los Angeles, a trend viewed as problematic by many do-it-yourselfers (and others), may have some roots in corporate greed and government collusion,[21] but since the mid-20th century it has been as much a matter of mainstream public culture as any diabolical policy or plan. As an LA bicycle planner explained, "A society has a value for something and then the government takes on that value and becomes an instrument of it, you know? So this has been an auto-centric place, this is what people have been wanting."

Most of the other conditions that DIY urban design responds to—outright punitive tactics directed at the poor notwithstanding—are consequences of broad funding crises among public agencies and a slow redistribution of decision-making power and service provision to private and quasi-public organizations with uneven resources and priorities. The party responsible for a neglected piece of property or an insensitively outsized development may be obvious enough too, but less so the causes of maladies such as insufficient signage, greenspace, seating, or maintenance. These things may be effectively systemic, especially in cities facing heightened fiscal austerity. If DIY urban design is, as I argue, a response to but also a product of neoliberalized planning policy, it is in fact a response to and a product of contemporary urban culture, historical development and design trends, everyday urban governance, and global political-economic processes all at once.

These too are things many do-it-yourselfers recognize. Some people I talked to spoke of the need not only to fix problems but to change the culture of planners and their fellow citizens. And, as we have seen, many recognize how systemic and seemingly intractable a position their city governments are in, saying as Jenny did that it is "unrealistic" to expect more of them. In the words of a DIY urban designer named Clint Sleeper, who began surreptitiously repairing benches and playground equipment in Reno, Nevada, and other cities in the North American West in 2011, "Nobody can pay for anything. Nobody can look after these—I mean nobody can look after themselves, so these kind of public spaces are victims." One result would seem to be a growing presence of those like Clint, like Jordan, Ken and Jenny, and all the guerrilla bus stop bench builders of the world, who feel like maybe their acts of civic-minded creative transgression are a solution.

A conclusion here then is that personal and cultural micro-practices in urban space cannot be separated from macro political-economic structures and processes. Many features of 20th-century urban policy and planning—from a dominant autocentricity dating to the 1920s to the joint public-private deterioration-through-commodification of public services in more recent years—produce not only the physical conditions to which many DIY urban design interventions respond but an ideological environment that they in many ways embody and embolden. The creators of these "improvements" are acting in the context of urban governance that has been effectively neoliberalized, yet they are simultaneously indicative of an effective redistribution of local placemaking responsibilities to individual private actors. In other words, uneven development and neoliberal planning not only produce conditions that inspire do-it-yourselfers to act but also normalize the idea that the world is their playground.

There are dozens more examples to accompany the cases described above: planting and landscaping work on neglected tree wells and traffic medians, faux-official signs and alternative development proposals, guerrilla crosswalks and other street-calming efforts. All are undertaken as attempts to bring care, investment, and human-centered planning to streetscapes where do-it-yourselfers believe that landowners or city departments are failing, or that a market-driven growth agenda has overlooked local use values. In this sense, probably a majority of DIY urban design interventions can be described as responding to perceived failures of urban policy and planning processes as they play out under contemporary political-economic conditions. Yet the same systemic policy ideologies and vacuum of authority and service provision open up the possibility of more selfish, undemocratic forms of unauthorized alteration as well. As we have seen, one person's personal "improvement" may be to the wider public's detriment. Indeed, it could be as much a contributor to service deprivation, public space enclosure, or uneven investment as any more official aspects of urban policy.

Placing DIY urban design in this context of the imperfections of late modern urban planning suggests a number of more immediate questions as well. Of society and the public, do we no longer "trust" government agencies, private interests, or the "system" to provide necessary infrastructure or amenities? Of the exalted yet much-maligned democratic planning process, are its more noble principles embodied and expanded or undermined and conflicted with by informal intervention? And of the do-it-yourselfers themselves, in creating these improvements, are they effectively doing jobs and providing services that somebody else used to, diminishing governmental authority and furthering the redistribution of responsibility to private actors?

In this sense, again, even the most well-meaning do-it-yourselfers must be viewed as rather quintessentially neoliberal actors, and their approach

People waiting at a bus stop without a bench or shelter in San Francisco, 2014. Photo by the author.

of creative transgression, with its individualization of civic responsibilities, ironically a perfect model of labor in the help-yourself city. If it really is increasingly up to these individuals to make needed or desired local improvements, we might consider whether in this sense the most meaningful difference between "typical" market-driven urban development schemes and DIY urban design activities is that the state has officially ceded decision-making power to private developers and corporations, but not to individual citizens. Whether DIY urbanism still offers a more hopeful direction, from local benefits to broader cultural implications, has much to do with the actions of these individual citizens themselves, and whether access to the opportunity to make DIY improvements is any more democratic than the alternatives.

# "I'm an Expert on Public Space"

*Professional Knowledge at Work*

*in DIY Urbanism*

About two years into my research on DIY urban design, I found myself standing one evening by a table in a popular bar in Brooklyn's Cobble Hill neighborhood, surrounded by urban planners, architects, and design professionals. I had been invited to this casual networking get-together by one of the organizers, an informant of mine who had become a friend after I interviewed him months earlier. The crowd was a sort of who's who of young progressive urban thinkers and doers in New York. People discussed each other's work, opportunities for collaboration, one attendee's recent "Ted Talk"; conversations were peppered with references to controversial local development proposals, the comparative benefits of bike-share systems in different cities, and the urban design theories of William H. Whyte. From landscape architecture consultants and transportation planners to students and open space advocates, nearly everyone in the group possessed what could be described as a sophisticated command of city policy, planning jargon, and academic urbanism. They were experts and professionals. More than half of them were also in some way connected to the world of informal urbanism, using their knowledge and skills to make unsanctioned streetscape contributions in their communities.

That same winter, I took part in an analogous gathering in Mexico City. At a table outside a hip bar on a lively pedestrianized street just south of the *zócalo*, I sat chatting in a mix of Spanish and English with a group of the city's foremost do-it-yourself urban designers. Members of a self-described collective called Camina, Haz Ciudad ("walk, make the city"; just Haz Ciudad for short), my gracious hosts told me about their various DIY projects in the capital, which we would set out by bike to see the next day. They have painted bike lanes and bike priority symbols, bright striped crosswalks, even a whole improvised sidewalk, along with complementary signage, to make a place for pedestrians who must cross a dangerous bridge designed only for cars. Yet every one of these do-it-yourselfers could be described as a professional urbanist, holding jobs with the city and local design offices, and their interventions are informed by official standards and regulations.

My five drinking companions, and soon-to-be tour guides, were interested to hear about people in other cities making similar DIY efforts. They asked me what I'd learned about the people, the projects, how much they cost, if anyone gets in trouble. For their parts, they were frustrated with Mexico's inadequate infrastructure but viewed it as an opportunity for creativity, to "make something out of our loss," as one of them put it. They were also very aware of the deep local tradition of informal urbanism in the chaotic metropolis of more than 20 million. "We are not the first in doing DIY urbanism because there is informal commerce, there's like some areas of the city that are just land where people started living there and

A man rides in a guerrilla bike lane painted by members of Collectivo Camina, Haz Ciudad in Mexico City, 2012. Photo by the author.

they made the streets and everything," one of them, a man in his 30s, told me. But the people I was sitting with were experts. Several of them work together for an urban planning and policy think tank that has consulted for the government. One was employed by the city's bicycle program, another told me she was literally "doing the manual for pedestrian infrastructure" at her job. Looking around at her friends and colleagues, many with formal training in architecture or planning, this woman in her late 20s laughed. "We're like undercover agents," she said.

This chapter, along with the next one, further complicates our thinking about just who engages in DIY urban design and the wider implications of their activities by giving attention to the biographical backgrounds of typical do-it-yourselfers. I begin here with a particular focus on the considerable degree of formal knowledge that they bring to this informal practice. I argue that this knowledge enables and to some extent inspires them to act, and provides part of their justification for doing so. We have seen that even official-seeming streetscape design elements may be far from official; I show here the degree to which unsanctioned and outright illegal placemaking can come from a background of professional and scholarly experience, and sometimes even from professional placemakers themselves.

## THE PROFESSIONALIZATION AND DEPROFESSIONALIZATION OF URBAN PLACEMAKING

The "right"—or privilege, or responsibility—to make and alter the urban built environment has shifted, legally and normatively, across history and geography. Degrees of formality and informality in placemaking have differed widely. And the suggestion that planning decisions ought to be made by communities rather than, or at least in addition to, professional planners is not a new one—even if such calls have been more about making the work of professionals more responsive than truly turning this work itself over to lay people.[1] Certainly though, if we take the historical long view, in Europe and North America (and to some extent the world over) the general trend since the beginning of the modern era has been toward standardization and professionalization of urban placemaking.

Even some ancient cities, despite often being described as "unplanned," show archaeological evidence of coordination and rationalization in their layouts and functions. A degree of centralized planning is clearly visible in the cities of classical Greece and Rome, Imperial China, and pre-Columbian Mesoamerica.[2] The medieval city, popularly rendered as a dark, muddy, violent free-for-all with a castle in the middle, had its strict regulations, including controls over land use and the freedom to physically alter (or even move about in) the urban environment. If the overall appearance was indeed fairly organic and chaotic, the existence of any particular buildings, features, or services was basically organized by a combination of commerce, religion, and martial authority. The profession of "architect-planner" emerged in Italy during the Renaissance and by the late 1500s the organization and form of the city and of its governance had shifted significantly. The concept of "urban planning"—in a formal or professional sense—dates to the late 18th century if not before. There is considerable ambiguity as to when actually, but experts broadly agree that formalized planning, like the highly rationalized and controlled state in general, came about in the sweep of European history from the Enlightenment to the Industrial Revolution.[3]

During this time, Europe's great capitals witnessed the grand redesigns of imperialism and the explicit wish of "rational" men (and the monarchs they served) to impose order on their cities through regulations, building codes, and grandly commissioned improvements. Meanwhile, as the pursuit of trade and discovery brought Europeans to the "New World," most colonial cities and towns were rigidly planned and designed from the outset. Although the earliest English and Dutch settlements in North America were little more than muddy encampments, seminal highly formalized American city plans such as those for Philadelphia (1682), Savannah (1733), and Washington (1791), date to their foundings, drawn up by educated, elite men of high regard. In Philadelphia, "surveyors and regulators" were granted power as early as 1721 to determine the layout of streets and buildings.[4] Alexis de Tocqueville famously recognized in early 19th-century America the chaos of a "thousand simultaneous voices" demanding they be heard, but also, emerging from it, a participatory planning tradition.*

Perhaps the most dramatic symbol of the great formalization of urban design under modernity was the *"rénovation"* of Paris under Baron Georges-Eugène Haussmann. Beginning in 1853, by commission from Napoleon III, Haussmann oversaw an unprecedented imposition of top-down, ultra-rationalized planning on the city, from wide, straight boulevards carved through the dense warrens of medieval Paris to sewers, parks, and monuments, as well as a host of orderly building regulations. (It has also been famously noted, by Haussmann's contemporaries as well as observers today, that many elements of the plan were efforts to impose social and

---

* In the very same passage as his remarks about the "confused clamor" of American individualism, for instance, Tocqueville (1956 [1835]: 108) evoked a montage of collective planning activity: "here, the people of one quarter of a town are met to decide on the building of a church; there the election of a representative is going on; a little further, the delegates of a district are posting to town in order to consult some local improvements; in another place, the laborers of a village quit their plows to deliberate on the project of a road or a public school." Formalized yet seemingly quite participatory planning and policymaking at work.

physical order on the city, with the boulevards facilitating military policing and making urban unrest easier to control.)

To be sure, in places like the rapidly exploding new industrial cities of late 19th-century America, there was still, as Anthony Sutcliffe (1981: 96) describes, a "virtual absence of controls over building, advertising, overhead wires and other causes of ugliness and disorder." Even in older East Coast cities, and despite early building codes in Baltimore and New York in the 1850s, "the core areas, which retained a degree of dignity, were swamped after mid-century by undisciplined development." This included the great squalor—and great do-it-yourself informality—of tenement housing blocks, even as it was also the era of America's great municipal parks and the rise of landscape architecture as a profession as well. From this state of affairs, another sort of DIY urban design trend blossomed among the wealthy urban (and already increasingly suburban) elite: the "city beautiful" movement. Combining Progressive Era social reforms aimed at the immigrant poor with a design emphasis on cultural and aesthetic improvements, this concern (like the contemporaneous "garden city" movement in the United Kingdom) ultimately influenced official planning, design, and governance quite significantly.

At the turn of the 20th century, the cities of the advanced industrial global North were moving toward an increasingly civilized and ordered—if still not always civil and orderly[†]—existence. Sophisticated, regulated, and technically informed planning became more common, and civil engineers, architects, lawyers, and others began working together as a professional class of town planners in a wide variety of contexts. The first university courses in planning were offered in 1909 at Liverpool and in 1924 at Harvard. Le Corbusier became famous as an architect and designer for his visions of an idealized, modern, highly planned city. The development of housing tracts and tidy railroad suburbs, the first (imperfect) accommodations for the automobile, and the rise of the skyscraper all meant ever more codes and certification and agencies and professionals whose

---

† For example, even as laws were increasingly adopted to accommodate the widespread introduction of automobiles to the streets of American cities in the 1920s, "the scale of death and dismemberment on roads and streets in America grew fast" (Norton 2008). The classic grid plan was viewed as part of the problem and the concept of an ostensibly more pedestrian friendly "superblock" pattern (with local residential streets internalized by a few surrounding arterials) was promoted as an alternative in cities such as Los Angeles. Of course this plan still favored the car and, in the end, left many neighborhoods in LA and other cities isolating for pedestrians (see Christoforidis 1994). Throughout the 20th century, the urban design of the American city was profoundly influenced by this particular piece of industrial design from Detroit.

jobs were to design, build, and manage it all. The term "urban design," first coined by the British architect and town planner Patrick Abercrombie in the 1910s, emerged as a professional term in Europe and North America following the Second World War, reflecting the further specialization of this work as an act of creative expertise. Harvard's Graduate School of Design popularized the term with a series of colloquia in the 1950s, leading to the founding of the first professional program in urban design there in 1960.

As I have argued, do-it-yourself urban design shows us that the people making unsanctioned alterations to streetscapes, signage, and private property are not always the scofflaws or radicals one might assume. Though certainly there are many of all of these, there are others at work, acting without permission to make what they see as functional, beneficial improvements to the built environment. In this chapter, I show that many do-it-yourselfers employ learned professional skills to create informal improvements that replicate formal design features impeccably—for example, Los Angeles artist Richard Ankrom put years of professional sign-making experience to work "fixing" a major freeway sign so well that his changes remained in place for eight years. These individuals can pass fluently in the worlds of city bureaucracy, professional design, and neighborhood activism alike—I met Gil, the man behind the conversion of an overgrown railroad easement into a squatted urban farm, talking shop at a reception for New York City's "Urban Design Week" in the showroom of a high-end publisher and have since accompanied him to meetings with lawyers and city officials. In conversation, many do-it-yourselfers can quote statistics and planning theory to stand civil codes on their heads, and reference unprovoked the ideas of deceased theorists and contemporary urbanism. Many are, for these reasons, confident that their efforts are unqualified improvements to urban space.

I describe in this chapter the role that this learned and sometimes professional familiarity with urban theory, planning, and design plays in the actions of DIY urban designers. The features of professional and scholarly urbanism presented do not apply equally to everyone I have classified as a DIY urban designer: degrees of familiarity with the official system vary considerably. However, a large majority of the do-it-yourselfers I interviewed—individuals representing 63 of the 75 DIY projects in the sample—make use of one or both of the following broad categories of formalized knowledge that I refer to throughout: *technical knowledge*, a familiarity with local governance and policy, development history, planning practice, and professional tools, materials, and methods; and *scholarly knowledge*, a command of critical urban studies discourse, broader planning and development theory, and other academic urbanism. Examples from my study demonstrate some of the ways that do-it-yourselfers employ this knowledge and allow us to explore how their relationship to formal or official urbanism influences their actions, justifications, and impacts.

## "WE HAD TO LEARN ABOUT URBAN DESIGN"—UTILIZING TECHNICAL AND SCHOLARLY KNOWLEDGE

The basic demographics of the do-it-yourselfers I spoke with and observed—predominantly white, middle class, and adult—go a long way on their own to challenge our stereotypes about people who make illegal alterations to public space. As noted, many do-it-yourselfers are well educated, with undergraduate degrees and even graduate and professional certifications fairly common. And they tended to have an in-depth knowledge of urban issues, design, and public policy.

Now, considering their typical education levels and preponderance of careers in the "creative" industries in urban areas, some familiarity with professional and scholarly urban planning thinking is not so surprising. What Brendan Gleeson (2012) has called the "new genre of popular 'urbanology,'" in which urban design, urban culture, and the so-called Urban Age are of broad interest, is testament to the culture of popular urbanism in the United States and beyond (and perhaps to the perceived elitism and cultural distinctiveness of these places from their rural hinterlands). Topics like gentrification fairly dominate everyday conversation in many American cities—perhaps especially among gentrifiers. Jane Jacobs's *The Death and Life of Great American Cities* can be found on many a nightstand. Progressive planning ideals around sustainability, urban agriculture, and the value of bicycle and pedestrian spaces are today common social concerns among the urban "creative class," as visible in the popularity of websites like *Atlantic Cities, Curbed, Guardian Cities, Streetsblog,* and the *Gothamist* family of local news and culture blogs. Street art, activism, and the hacker and maker cultures are likewise celebrated in this cultural milieu, which makes room for many acts of creative transgression, at least if they do not transgress mainstream values and aesthetics too far.

Even so, most of the do-it-yourselfers I spoke to have a next level knowledge of, proficiency with, and connection to professional urbanism that goes beyond this cultural literacy. Some do-it-yourselfers literally work day jobs in urban planning and design (and I return to them below). And even many of those without this professional affiliation or background are closely familiar with the ideas and the worlds of urban theory, planning, and design. I argue that this knowledge is a large part of their motivation and willingness to engage in DIY urban design, and they put it to work while creating unauthorized and sometimes illegal alterations to public space and private property.

Consider Stephen Box, a long-time organizer of "Park(ing) Day" in Los Angeles—a now-global event that began in San Francisco and involves turning parking spaces into temporary parks—along with a number of other DIY pedestrianizing projects. In conversation, he has convincing command not only of the social and economic implications of urban parking and open space policies but also of transit usage and neighborhood park acreage statistics in his community. Well versed in planning public relations lingo, he prefers the term "street-opening" (i.e., to pedestrians) to "street-closing" when discussing traffic-calming efforts, joining this onomastic debate in planning circles. While speaking to me at a coffee shop near LA City Hall, he heckled a group of city transportation engineers within earshot of our table for designing "for cars not for people," and then proceeded to tell me about Baron Haussmann's 19th-century redevelopment of Paris. Stephen is a white man in his 40s, a filmmaker and community organizer by day. A known figure around city hall, he enjoys engaging in legalistic arguments with city planners and police officers and has even run for local office himself.

Jordan, the man behind the campaign to rid New York and other cities of corporate outdoor advertising, serves as another example. He likes to quote the American Planning Association's definition of good public spaces. He references David Harvey and other critical theorists when discussing his work. Months after accompanying him on a late-night mission replacing corporate advertising on payphones with anonymous art pieces, I ran into Jordan at an urban studies workshop at the CUNY Graduate Center (to which he has no affiliation). As for the visual pollution that he sees as his target, Jordan also casually drops figures about the advertising industry, including annual expenditures and revenues for outdoor ads. He knows city codes and ordinances so well that much of what he targets actually is illegal—the repetitive smattering of posters and handbills known as "wild posting," as well as unpermitted wall sides and billboards. He has acquired the technical knowledge and purpose-built tools needed to open up advertising frames on bus stops, payphones, and subway stations, investing in the same custom key that advertising companies use. And he does so with casual confidence, sometimes in broad daylight.

When some of the various (and actually largely unaffiliated) individuals who have been referred to as the "Los Angeles Department of DIY" began painting their own bike lanes in the city in 2008, they started by consulting planning documents and city codes. Then, they researched how the city installs bike lanes (usually with specialty road paint or thermoplastic laid by a small team riding or walking behind a truck along a route lined with orange cones) and thinking about what it would take to create their own. "We talked about a lot of materials but all of them were too expensive really," explained one person who was involved, a white man in his late 40s. "So we decided on a lane-painter, a parking lot striping device, which you can buy at Home Depot with many different colors of paint. That device cost about a hundred bucks and paint's about ten bucks a can and came in various colors."

Another member of the group, a white guy in his 30s, told me how he impersonated a member of the Los Angeles Department of Transportation: "When I was in the hardware store, I just told them that I was a manager at the Department and we needed to do something to the curb, and they showed me the best [lane striper]." His group also bought orange work vests to wear on the job. A third person, a graphic designer, worked to carefully craft accurate stencils of cyclists to put in the lane. The first man, who had no prior sign-making experience (but does describe himself as having "good research abilities") designed signs to accompany them on the side of the road:

> I worked on designing the signs, the actual metal signs that were an exact duplicate of the Los Angeles bike lane signs, except they said "DIY" at the bottom of them instead of "DOT" for Department of Transportation. We had those professionally done, I did a mock-up and then took it to a sign shop. [ . . . ] And I had to buy some of these straps that they use [to secure signs to poles]. We wanted the signs especially to look really official because it was the only part of this where we could actually use the genuine equipment. [ . . . ] I wanted them to really look real.

Elsewhere, to encourage turning a central LA street corner into a park rather than the condo actually planned there, some of the same people created a massive, painstakingly official-looking "coming soon" sign for their hypothetical greenspace. The sign was a visually and technically accurate recreation of a city planning announcement, right down to contact information for real public officials and standard tri-lingual presentation in English, Korean, and Spanish. The local sign maker they hired to print it thought he was scoring a city contract.

These people, who see problems that they are driven to respond to with unauthorized interventions, have taken the added step of bringing

A sign announcing a hypothetical "Park for the People" on a Los Angeles corner actually slated for condo development, in English, Spanish, and Korean and designed to look like an official City of Los Angeles project, attributed to the "LA Dept. of DIY," in 2009. Photo by Stanley Cousins.

knowledge of technical planning and scholarly urbanism to make them better. In the first case, a formerly apathetic community member does not just speak up when he notices the planning process is out of balance but learns the planning doctrine and starts changing things. In the next, a trained artist, troubled by corporate advertisers cluttering and financially exploiting the city's public spaces, reads the law and takes matters into his own hands. In the last, Angelenos of different ages and occupations, tired of waiting for the city to improve their streets, decide to learn how the city does it and do it themselves. These do-it-yourselfers are making the changes that they want to see happen, and doing so with savvy, knowledge, and skills that reveal a sophisticated awareness of formal planning and design.

Most of these individuals—those in the examples above, and a majority of all my interviewees—have essentially sought out this knowledge as part of making their improvements, whether to improve the functionality of the intervention, or with hopes of greater legitimacy (for themselves and the work), or simply because they enjoy learning about how to "do it right." As one member of LA's so-called Department of DIY put it, "we had to learn about urban design. [ . . . ] [W]e had to learn about where a good place for a bike lane would be." Time and again I heard this sort of thing, including references to specific cities' planning manuals and efforts to build or paint something "according to the law."

Clint, an artist and teacher with a background in media and advertising, had no particular skills for the task when he began making small repairs to playgrounds, parks, and other public spaces in Reno, Nevada. "I didn't even seem like a knowledgeable do-it-yourselfer," he laughed. "Some people really look like they know what they're doing; I wasn't giving that impression so much." He continued:

> I needed to actually learn something about maintenance. And about coarse threads and fine threads and the ratings of bolts. [ . . . ] It's all those things that you learn, especially having that media background, and having that kind of "just Google it" approach to learning things, is then extended outward into these spaces and into this other kind of work that I'm doing—OK I just need to figure out what a circular saw does. I needed to figure out what the tension of these bolts is, what the kind of torque specifications are. I probably don't look like I know what I'm doing any more than I initially did, but I do.

For a number of other DIY urban designers, it is the formal knowledge and skills that come first, followed by an inspiration to act informally. One of the best examples of this is Richard Ankrom's 2001 freeway sign mentioned earlier. He put his years of professional sign-making experience to work "fixing" a confusing Downtown Los Angeles freeway sign that left some motorists in the wrong lane for an unexpected exit on the left. The story of what he called his "guerrilla public service" intervention speaks volumes:

> I had gotten lost twenty years earlier when I didn't live in the neighborhood. And then when I moved here and drove under the same [sign] I realized, Oh well that's why I got lost! [ . . . ] Since I'm in the business I realized of course who else is gonna do it? Who else is more qualified? And who could actually just go install, with no question, just get it done. [ . . . ]
>
> So I did a bunch of homework on it first, to make sure if that [missing information about an upcoming exit] did belong there. There may have been a technical reason why they left it off. I couldn't find it, so I went ahead with the project. [ . . . ] It was important because I didn't want them to have any excuse to remove it! Not because of shoddy material, not because it was improperly fabricated. And also too just the skill set that I've learned in the sign business, of what materials you use, and why. So I did the homework and I checked the engineering specs. And I also checked in the field because they don't always match. So that's, I mean, I just basically followed directions like I would any other sign.

Richard's efforts to produce a technically accurate improvement paid off. Even after his additions were acknowledged by the California Department of Transportation two years later, the sign was left untouched until routine updates in 2009 facilitated its replacement—and then with his design ideas included in the new sign.[5]

Ali Pulver, a Google employee with a master's degree in industrial design and a background in new product marketing, put her skills to use creating a series of portable tables, seating, and accessories that exploit features of the existing urban landscape to make it easier to sit and eat on the streets of New York. Baltimore artist Graham Coreil-Allen draws on his schooling in architecture and urban planning as well as the arts to create public walking tours, published guidebooks, and information kiosks that highlight and critique overlooked public spaces. And in Phoenix, the woman behind the collaborative aspirational urbanism project in which community members write their sustainable planning ideas on a chalkboard, is also the director of an environmental quality consulting and public relations firm.

This goes further. As described at the beginning of this chapter, I also found instances of professional urban planners, designers, and policymakers enacting some of the improvements they wanted to see through DIY tactics. Atlanta's Mad Housers, who have been building wooden shelters for those without since the late 1980s, do so using designs by the Georgia Tech–trained architects and engineers who founded and lead the group. They offer several "hut" designs to match the needs of the people they consider their "clients" (some with sleeping lofts, others intentionally low-lying to reduce visibility) and have even developed a "cogeneration power plant" that uses a car engine to generate power and heat water at an encampment—among the most high-tech DIY interventions I learned

Ali Pulver's Fire Hydrant Table, part of her "Pop-Up Lunch" project in New York City, 2009. Photos by Ali Pulver.

about. The group make blueprints and 3D models of all of their designs available for free on their website, and they also view teaching technical skills to the people they are helping as a core part of their mission.

DoTank, the Brooklyn design collective known for activating urban spaces with homemade chairs, interactive public message boards, and improvised community spaces, was composed entirely of people who work day jobs in urban planning, design, and policy activism. (They organized the networking get-together described at the beginning of this chapter.) Professional architects and university faculty are among the members of the Hypothetical Development Organization, who in 2010 posted illustrated project designs for unused sites in New Orleans as a "public service." Guerrilla gardener Jay Griffith, the so-called Johnny Appleseed of Venice, is a high-profile landscape designer in Southern California. And again, many of Mexico City's most ardent painters of unauthorized crosswalks and bicycle lanes have worked directly for or with city government there.

As these examples demonstrate, the application of technical and scholarly knowledge to DIY urban design projects occurs in two ways. Practical and academic urban planning knowledge is sought out by everyday community members in order to better effect the change they want to see. Others see a need that their existing skills and even professional occupations find them well-positioned to address and then choose to act informally. Whether talking to a do-it-yourselfer who fully "daylights" as a design professional or another who has simply acquired the information to make functional improvements, I found that formal knowledge is a central feature of this informal intervention. As I show next, this knowledge also informs their motivations and justifications for acting, in sometimes contradictory ways.

### "If You're a City Planner, There's Only so Much You Can Plan For"—Filling in for Bureaucracy

The DIY urban designers I spoke with almost always described their most basic motivations or justifications for acting as seeing a "need" or an "opportunity" to make what they viewed as an improvement to the built environment in their community. In acting, they often see themselves as stepping up where the local government or a private property owner has dropped the ball. But rather than writing a letter to the city council, DIY urban designers do it themselves without authorization and, as we have seen, with some degree of professional know-how. To understand why these individuals are going to these lengths themselves, walking the line between unauthorized actions and official methods, their familiarity with official regulations, planning codes, and especially the workings of civic planning and policy bureaucracy is a central consideration.

A common feature of many DIY urban design interventions is that they effectively "propose" improvements that their creators feel the city or other official development actors ought to be making. Some told me they would prefer the city just did it, effectively so they would not "have to." Such preferences aside, however, there is also a strong feeling that this is wishful thinking. Like Jenny, the SignBench designer in Los Angeles who felt it "unrealistic" to expect the city to spend limited resources on sidewalk improvements in her neighborhood, they demonstrate well-informed awareness of inadequacies in urban planning at structural and policy levels. Most do-it-yourselfers I spoke with also believe on a more basic level that their local government's policies are wrongheaded and that the bureaucracy is too slow-moving to do it right anyway. This is an assessment clearly informed by the frustrated experience many have with the formal planning process, which perhaps contributes to a broader, help-yourself attitude toward the city.

Matt Tomasulo, a Raleigh, North Carolina, resident, was a planning student there when he became frustrated with the lack of official interest in community mobility concerns that he felt could be successful in the city. So he designed and installed his own series of "guerrilla wayfinding" signs for pedestrians in a project he called Walk Raleigh. Describing how his training as a planner motivated him to act, he remarked, "We know why things are so black and white and why they take so long to get done. [ . . . ] A lot of our standards are old and opaque and very traditional and built for a world that's much different than what it is today." He contrasts his own project directly with a comparable official effort in Raleigh:

> Raleigh spent $1.3 million and three years planning a wayfinding system for Downtown that installed the same year as Walk Raleigh. And, you know, they're like ten feet high and they point to maybe six different destinations, and they're only on a few main corridors, and that's it. [ . . . ] I installed 27 signs for $300 a year and a half ago. And that compared to 140 signs for $1.3 million over three years, you know, it doesn't really make too much sense.

Stacey, the woman behind the Phoenix Chalkboard, knows from experience consulting with local agencies that "it's easier to just do things rather than deal with the bureaucracy." A young woman member of Haz Ciudad echoed this sentiment, saying "everyone is waiting for the government to do its job, but the government does not have all the answers. We have, like, our crosswalks aren't painted? So we can paint them." Indeed, one of the founders of Dallas's DIY community improvement phenomenon "Better Block" was a professional city planner who only after *leaving* that job found himself physically creating needed street improvements for the first time; he and his collaborators printed out the city codes they were violating and hung them near the planters, awnings, bike lanes, and other offending additions that they made to the streetscape.

Thinking of the many improvements he feels are necessary around Los Angeles, another do-it-yourselfer involved in creating unauthorized bicycle infrastructure said he simply was "not sure if the city would be capable of it" due to their lack of familiarity with community needs on this level. Whether or not he is right, this concern is one of his justifications for taking matters into his own hands:

> Like how many of the people who work for the Department of Planning live in Los Angeles, like LA proper? I'm sure they don't live in my neighborhood. And I think it takes that like on-the-ground acting and moving to see what can be done and what needs to be done.

Joe, of the LA EcoVillage echoed this sentiment: "The city tries to do a one-size-fits-all thing that applies to all neighborhoods and it's like, that's not our . . . whatever, it just doesn't serve us in all cases."

It is perhaps for similar reasons that Stephen, the pro-pedestrian do-it-yourselfer and Park(ing) Day participant, is no fan of formal design work and has a pretty low opinion of professional planners to boot. As we sat talking in a Starbucks near City Hall, he referred to private design firms as "bourgeois commercial pig dogs" and derided city planners as "well-trained fleas" who "are really busy drinking coffee and shit." Indeed, while he laughed and emphasized that he does have friends in the Planning Department and sympathizes with their bureaucratic constraints, he suggested at one point that they could still be complicit in "fucking up our city" by doing too little. (Years later, Stephen actually works for the City of Los Angeles in its Department of Neighborhood Empowerment.)

Ali, the aforementioned creator of a series of tables, seating, and other infrastructural add-ons she calls "Pop-Up Lunch," summed up what she views as the driving forces of bureaucratic inertia this way:

> If you're a city planner, you're like, there's only so much you can plan for. You can't do a focus group around how people are going to use the city! [ . . . ] Because

we'd never get anything done! [ ... ] It's like, one, it's so slow, but two, there is this notion of people will fight it until they see it! And then you have to show them what it could be. They could be pissed off, but you have to do it, because you can't just keep talking about it.

Another interviewee in Los Angeles suggested that the city should just allow improvements to be made by people like him, to its own bene- fit and following official standards: "Members of the public should be allowed to look at the bike plan, and if there's a place where we can do it [ ... ] up to spec and everything, we should be able to put it in ourselves." This is, like many of the examples given above, indicative of considera- ble hubris from DIYers who believe their improvements are unquestion- ably valuable and of a high quality. Their knowledge of urbanism not only informs their actions but it also gives them confidence that they are effectively qualified to do so and that their interventions are the right thing for the city.

It is in this spirit that a spokesman for Toronto's Urban Repair Squad, among the first groups anywhere to begin illegally installing cycling infra- structure, went so far as to argue that "the group kind of fulfills an official function." With the city unwilling to build bicycle infrastructure, some- one had to do it. Jordan, with his efforts to remove illegal advertising, would agree that he too is doing an official service that the city ought to be applauding, as would Richard, whose freeway sign improvement was so effective that the California Department of Transportation gave it implicit approval. As we have seen, many of the do-it-yourselfers I spoke to do feel that because their projects are needed substitutes for services that local government clearly should be providing, they really are doing something that anyone, including local authorities, should be grateful for.

It could be that there's something to this. When Matt designed and installed his series of DIY walking signs and maps throughout Downtown Raleigh, they were quickly removed by authorities. But online attention and local outcry led to their restoration some weeks later as a civic ini- tiative. Today, Matt's "Walk Your City" program has been contracted by more than a dozen other communities and utilized by many more unof- ficial efforts as well. Matt has since run (unsuccessfully) for city council and was appointed to the Raleigh Planning Commission. As I describe in greater detail in Chapter 6, this sort of recognition and formalization of certain DIY projects is not uncommon. Yet for other do-it-yourselfers, also informed by the law and scholarly urbanism, the very lack of formalization is another part of their projects' value.

A Walk Your City sign, from the program created by Matt Tomasulo, installed in downtown San José. Photo by the author, 2016.

### "Maybe I Really Should Be Allowed to Be Doing What I'm Doing"— Legal Knowledge and Urban Theory as Further Justification

The diffusion of scholarly and professional urbanism among DIY urban designers and the self-confidence with which it seems to be accompanied is also evident in another justification that many gave for their tactics: a belief in the inherent value of unauthorized or bottom-up intervention itself. While some say they wish the city would just do it, many of my interviewees view citizen-initiated efforts as important components of a more dynamic, democratic, and locally sensitive approach to urban placemaking that they desire. Though their individual actions are small, they hope to inspire others to look at things differently and question the potential value of informality in the city.

"Why not do it formally?" asked a member of DoTank, repeating my question, "I think seeing something without the lens of like 'Oh this is sponsored by this group,' [ . . . ] that works against the idea of trying to have others repeat it." Ali picked up on this:

> There's something wonderful in the bottom-up approach. [ . . . ] It almost might seem inauthentic if—like, as the city, you're setting up the framework, you're

setting up the structure. I want to see what people will do with it. And just like being a bit more fun or [ . . . ] supporting the things that people are doing on their own.

Joe, of LA's Eco-Village, likewise values the creative, communitarian value of a DIY approach:

You know, you don't need to wait for the city to do it and you probably don't want the city to do it, because they probably won't do it with creativity. And by doing it in the neighborhood you—we—develop a sense of ownership and stewardship of it, and we keep it up.

This sort of thinking is informed by progressive planning and community participation discourses, in keeping with themes in academic urbanism and the critical Marxian spatial theory of the past half century. One creator of LA's aspirational "Park for the People" sign professed admiration for the ideas of Guy Debord, principal thinker of the Situationists, and another 20th-century philosopher of transgressive practice, Michel de Certeau, heralding the value of "These little things, that if you make these little things better for people, they might not even notice them, but it encourages them to act differently." Clint connected the value of even his minor repair efforts to the ideas of the social practice artist and scholar Ted Purves: "He has this great kind of one-liner that generous acts are blows against the empire."

Another Angeleno I met, responsible among other things for signposting concrete traffic islands as "National Park" land to encourage their use as public spaces, referred me to the book *Everyday Urbanism* by University of California architecture and planning scholar Margaret Crawford. A Baltimore man who helped found a community farm and park on a vacant lot there referenced Henri Lefebvre, another French theorist, several times in our conversation. A member of Mexico City's Haz Ciudad told me about the writing of the social psychologist Pablo Fernández Christlieb, whose work on "the spirit of the street" and the collective nature of "everyday culture" inspires his own actions; another keeps a signed copy of Lefebvre's *Right to the City*. And Stephen, in defending the prospect of occupying a metered parking space as a place to live ("it's the best real-estate deal in town!") cited the work of the economist Donald Shoup: "He wrote *The High Cost of Free Parking*, used to be a professor at UCLA."‡

‡ At the time of writing, Shoup is still a professor of urban planning at UCLA.

Jordan offered an especially thoughtful example of all this that brings in the other elements described above as well:

> Often we have this notion that things are not really ours, or changeable, these spaces. And what David Harvey was saying [ . . . ] that we're all participants in the creation of these spaces, and really embodying that and accepting that it's one of your responsibilities as a public citizen to go out and kind of create the environment in which you want to exist. [ . . . ] And just by going out and physically doing something you gain a political power, that the resisting forces are really gonna have to pose a better argument, you know, why should you be allowed to be doing that? When you start to get into that conversation, maybe I really should be allowed to be doing what I'm doing. And by virtue of just doing it, I kind of prove that.

More practically speaking, do-it-yourselfers' familiarity with official practices can also help them to skillfully navigate interactions with authorities or avoid getting caught. When a Los Angeles group organized a huge effort to install hundreds of "pass with care"/"*pase con cuidado*" road safety signs at intersections throughout that city, they instructed everyone only to paste them onto city street light signal boxes ("They are not to be put up on private property, they're not to be put up in any locations other than signal boxes," one leader of the effort emphasized). This was a smart plan not only because there is a signal box at every intersection that has a light, but because he knew that

> the signal box is a public piece of property, and those are the places where messages are posted by the LAPD. I've seen LAPD messages posted on there, you know a rash of burglaries, or, you know, public notices are typically put on those signal boxes. So at the end of the day, if it really came down to someone's door getting busted down and that person getting arrested, the defense is, Hey this is public—it's something that's been happening in America since America was born. [ . . . ] So we've kind of found that threshold where, you know, it is quasi-legal . . . it's kind of illegal, but then again it's kind of not.

Some do-it-yourselfers even dress as city road workers, tour guides, and other officials when creating their improvements. Costumes help them to avoid scrutiny when engaged in unauthorized activities. "We have hardhats and reflective vests and clipboards," explained Nick, president of the Atlanta group that builds and installs shelters for the homeless; "nobody ever asks you anything if you've got a clipboard." Likewise, painting well-researched bike lanes, intersection bike boxes, and other such infrastructure while sometimes "dressed up as city workers," Toronto's Urban Repair Squad claim to have "fooled the city many times" and "fooled a lot of people many times, just thinking that it was done by the city." The use of uniforms and professional tools also plays into DIYers self-conception of legitimacy. As Graham put it, tongue only slightly in cheek, "I wear a uniform [when leading walking tours] because I'm an expert on public space."

There are, then, a variety of interconnected motivations, backgrounds, and tactics, from the pragmatic to the almost whimsical, which help explain why and how these individuals act to "improve" the built environments of their communities without permission. To varying degrees though, familiarity with planning, design, and academic urbanism regularly plays a role. A final case helps illustrate the interworking of many of the different applications of technical and scholarly knowledge in DIY urban design. It also sets the stage for a further consideration of the varying degrees of official acceptance of informal tactics. This example of aspirational urbanism takes us back to the contested public spaces of Southern California.

## "We Think a Lot about the Privatization of Space All the Time"— Another Form of Tourism

Sara Daleiden, an artist originally from Wisconsin, is a founding member of a group called the LA Urban Rangers. She is involved in several related projects that have in common what she describes as "offering another form of tourism, or a critique of tourism" through leading tours, publishing maps and other information, and staging events that draw attention to things like privatization and overdevelopment in Los Angeles. Her work demonstrates how knowledge of urban policy can point to DIY urbanism as a response to the shortcomings of market-driven planning and to the dangers of private actors taking urban planning into their own hands. While explicitly critical of some politicians, developers, and other unauthorized actors, Sara's projects are ideologically in step with the goals of more socially minded public agencies. They are informed by the law and have received some approval from some official actors.

A particular focus of the Urban Rangers, for instance, has been public access on beaches in places like Malibu. Sara explained:

> It's a city that's like 25 miles long, it's a long piece of land along some of the most gorgeous coastline I've ever seen. And it has extremely wealthy residents, often their second home, which is a beach home, and it just lines the whole coast. And we just work from the premise that the state Coastal Commission

reinforces that there's basically a public sidewalk of space that runs the entire coast of California. [ . . . ] Then there's also what are called public easements, that when homeowners take their beach cabins and turn them into multi-million dollar homes that max out the property? The state says well you have to give up this whole chunk of beach in front of your property. So there's this kind of interesting varying line of public space on the beaches out there.

Malibu homeowners practice what Sara described as "any number of what we figure are somewhat territorial behaviors" on the beach, including posting unsanctioned signs and barriers, which the state has traditionally done little to rectify.[6] And they even seem to think they are in the right: "These homeowners threaten lawsuits all the time," Sara continued, "just because they think you're blocking their view of the water."

The Urban Rangers, citing the law, have taken it upon themselves to open the beaches. "We're out there to just gently reinforce that it's public space and to show people how they can get there, but also how they can spend time there." She described some of their interventions: "One of the activities we run is called Stereotypic Beach Activities, where people are invited to sunbathe, sand castle building, yoga, in these public easements. So we actually teach them how to read the Coastal Commission's maps to know where the public space is."

The Urban Rangers have also published their own maps and guides to walks and trails that promote public access. They leave them alongside official materials in tourism bureaus and information kiosks—and have built kiosks of their own—as a sort of aspirational urbanism project, informing and encouraging people to use the beaches as they are meant to be used. Like Jordan's efforts to remove illegal advertising from the streets, where state policy enforcement has failed in this case too it is essentially vigilante versus vigilante. Yet while Jordan's work has been met with arrests, Sara's have attracted favorable attention from various environmental and conservation agencies, including local National Parks Service rangers who are interested in learning from the Malibu actions.

Across the region, in Downtown Los Angeles, a project of Sara's called "Being Pedestrian" disseminates information about walking and local wayfinding in response to concerns of hyper-commercialization, corporate megaprojects, and the general pro-development "boosterism" practiced by city leaders, the Community Redevelopment Agency, and the Chamber of Commerce. Sara is concerned that these groups' efforts, from large-scale investment to official versions of the very sorts of walking tours that her group leads, are largely about promoting consumption and commercial development. She feels they want to construct neighborhoods and community identity "way too much for a tourist mentality," at the expense of local residents and ignoring more important problems. Sara went on:

> Sometimes I go out and walk around and I see [ . . . ] all these other layers and political questions that are like right in front of my face in the landscape, but the Tourism Bureau isn't pointing those questions out. They're not going to. They're going to keep painting a picture that this is a livable place. Well where isn't it livable? Or where is it about a different agenda than the one that's gonna encourage a large corporation to move to that neighborhood or encourage a tour bus to come through?

In contrast, through their own guided walks, street signs, maps, and other information, Sara and her collaborators create "projects that are promoting a form of tourism that's about wandering and noticing what's there, even in terms of redevelopment, rather than needing a destination to arrive at." These interventions too have been conducted with cooperation from public agencies that support these ideals. In general, she says she makes an effort to recognize the tendencies and processes at work in the city, and tries to respond to them through her interventions:

> So if we're looking at a vacant lot, [ . . . ] what will be the intention of the human development of that site, and what type of human development should be prop-agated? I guess I'm just trying to get at how questions of control of land and control of space come back to a question of like how human construction gets valued and determined. And who's doing the determining is another part of that too! That's what I mean about development. I mean we might not need to ask all these questions so much if we felt like we were in a political system that has transparency and flexibility to it in terms of, you know, in terms what values got implemented in policy. But I mean, in Los Angeles it's definitely a huge part that we think a lot about the privatization of space all the time.

Sara's efforts aim to address what she views as systemic failures of policy, regulation, and economic ideology in her city. She is well informed of the contexts and consequences of these failures, their everyday realities and their more theoretical implications. Unlike some, Sara does not have a professional background with these issues per se (she has a master's degree in public art studies and is a professional artist and arts educator), though she has worked in community organizing and with the Center for Land Use Interpretation, a nonprofit organization dedicated to research, art, and advocacy around urban and rural land use. But through her practice and her personal passions Sara has become an expert, affecting changes to the uses and perceptions of public spaces in her city and even earning the respect of official actors. In the process, like so many do-it-yourself urbanists I met, she is blurring the line between informal and formal in urban design and community placemaking.

• • •

Cultural context and social positionality matter a great deal for determining the kinds of work people do. By looking at the backgrounds of DIY urban designers, especially their familiarity with relevant knowledge of urban policy, design standards, and scholarship, we further complicate our understanding of the motivations, justifications, and cultural contexts of their actions. Do-it-yourself urban design challenges the norm of a controlled urban landscape open only to professional alteration or criminal vandalism, demonstrating instead an informal gray area of unsanctioned but civic-minded would-be contributions. And, as this chapter has shown, many do-it-yourselfers intervene using the same tools, guidelines, and broader considerations *as* professionals. Some of them literally *are* professionals.

I demonstrated first how surprisingly "formalized" types of technical and scholarly knowledge feature in the creation of these otherwise informal interventions. Some interventionists make use of technical skills and purpose-built tools. Many learn about the appropriate places, materials, and even design guidelines for the types of additions they want to make, and the codes and laws that govern them. Still others call upon the ideals of planning theory past or present, or reference the ideas of academic urban studies theorists.

The diffusion of relevant professional and academic knowledge occurs in two related ways: with everyday community members seeking information in order to more effectively make changes themselves, and with actual design and planning professionals seeing an opportunity or need and then bringing their know-how to the streets. Particular DIY urban design responses are also often directly inspired by their creator's own skills, interests, and backgrounds. In other words, these are not your average community members or your average bureaucrats, but well-informed interlopers somewhere in between who learn the facts, use the tools, and quote the rationales of professionals and scholars to inform and justify the unauthorized improvements that they make. The handful of do-it-yourselfers I met who have direct familiarity with formal planning processes through schooling, careers, or engagement in local politics intervene in ways that are clearly informed by this knowledge. These activities not only make clear that forms of potentially constructive informality are at work in the physical shaping of American cities and others in the global North, they also introduce valuable ambiguity to the idea of a formal-informal binary in the first place.

In the context of community development, do-it-yourself urban design is a very different sort of "neighborhood development from below" than that of the community groups, local businesses, and grassroots activists documented and advocated for by sociologists like Gerald Suttles or Richard Taub, equity planners like Robert Goodman, or influential community organizers like Jane Jacobs. Certainly, it is miles from the work of formalized community boards or neighborhood councils. It is also the product of individuals and groups getting much less outside professional assistance than is envisioned by well-meaning advocacy planners or public sociologists.[7] Yet DIY urbanism can have similar intentions and sometimes even comparable influence on policy and the resulting landscape. In no small part, it would seem, this may be due to do-it-yourselfers arguably having all the expertise needed.

Is the possession of some degree of technical or scholarly knowledge *necessary* for the creation of DIY urban design interventions? The simple answer is no, there are exceptions among the projects I studied. But the answer is not a simple one. Among the minority of projects that are not obviously products of *some* technical or scholarly background knowledge, all are of the subtypes I describe as guerrilla greening or aspirational urbanism (so, none of the most directly physically impacting streetscape interventions) and most are on the more ornamental end of these types to boot. They include things like "yarn bombing" (enlivening banal urban infrastructure with knit coverings) that sit on the edge between what qualifies as DIY urban design and something less clearly functional or civic minded, like street art. Most interventions I learned about, and all of the instances of what I've called "spontaneous streetscaping"—signage, road markings, sidewalk seating—came from do-it-yourselfers who either learned explicitly about professional standards and techniques or had professional backgrounds going in.

This knowledge not only inspires and enables do-it-yourselfers to act, but, crucially, gives them considerable confidence in the quality and legitimacy of their unauthorized contributions. The people I spoke to had faith in the validity of their "improvements" because they believe they are necessary, essentially as good as the real thing, and even that there is added value in their very informality. The use of technical and scholarly knowledge may well make their efforts more thoughtful and intentional, and potentially that much more functional and positive in their impacts. In some cases, it leads even to tacit approval from officials, something I return to in Chapter 6.

But what does this portend for local communities and the role, cumbersome or not, of the official planning process? It implies some limits to who has access to participation and who truly has a say in the shaping of their communities. In these ways, it might be viewed just as much as a grassroots continuation of the technocracy of scientific planning as a punk rock upending of it. And yet it is no better in terms of the fundamental problems it may introduce simply by being unplanned and unaccounted for. Furthermore, one begins to wonder what *obligation* a familiarity with the principles of urban planning, knowledge of city codes, and claims to be doing the city's work for it might also demand of do-it-yourselfers—not only to do good in the abstract but also to take local sensitivities and priorities into account if these projects are truly to be viewed as beneficial and welcome. The confidence that these lay experts have in their work raises questions about how reflexive they can be about their social positions and how conscious of their own culpability in any unintended consequences their actions may have.

This problem is complicated by another fundamental characteristic of many do-it-yourselfers, one that underlies their knowledge of technical and scholarly urbanism. The vast majority of do-it-yourselfers I spoke to and observed operate from a more immutable position of sociocultural privilege as well, raising questions of access to participation in DIY urban design at a more fundamental level. I extend this analysis of do-it-yourself urban designers' social context in Chapter 5, examining the issue of race and class privilege and how easy it is, as a result of this, for DIY urban designers to overstep their welcome in the very communities they aim to improve.

5

# The Spatial Reproduction of Inequality

*Social Privilege and Hubris in Creative Transgression*

One night, in April 2012, I was staying with a friend in Pittsburgh while conducting research with do-it-yourself urbanists in the hilly, enchanting old city. Around 10:30 in the evening I headed out back through the alley to take my dog for a walk around the predominantly white and blue-collar (but increasingly hip) neighborhood, called Bloomfield, where quiet streets of modest row houses terrace the low hillsides. This is (or was still, then) the kind of place where Italian American grandmothers peer out their windows at interlopers like myself, and where you can go to a Saturday night square dance in a converted old church that is both attended and performed by an even mix of working-class old-timey musicians and trendy youthful converts. After a few blocks on our walk, Calle and I came to a park and the unexpected sound of sawing, hammering, and power-drilling.

In one of the rectangular park's small circular plazas, two young men—both local college students, I came to find out—were hard at work under the light of the street lamp above with building tools and the remnants of a few shipping pallets. What were they doing? "Just building a bench." A bench for this park? (There were already more than a few actually.) "Yeah, to put in the park, or put anywhere really," one of them told me. He wasn't sure. They told me they were both Carnegie Mellon University students who lived nearby, one in the five-year architecture program, the other soon headed to graduate school to pursue his interest in medical technology. And they like to build stuff. They had found the materials in an industrial area farther south of where we were and figured they could use it to make a bench to leave somewhere useful as their own little addition to the streetscape.

Two men construct a bench out of found materials in a Pittsburgh park, 2012. Photo by the author.

It is also worth noting that, like a majority do-it-yourselfers I met, these two young men are white. One could imagine an encounter with two young men wielding construction tools in a city park in the middle of a quiet night going differently, or, moreover, being received differently—by others walking through the park, by residents of the homes across the street, by the police, and yes by your trusty ethnographer—if everything had been the same except for the skin color of the men themselves. We needn't find a counterexample or postulate an elaborate thought experiment; we know from voluminous sociological research and everyday experience that the circumstances might likely have been very different had these two students been young men of color.

Continuing the investigation of DIY urban design, this chapter further complicates our thinking about who engages in the practice and the wider implications of their actions by focusing explicitly on race and class and introducing questions of privilege and entitlement. There are two primary ways (in addition to many everyday ones) that race, and to a slightly less obvious extent class, matter in understanding DIY urban design. The first is the degree of social privilege experienced by do-it-yourselfers—in public spaces, in interacting with authorities or pushing legal boundaries, and in their everyday lives—based on their race and class categories, which I argue fundamentally influence their willingness to engage in these practices. The second is the way that race and class differences affect how others perceive the actions of do-it-yourselfers in the neighborhoods where they intervene. I take each of these concerns in turn, following a brief overview of the enormous corpus of sociological work on race, prejudice, and privilege in public space.

## PREJUDICE AND PRIVILEGE IN URBAN SPACE

Sociological research has documented how prejudice leads to stigmatization by race, ethnicity, gender, age, and class and the effects of living with such stigma on the attitudes and actions of members of these groups, particularly in terms of how they behave in public. These findings must inform our interpretation of how such social status categories affect individuals' decisions to engage in DIY urban design.

Especially influential in this discourse is research by the ethnographer Elijah Anderson. Studying a gentrifying, mixed-race neighborhood in Philadelphia in the 1980s, Anderson (1990) found that residents—both black and white—were afraid of young black men on the street. As a result, African Americans of any age, aware of this prejudice, would go out of their way to convince others of their commitment to "civility and law-abiding behavior" and adjust their interactions, self-presentation, and other conscious negotiations of social cues. Anderson found this to be especially true around issues of illegality and the police. Whether or not he has ever broken the law, a young black man knows he "exists in a legally precarious state" where he can get into trouble simply for being in a public place at the wrong time. And even if unwarranted stops, interrogations, and arrests tend to occur less often after black men reach a certain age, they are acutely aware that they remain objects of scrutiny by police and others.

Anderson's findings are based on ethnographic work in one area of a single American city conducted some three decades ago. Today's rapidly changing "inner-city" neighborhoods are drastically different places. But many of the basic assumptions of—and realities faced by—people of color in public space sadly remain. African Americans and Latinos are more likely to be hassled by police, arrested for drug offenses and "quality of life" policing, targeted in "stop and frisk" searches, and more. A simple gathering of black or Latino men in the wrong place at the wrong time can be sufficient for being labeled "gang activity."[1]

As Anderson (1990: 208) puts it simply, "the experiences and problems on the street of a person with dark skin are very different from those of a white person." The cumulative experiences with prejudice experienced by many people of color, and by African Americans and Mexican Americans in particular, can result in psychological trauma and shape everyday decision making, especially around interactions with police and willingness to attract police attention.[2] Other indicators of social engagement, from political participation to survey response rates and willingness to take advantage of assistance, are also diminished in Latino communities, where concerns over citizenship and immigration status may be an issue. In the United States today, immigration enforcement crackdowns and the specter of deportation haunt the daily lives of people living in immigrant communities regardless of their individual status.[3] There is some evidence that social class produces or compounds many of these attitudes as well.[4]

We also know that white privilege is very real and very prevalent. Research has identified and discussed the occurrence of systemic sociocultural advantages and opportunities associated with being white—and all the more so with being an affluent, heterosexual, white male. The feminist scholar Peggy McIntosh (1989) famously described white privilege as "like an invisible weightless knapsack of special provisions, maps, passports, codebooks, visas, clothes, tools and blank checks." In addition to numerous cultural and material benefits (from wages and career opportunities to social capital, political power, and generations of relative freedom and affluence), scholars have noted more subtle psychological advantages to whiteness including feelings of superiority and membership in the societal norm.[5] These confer a considerable, if perhaps subconscious, feeling of confidence and comfort in the day-to-day living of life that those without privilege do not enjoy. As Shamus Khan (2011) puts it, "privilege means being at ease, no matter what the context." (These advantages of white privilege can largely be extended to male privilege as well, although the impact of gender on one's ability to break the law or act freely in public space is more complicated.)*

---

* We might consider whether the women in my study operate with additional relative advantage or disadvantage due to gender stereotypes. The relevant research here is inconclusive. Women commit far fewer crimes than men in general and are broadly assumed to be less likely and less inherently prone to do so (see Heidensohn & Silvestri 2012). There is also some evidence that women may be less likely to be reported, charged, or convicted of some offenses; in studies of juvenile offenders across all types of crime, Elliott and Voss (1974) and Armstrong (1977) found that police treated girls more leniently than boys. Yet a large number of studies have argued that juvenile girls are actually more likely than juvenile males to be charged with status offenses, traffic violations, and other "less serious crimes" (Krohn et al. 1983; Horowitz & Pottieger 1991). In perhaps the most analogous (if still imperfect) case for comparison, Snyder (2009: 5) found that female graffiti writers are "less likely to be roughed up or harassed by cops or male writers," but they still "face enormous challenges negotiating dangerous streets alone at night." None of my female interviewees reported any direct interactions with police, and, while some were fearful of getting caught and others

As a result of all this, the privileged also have greater freedom to choose whether to go along with or object to the status quo. Stigma and privilege thus have direct implications for understanding a person's ability to act outside the law and engage in creative transgression in public space. For example, in her studies of local organization and neighborhood change in a predominantly African American Chicago neighborhood, Mary Pattillo observed how community members and the police conflate a number of seemingly innocuous (and not even illegal) creative uses of public space— some of which, like having a party and barbecuing in a public parkway, could be analogous to DIY urbanism—with deviant behavior when those involved are perceived to be poor or otherwise unwelcome.[6] In certain contexts of hip urban cultural production, however, these very same uses of public space, and a number of far more transgressive and even illegal ones (such as graffiti), are celebrated as signs of creativity and vibrancy and appropriated for economic development.[7]

In his 1999 study of sidewalk vendors on the streets of New York City's Greenwich Village, Mitchell Duneier found telling differences in the ways that different groups are perceived and treated based on their race and social status. He compared the experiences of predominantly African American book and magazine sellers to a white family selling Christmas trees nearby. Both groups were regularly present and recognizable "public characters" occupying similar roles as informal sidewalk vendors yet were received very differently by other locals. The book sellers, who are predominantly (but not exclusively) poor, under-educated, black men without regular housing, were routinely hassled by police and viewed as "indecent" and "deviant" public nuisances. The white family, who live in Vermont but come to the city annually to sell trees while living out of a mobile home, were quickly made part of the community, welcomed into local businesses and given keys to people's apartments, beseeched by some to find a way to vend year round. As Duneier argued, a combination of race, class, and public behavior make it much more difficult for some people to be viewed as helpful or "decent" and less likely to be given any leeway by other community members or the police.

were not, neither these attitudes nor any other experiences or personal concerns they described suggested gender-based privilege or stigma around their DIY urban design activities that could be clearly separated from other elements of their social status. But Western notions of masculinity nonetheless weigh heavily on cultural norms around risk-taking and law-breaking, and women certainly face a number of obstacles to acting and existing freely in public space in general, including the threat of harassment, objectification, and violence. Women and girls have also historically been subject to horrific public punishment for gender-specific moral offenses. It is not surprising that the majority of do-it-yourselfers I met or learned about are male.

This research on the effects of stigma and privilege on public perception and treatment by law enforcement is of direct relevance to understanding the legal gray area of DIY urban design, including what it suggests about people's willingness to step outside the law in the first place. Interactions that Duneier himself had with police officers while tending one of the sidewalk book stands he was studying are even more analogous to the DIY urban design context. Although still hassled by the police for the quasi-illegal activity, Duneier entered these interactions well informed about his rights and various other social and legal factors at play in the situation. He welcomed the exchange as an opportunity to test this knowledge and test the way the police respond. He is also a white university professor who had little to fear even if the situation had gone the wrong way (whatever the difficulties it incurred, his arrest would surely have resulted in minimal discomfort and provided additional valuable ethnographic material). In the same way, the typically white, middle-class, and well-informed do-it-yourselfer is in a stronger position to push legal boundaries and often has comparatively little to fear from attracting police attention.

All in all, we can see how this could make black and Latino community members less likely to feel comfortable creating unauthorized interventions in urban space. Why risk breaking the law to alter the urban environment when so much is at stake? As Greg Snyder (2009: 4) noted bluntly with regard to the impact of race on a person's decision to become a graffiti writer: "White folks do not have to weigh the issue of whether or not they will be beaten or shot by police for their misdemeanors." And why bother making a small improvement when one's very ability to be perceived as helpful is in doubt? To draw again from Anderson (1990: 182), "The public stigma is so powerful that black strangers are seldom allowed to be civil or even helpful without some suspicion of their motives." Blacks and Latinos—and especially younger or poorer blacks and Latinos—experience substantial stigmatization in urban space, in ways that have direct bearing on their likelihood of feeling comfortable acting outside of norms or legal boundaries in public. Middle-class white folks, meanwhile, essentially "get away with" more, and therefore feel more comfortable taking such risks.

## 'DON'T BOTHER WITH THOSE, THOSE ARE NON-OFFENSIVE'— WHITE PRIVILEGE AND CREATIVE TRANSGRESSION

The typical do-it-yourself urban designer—the vast majority of those I spoke to or learned about—is white, middle class, adult, male, and possessing of some degree of familiarity with professional or scholarly urbanism.

In comparison to would-be do-it-yourselfers of color, whites operate from a position of considerable privilege, not least in terms of their relationship to authorities and common assumptions about their motives in urban space. As members of the urban "creative class," they also exist within a popular culture and mode of production that tends to celebrate graffiti art, protest, hacking, and other practices of creative transgression. These factors strongly influence their willingness and ability to push legal boundaries in public space and thus to participate more freely and fully in DIY urban design activities.

In many cases, white, educated, middle-class do-it-yourselfers act with great confidence and even entitlement when making changes to their surroundings, acting as experts and feeling they are unlikely to face any real consequences. Although a handful of the white and Asian do-it-yourselfers I spoke to were worried about legal repercussions—notably many of those involved in DIY bicycle improvements in Los Angeles—actual run-ins with the law that my white interviewees described always ended without arrest, even during quite flagrantly illegal interventions. Some even feature congenial conversation.

Jordan told me of an occasion on which police approached him while he was removing an advertisement from a Manhattan bus stop; he explained exactly what he was doing and received a friendly "carry on." A man of mixed white and Asian descent recounted a time that he and several others were stopped by police while painting bicycle share-the-lane arrows on a major Los Angeles street in the middle of the night and were simply told to go home. When I was accompanying do-it-yourselfers while they were installing projects in public space both day and night we never had any encounters with police, though sometimes they would drive past. In comparison, an African American do-it-yourselfer I interviewed in Oakland, Larry, recounted several stories of police harassment, even when he was doing nothing illegal at all. He viewed this quite explicitly in racial terms. Standing on a busy street near his home, he gestured toward another black man waiting for a bus near the DIY bench Larry had built and noted pointedly that "they'll harass us, but," looking back at me, "they won't harass you."

Stephen, who is white, actually welcomes the opportunity to speak with the police during his interventions. When occupying a parking spot on an LA street with an impromptu park, he was eager to have what he described as a "land-use discussion" with the police who showed up:

> So we get to have a discussion about, seriously, who do the streets belong to? And why do we have space allocated for parking? So that you can store your

personal property? [ . . . ] But what about 20 bicycles? What about me? I think I'll live here. [ . . . ] So, now we're having a conversation. And by the way we won, with [the police].

In this case, Stephen is comfortable engaging in such a debate with the police in part because he knows the law. But he also has the confidence to do so that comes from a history of interacting comfortably with authority and participating in culturally acceptable forms of creative transgression such as Park(ing) Day and Critical Mass bike rides. There are clear parallels here to Duneier's interaction with the police during his ethnographic research. With a convincing command of the regulations at play and relatively less to fear even if he were arrested, Stephen too can afford to see his interactions with police as opportunities.

Familiarity with the law and comfort with their own rights and privilege can give the typical white, middle-class, and well-informed do-it-yourselfer a sense of superiority and thus confidence in practicing creative transgression. Individuals without this knowledge or from a less privileged background could not expect the same opportunity for "conversation" even if they had the confidence to try. And a more confident, above-board attitude can, in turn, help illegal activities avoid opposition. A Los Angeles man in his 30s who was involved in designing and placing the hundreds of "pass with care" road safety signs at intersections throughout that city described his experience with the project and its illegality:

> The LAPD comes onto our website, they get invited to our rides. I do work with the LAPD bike task force, they know who I am. [The "pass with care" signs are] one of those little areas where it just doesn't get discussed because I think it was done in such a respectful way that . . . I've personally talked to members of the buffing squad—you know the people that remove graffiti—and I have a friend actually who does this for a living, and you know I was having a beer with the guy and I was like yeah, blah blah blah these posters . . . and he said that his boss said, "Don't bother with those, those are non-offensive!"

Perhaps most significantly, most of the white do-it-yourselfers I spoke to were simply not worried about the police at all. They were more often concerned about someone being injured as a result of a physical flaw in their work, or about suboptimal design for functional or aesthetic reasons. Between their structural privilege and their knowledge of the system, most do-it-yourselfers pay the legally precarious nature of their craft little mind.

This lack of concern about legal consequences may also provide an answer to another question raised by the findings above: why do these individuals, who by and large possess considerable political, social, and economic capital, choose to make improvements themselves and often illegally? The effort to place benches and planters at some neglected bus stops and street corners in South Los Angeles was organized in part by the highly regarded and well-connected pastor at St. Michael's Parish Church. Stephen is a known face around city hall and recently ran for city council. Surely based on race and class alone, privileged individuals have more ability than most to seek the changes they desire through formal channels. Research has documented that local government tends to be more responsive to the concerns of white, wealthier citizens, and these residents are more likely to feel taken care of as a result.[8]

So why risk breaking the law to make unauthorized improvements? In addition to their faith in the quality of their contributions and the inherent value some see in grassroots citizen participation, their privilege means that there is little risk involved at all; they needn't take advantage of their political capital through formal channels because their social and cultural capital let them do what they want anyway. Privileged do-it-yourself urban designers have their motivations, and essentially nothing is standing in their way. For black and Latino do-it-yourselfers, however, concerns about legality are never far from their minds.

## "WE DON'T WANT TO RISK BEING CALLED ILLEGAL"—LEGAL VULNERABILITY FOR DO-IT-YOURSELFERS OF COLOR

The architect Steve Rasmussen Cancian has been working since the early 2000s with people in underprivileged parts of Los Angeles and Oakland to help them improve the public spaces in their neighborhoods. "For the majority of the low-income communities I've worked with," he told me, "people are particularly concerned about doing things that are unauthorized because they're legally vulnerable." As we walked through several of these communities together, meeting Steve's local collaborators on the DIY projects and the everyday residents who make use of them, it was apparent that many working-class, predominantly Latino neighborhoods such as these could benefit from streetscape improvements. And people there are eager to see such things happen. But a series of anecdotes from two of the groups Steve has worked with in LA are especially telling in terms of how concerns about breaking the law factor into decision making around DIY urban design among people of color. Steve continued:

> Most of the people I work with in LA wouldn't feel comfortable breaking the law. Either they're immigrants without documents or, in the African American community, the elders respect the law and then the younger folks have too much at risk with police. You can't hang out on an illegal bench, it's not viable.

Among the Latino community groups involved in DIY urban design activities in Los Angeles (which are significantly more organized and established than the individuals or informal groups that I otherwise observed), there are effectively two perspectives toward unauthorized actions, and they have much to do with understandings of local legitimacy both internal to the community and in the eyes of authority. On the one hand are groups like Union de Vecinos, in East LA, who create unauthorized improvements from their own position of relative privilege as an established and well-connected community organization dating to 1996. As Steve explained,

> They're this really active group of people, and not only do they have social capital, well-educated, but also they have a predisposition to be risk-takers. And not just to do things unauthorized, but to meet new people and join projects.

On the other hand, the group Acción Westlake, based near Downtown LA, is "oh, 90 percent Latina moms? So they don't ever work with the folks who do the unauthorized stuff." Members of this group believe they have more to gain from staying above-board and working through the official networks that they have worked hard to build. "You know, access to power," one of them answered when asked what they had to lose. "So why would we do something unauthorized?"

Some do-it-yourselfers in disadvantaged or stigmatized neighborhoods are also wary of working with other members of their own community when such would-be collaborators are viewed as potential legal liabilities. For instance, I heard how an internal dispute had erupted within Union de Vecinos' membership over the prospect of working with a gang-affiliated group of men on converting a neglected alleyway into a handball court. Although mostly older men, they were still known as "bad gang kids," so the organization's more conservative members feared being affiliated with them. (Those with criminal backgrounds and less political capital of course have plenty to gain from being affiliated with the more established groups.)

Concerns over legal repercussions impact how far, how visible, how flashy these groups are willing to get with their DIY efforts as well. Although "you'd have to be a real bureaucrat to bug someone about a bird house, something that sticks out six inches," said Steve, "if we want to build benches or planters or hanging lighting? Well then, if we don't want to risk being called illegal and [authorities] trying to take it down or take action against us, you have to ask for permits." This helps explain why it is that, although all manner of small-scale improvements and informal ways of making do can be found in low-income communities or in social housing projects, I found so few examples of the sorts of flashier public streetscape improvements and visible signage that more privileged do-it-yourselfers tend to create. The main exception to this is sidewalk seating, which I saw everywhere I went, perhaps even especially in poorer neighborhoods, where crates, boxes, or household chairs arranged out on the sidewalk are all commonplace sights occasioned by the living of life outdoors in areas with few official places to sit.

For people and communities of color, the prospect of engaging in DIY urban design is made more difficult and less likely by the racialized realities of their relationship to authority and the pursuant wariness within these communities around law-breaking. Stronger reactions from the police are more likely and personal risks to the culprits are considerably higher, turning off some potential participants and making it harder for others to gain traction. Yet clearly some people in such positions *do* participate in DIY urban design. We could ask the same question that we asked of more privileged do-it-yourselfers, if under very different circumstances: why risk breaking the law to make local improvements? From the few telling cases in my research, the answer is essentially that they do it when they feel they "have to" (the need is great and an official solution is unlikely), when the risk is assessed and considered acceptable, and then often still from the relative safety of some sort of organizational legitimacy.

When legal repercussions are a real possibility, weighing these risks is central to the process of considering a DIY intervention. Decisions are made based on how much risk people are willing to take. When the need is viewed as great enough and official involvement or approval is viewed as too cumbersome or unlikely, then, despite the risk, the unauthorized route can still win out. With Union de Vecinos' efforts to convert their alleyways into much-needed public spaces,

> we brainstormed out what was possible and then people voted what they wanted to do, and chose the highest-risk alternative, which was let's go ahead and repave the streets. Because it's like, that's what we need. [ . . . ] The rest of it's a waste of time, if you have these huge potholes and it all looks ugly, why would we do everything else [make smaller-scale improvements]? [ . . . ] If we wanna do stuff in the middle of the street, basically they're never gonna let us.

In East Los Angeles, a fairly typical alleyway, at top, and one converted into a public gathering space by the group Union de Vecinos, including a mural, basketball hoop, red-painted "plaza" cement (in progress), electric lighting, and painted mobile barriers at both ends. Photos by the author, 2012.

And so, in this case, Union de Vecinos, working with Steve, started with a small stretch of alley ("maybe 150 feet") and began filling the potholes. Next, they applied a slurry coat of red asphalt, and built two eight-foot-long planters with wheels that could be rolled out as necessary to "close the alley and make it a public space." An artistically inclined teenager from the neighborhood designed a paint scheme for the planters and the walls, and the community finished it all off with a basketball hoop and some lighting—all without permission.

Standing in this alley-cum-plaza with Steve and several longtime community members on a sunny December afternoon, a feeling of hope and accomplishment was palpable among residents. And the difference between this place—still a work in progress when I visited—and the untouched, litter-strewn dangerous alleyways nearby was stark. Union de Vecinos' plan was to invite their city councilman to see the finished product, and when, they imagine, he is impressed and asks what city department is responsible, they would say:

> No, actually, look at the alley across the street—that's what a city alley looks like. We did this. And, you know, shame on you that we, you know, folks who are not of means, had to come out and do all this. You guys, you gotta get your shit together and fix the other alley, and the next one and the next one! Because we can't fill all the potholes!

Several groups throughout East LA have now taken the improvement of their plentiful back alleys into their own hands in different ways. One group decided to create "a vertical garden up and down the alleys" by hanging organic pouches full of soil and seed on their alleys' walls; another created a large plaza; still another runs an informal street market in their alley and had plans to install retractable canopies to provide shade for it. Union de Vecinos has also painted street intersection plazas in the style of Mark Lakeman's efforts in Portland and the EcoVillage in Central LA; the group can now take credit for transforming some 15 different public spaces. (They have also played a leading role in recent protests targeting art galleries and other signs of gentrification in their rapidly changing community.)

All of these efforts are those of established community organizations, acting after careful consideration of the potential legal consequences of their actions. Some African American do-it-yourselfers I met in Oakland likewise make their unauthorized improvements as a recognized (if not quite legally established) community group called Hood Builders. Affiliations like these can provide a small but important layer of added legitimacy to those who might not otherwise be given much leeway by authorities. In sum, while I certainly saw examples of DIY urban design in low socioeconomic status communities, participation tended to feature far greater consideration of legal vulnerability and the unauthorized nature of the practice. While he showed me around the sites in Central and East Los Angeles where he has helped groups to build benches, tables, and other "community living room" amenities, Steve also summarized the relative positions of privilege and disadvantage between himself and these communities:

> I think with a lot of the immigrant neighborhoods, people really want [DIY improvements] permitted. Because the idea of doing something that's overtly illegal . . . a lot of folks don't have documents, they can't afford the risk, and also the culture: it's not cool to break the law. So, I think that's an interesting question that, if you were to describe it sharply, it's only cool to break the law if in some ways you're personally above it. So, I can break the law! What are they gonna do? I've been in jail before, lots of times for protests, nothing's really gonna happen. But if going to prison is a real issue in your life? You are not gonna break the law for some urbanist project. So that's a real limiting factor.

Steve is wary of the whole prospect of DIY urban design because of this unequal access to participation. "I think it needs to be accessible to people who don't feel comfortable breaking the law," he said. Without equal access, only those with privilege will be able to have this sort of say in the planning and design of their communities.

A lack of privilege does not automatically prevent people of low socioeconomic status from living their lives in public spaces or acting to improve their communities, nor does it automatically lead authorities to target their actions. Indeed, some sorts of informal urbanism are unquestionably more common in underprivileged communities, from workaday alterations that make shared dwellings feel more like home and community murals and monuments that project neighborhood identity, to whole informal economies of getting by and making do. The urban planner and community activist James Rojas has identified a particular mode of cultural placemaking in California's Mexican American communities that he calls Latino Urbanism. Things such as parking lot religious shrines and other informal adaptations of the built environment for social or entrepreneurial uses (not to mention the tremendous tradition of street murals) are relatively common in East LA and other parts of the United States as well. The predominantly African American residents of St. Elmo Village, a self-described "place of creativity" and "mosaic of humanity" centered around the street

A shrine to the Virgin of Guadalupe in a parking lot in East Los Angeles, 2012. Photo by the author.

of the same name in central Los Angeles, have been painting, landscaping, and otherwise repairing and enlivening their street in response to "visual detrerioration" since 1969.[9] Photographer and visual sociologist Camilo José Vergara (e.g., 2016) has documented numerous informal adaptations, including benches and other sidewalk seating, in the extreme disinvestment context of Detroit. Again, I saw many instances of improvised street seating, as well as guerrilla gardening, in disadvantaged parts of Chicago, Los Angeles, New Orleans, New York, and Oakland.

And we might think of perhaps the most time-honored and commonplace do-it-yourself urban streetscape improvement: the opening of fire hydrants to cool off in the summertime, effectively turning this piece of emergency infrastructure into an amenity. Despite being dangerous and illegal in most circumstances, cities generally simply attempt to control this activity rather than enforce the fines and arrests that are on the books for it (more than 200 New York City fire hydrants were illegally opened in a single hot weekend in July of 2013, apparently without fine or arrest).[10] I observed—indeed participated in and enjoyed—this practice numerous times in New York, often in lower income and predominantly African American or Latino neighborhoods, and always unfettered (sometimes even enabled) by police.

But a willingness among everyday people to partake in culturally normalized practices like opening fire hydrants does not translate into a broad willingness to engage in unsanctioned streetscape alterations of the most visible or provocative type. This is an issue of one sort of legitimacy, the social norms and culturally accepted practices within a particular context or field. In the case of opening a fire hydrant or pushing a chair out onto the street, both the action and the likely police response (or lack thereof) are normalized and predictable. With less established and more visible or flamboyant types of informal urbanism, police responses are unpredictable, so informal action is carried out with great caution among those with more to lose or those who know they are under heightened scrutiny to begin with. I found such risks are taken rarely, out of some desperation and with explicit consideration of legal dangers, and then usually in forms that minimize unwanted attention and often under the cover of an established community organization that provides a small layer of added legitimacy. The DIY urban design interventions that seem to attract the most condemnation from authorities (and which had their creators most worried about arrest) are guerrilla bike lanes, all of which that I am aware of were created by more privileged middle-class do-it-yourselfers.

In these ways, although race and class are not defining elements of DIY urbanism itself (nor in most cases are they conscious considerations of its practitioners), race and class are undeniably and inextricably essential to how we understand DIY urbanism as a social phenomenon shaping our cities. People who are white, educated, middle class, and adult experience considerable privilege in dealings with authorities as well as in how they are perceived by others in public space. They begin with greater legitimacy in the eyes of authority and mainstream (white) society, and they achieve legitimacy in their actions through the cultural and symbolic capital expressed in their aesthetic choices as well. As such, white, educated, middle-class adults are significantly more likely to feel comfortable pushing legal boundaries with certain actions in public space—including painting a bike lane under cover of night, climbing a lamppost to attach a homemade metal sign, or ripping apart an old payphone to remove an advertisement or to convert it into a public book exchange. Marginalized actors begin from a place of relative suspicion in the eyes of authority and often rely on more formal institutional routes to mainstream legitimacy. Access to participation in DIY urban design is not equal.

What is more—and unlike groups like Union de Vecinos or St. Elmo Village or even the people of New York or Chicago who regularly open their local fire hydrants in the summertime—privileged do-it-yourselfers are more likely to feel comfortable engaging in design interventions anywhere they please. Yet this comfort—and, arguably, hubris—on the part of do-it-yourselfers does not mean they are always welcomed or accepted by others. This leads us to another important (and very much related) way that race and class privilege manifest themselves in DIY urban design: how do-it-yourselfers are perceived in different neighborhood contexts, and in particular why some interventions are celebrated while others are viewed as unwelcome. If race and class are less explicitly visible here, these categories are implicated just as strongly, as are other cultural norms and values. To explore these factors, I turn next to a case in which a seemingly innocuous guerrilla greening effort is perceived as unwelcome by longtime residents.

## CULTURAL CONFLICT AND LOCAL ILLEGITIMACY IN DIY URBAN DESIGN

On a rainy Saturday morning in April 2009, an artist named Deborah Fisher gathered together nearly 100 friends and other volunteers (mostly reached via a webpage she had set up) on a street near her home in Brooklyn's Bedford-Stuyvesant neighborhood. She gave some brief instructions and passed out custom tote bags full of wildflower seeds and local area map printouts from Google Maps. The eager volunteers then went to their designated zones (covering a total of about three square miles in the leafy, historic neighborhood) and spread the seeds in vacant lots, tree pits, and cracks in the sidewalk. In a matter of hours, Deborah told me, "wildflower seeds were sewn on every single neglected inch of Bed-Stuy."

A white woman in her mid-30s, Deborah had come up with the idea for this guerrilla greening effort out of frustration with the "dishonesty" and "inconsistencies" in her environmentally inspired art practice (and the "despair" and "self-denial" of environmentalism in general). She wanted to do something to actually improve the environment of her community, "just saying, I can affect my environment positively." Responding to what she described as "a lot of vacancy and blight" throughout Bed-Stuy, planting flowers in the vacant lots seemed like a good way to help.[11] "The amount of vacant space beckoned doing something with it, on a very basic level," she said. The project was inspired by other guerrilla gardening efforts in New York and beyond, including a history of guerrilla gardening dating to the 1970s in

Bedford-Stuyvesant itself.† It was also, as Deborah put it, an "homage" to the neighborhood's strong tradition of self-determination and self-reliance:

> I mean I walk in this neighborhood, [ . . . ] I see all of these beautiful instances of people caring, that are really, really awesome. My block in Bed-Stuy is a beautiful block. It was a beautiful block in the '80s. The people in the block association talk a lot about how they did that. You know, they're very eloquent about the way that they say this is about owning this street, and if you don't like this happening, say that you don't like it happening! They're making sure that everything is very clean and making sure that everyone is policed. [ . . . ] I was trying to appreciate that gesture of saying, like, this is my neighborhood, and I care about it.

Deborah set up a website seeking volunteers to spread seeds and donations to cover the costs of the project, which she called Bed-Stuy Meadow. Hundreds responded and she raised $2,000 in a few weeks—"enough to buy lots of seeds and these cool tote bags, and have a party afterwards."

Participants scatter wildflower seeds in front of a vacant building as part of Deborah Fisher's Bed-Stuy Meadow project, Brooklyn, 2009. Photo by Kate Glicksberg.

† For instance, Deborah made particular reference to Hattie Carthan, a Bedford-Stuyvesant resident and noted environmentalist and community activist, who was also one of Brooklyn's first guerrilla gardeners. She planted trees throughout the neighborhood in the early 1970s and helped to found both the educational Bed-Stuy Neighborhood Tree Corps and the radical Green Guerrillas group during this period. Carthan died in 1984 (see NYC Parks 2014).

The project was, in Deborah's eyes and on its own terms, a success: participants had fun and by the late summer, flowers were blooming throughout the neighborhood. In fact, because many were perennials, in some places they continue to grow today (if a new condominium building hasn't gone in on top of them). "Someone will walk by and say 'Isn't that beautiful? I walk by it every day and it makes me so happy,'" Deborah told me a year or so later, as we sat chatting in the window of a recently opened wine bar in the neighborhood, looking out at the relatively quiet, tree-lined street. "That's all I wanted, you know?" Yet the project was not so rosy in everyone's eyes. In the days that followed, the local media (and members of the community itself) presented the story in a different light.

Deborah had made an effort to raise awareness of her Bed-Stuy Meadow project by alerting various locally concerned blogs. In the end, even the *New York Times* covered her project in a local interest piece published the next day under the title "April Showers Bring Seed-Sewing Volunteers."[12] The piece described the fun that participants were having, including a photo of a child helping her mother scatter seeds in a tree well, and noted the nod Deborah hoped the intervention could make to the neighborhood's history and traditions.

But the article also noted, significantly, that the volunteers included "a sustainable-living consultant from nearby Prospect Heights, two Italian architects, [and] an industrial designer who rode his bike from Bushwick," in addition to some locals and community boosters. And it contained interviews with some residents who "seemed resentful, suggesting that it was impolite for outsiders to come into their neighborhood and try to change the way it looked." New York City's public radio station, WNYC, followed up with a story a couple of days later, revealing that many longtime Bedford-Stuyvesant residents had heard nothing about the project, while those locals who were involved were "mostly newcomers brought here by gentrification."[13] The recurring theme was that the event felt like "outsiders imposing their vision on the community."

I have described how many do-it-yourself urban design interventions are informed by sophisticated knowledge of professional planning techniques and ideas of scholarly urbanism. And we have seen here how the majority of do-it-yourselfers operate from a position of social privilege in urban space due to their skin color and socioeconomic status. These characteristics nurture among many do-it-yourselfers a potentially problematic degree of confidence in and even entitlement around their actions. And they portend further complications for the ostensibly democratic nature of DIY urban design. In this section, I explore these problems by analyzing cases like Deborah's where DIY contributions have proven controversial and unwelcome in the communities where they were made. I then consider the degree to which otherwise well-informed do-it-yourselfers are actually conscious of or sympathetic to local residents' negative perceptions of their interventions and how they might work to earn acceptance.

## "Before You Change Something, Become a Part of It"—DIY Urbanism Out of Place

Do-it-yourselfers are motivated, more or less, by a desire to make what they see as a positive contribution to the urban landscape. In so doing, however, they are physically imposing their values on the place, and by extension the community, in which they act. Problems can arise when a do-it-yourselfer's warrant for having such a say is called into question. This can happen for numerous reasons; myriad actors lay claim to the right to shape urban space, and such claims are often contentious. But probably the quickest way to raise a community's eyebrows in terms of urban development is to be viewed as acting "out of place."

Cultural identity is strongly tied to place, and a community's sense of place attachment is often connected to sentiments of permanence, authenticity, and cultural continuity.[14] "Outsiders" and "newcomers" are frequently suspect. New businesses, real estate developments, and individuals who seem inauthentic or in conflict with established norms or values may be perceived as illegitimate challenges to local identity, and thus as unwelcome.

Although some DIY projects are effectively generic, or universal, addressing a perceived citywide or even global problem—such as the advertising removal campaigns that Jordan has led all over New York as well as in Canada, Spain, and the United Kingdom—most are carried out by individuals in or near the neighborhoods where they live to address a particular issue there. This makes sense, and one might argue it is how it ought to be—residents of a neighborhood have a unique perspective on the needs of their community and a clear stake in positive outcomes, and as such they are more likely to be viewed as legitimate actors there. As a Los Angeles do-it-yourselfer put it confidently, "I know from like living and being in my neighborhood, in my area, like what improvements could be made to benefit lots of people in my situation."

When a DIY project effectively fits with the cultural context of the neighborhood where it is created—for instance, in neighborhoods known for youthful, artistic, and creative class subcultures where acts of creative transgression are celebrated along with street art, activism, and popular urbanism—they tend to go over quite well. The guys from DoTank installed their handmade chairs and other projects in trendy Brooklyn neighborhoods like Williamsburg and Clinton Hill, near where they were living. Stacey's "Phoenix Chalkboard" sits in easily the hippest urban arts district in that city. Much of the DIY bicycle infrastructure that has been added to Los Angeles streets is concentrated in a succession of gentrifying areas stretching from East Hollywood to Highland Park. In these places, DIY urban design is at home, authentic, often even celebrated.

Most of the DIY urban design interventions that I learned about were seemingly uncontroversial in community context. I observed many pieces of homemade street furniture being used just as intended. When talking with community members in numerous cities about the DIY signage or guerrilla gardens or free book exchanges that had popped up near their homes or businesses, I found that most were pleased or simply indifferent. Local media coverage, which I analyzed whenever a DIY intervention received any, was in the vast majority of cases positive too. And where I had no such information at all, it is safe to say the projects were probably all the more innocuous, usually being physically unobtrusive and very small in scale—sometimes basically unrecognizable. Many interventions, especially official-looking street signs and historical markers, have remained in place for years and years without attracting any attention at all, much less community opposition.

In the cases where communities did demonstrate opposition or apprehension around DIY alterations, however, clashing cultural values were universally apparent. These conflicts seem especially likely to occur when a do-it-yourselfer is a relatively new arrival to the place in which he or she is acting and does not match the dominant cultural characteristics of the area. If race or class sameness are fundamental measures of community belonging or cohesion, for instance, difference on these terms can serve as a clear indicator of otherness. In these cases, the do-it-yourselfers are perceived as interlopers without legitimacy as local actors, and their projects may be viewed as unwelcome intrusions (almost regardless of the intervention itself).

"I wanted the press to be about environmentalism," Deborah told me as we sat in the bar in Bed-Stuy, enjoying a bowl of guacamole and a couple glasses of wine. But instead, "all this press focused on race and gentrification." She viewed her seed-bombing project as a beautification effort, "a gift to a community," a "treat." She was shocked by the negative reaction—"Who's anti-flower?" she asked me. But local residents were more displeased with the cultural implications behind the action than with the action itself: "It's not so much about the flowers. It's about the idea," longtime resident Keith Henry told the *New York Times* that day; "Before you change something, become a part of it." Part of the problem was ineffective community outreach: by only posting the call on a blog oriented to urban agriculture enthusiasts, Deborah conceded she had essentially introduced an unwanted selection bias into who read about and participated in the project. But the story of Bed-Stuy Meadow, and its icy reception by many residents of the neighborhood it aimed to improve, demonstrates how easy it can be for one person's DIY urban design effort to be viewed as out of place and presumptuous in the wrong context, however well intended.

Another controversial DIY streetscape intervention occurred later the same year as Deborah's project and less than two miles away. Bedford Avenue, the longest street in Brooklyn, runs for more than 10 miles from the waterfront in working-class Sheepshead Bay to McCarren Park in ultra-trendy Williamsburg, and it is a major cycling route. In 2007, as part of Mayor Michael Bloomberg's efforts to improve cycling infrastructure in New York City, Bedford Avenue was given a bike lane from top to bottom. Along its course, in addition to passing through Bed-Stuy, the street forms the main commercial corridor for a densely populated Hasidic Jewish community in the South Williamsburg area dating to 1946. Religiously ultra-orthodox and socially conservative, the Satmar Hasidim have since the late 1990s found the borders of their insular enclave increasingly encroached upon, most dramatically by a certain class of predominantly young, secular, and socially liberal newcomers to its northern fringes—those who had, by the early 21st century, made Williamsburg synonymous with the word "hipster."[15] The Satmars' relationship to their neighbors was and remains a complex cultural conflict in one of Brooklyn's trendiest but also most diverse neighborhood crossroads. (Neighboring Latino and African American communities have also long had tensions with the Hasidim, and with the hip, predominantly white newcomers as well.) An insightful 2010 *New York Magazine* story by Michael Idov, spectacularly titled "Clash of the Bearded Ones," provides a detailed discussion of this history (an early flyer asked God to "please remove from upon us the plague of the artists") and of the 2009 conflict around the bicycle lane.

Suffice it to say that many of the newcomers are avid cyclists as well as provocative dressers, and when the bicycle lane seemed to further welcome them down Bedford Avenue, Hasidic locals viewed it as a cultural affront. They complained about what they considered the inappropriate clothing of some women riding through and the danger that scofflaw cyclists pose to children, and felt that the lane itself was an "intrusion" into the neighborhood. Like the Bed-Stuy flower bombing, this conflict was framed in terms of who was viewed as a legitimate actor in local urban space based on seniority. "How long have you lived in the community that you now want to make the rules and totally ignore my opinion, when I've lived here for 50 years?" one member of the Hasidic community told Idov, "You just got here." The Satmar community, which is well organized and politically influential, compelled the city to remove the most controversial segment of bike lane in December of 2009. What had been the longest continuous bike lane in Brooklyn suddenly had a 14-block gap.

Civic infrastructure having been undone by organized political participation, what happened next was much more DIY. Several nights after the lane had been sandblasted out through South Williamsburg, a small group of cyclists decided to re-stripe the missing lane themselves. Using spray paint and handmade stencils, they recreated the lanes and cycling symbols on the street over two nights. Though the effort was applauded by numerous bike blogs, it was, not surprisingly, viewed as yet another example of disrespect and "intrusion" by many Hasidic locals. And they had a do-it-yourself response of their own: the midnight lane-stripers were stopped and detained by the Hasidic community's informal police force, the *Shomrim* patrol, who held them, complete with sirens, until the NYPD arrived.[‡] Though they were released at the scene, two of culprits, both women, were ultimately arrested on criminal mischief charges and their new bike lane was once again deleted by the city.

The event inspired a "funeral procession" for the lost lane on the cyclists' side (and threats of a topless bike ride, which did not materialize) and even greater animosity between the two groups. Despite community forums aimed at reconciliation and the ever-shifting cultural geography of Williamsburg, the discord has only continued to simmer. Although the city has since constructed a major protected bicycle thoroughfare along the waterfront several blocks away, which yields plenty of cultural (and sometimes physical) collisions of its own, Bedford Avenue remains a popular bike route, even where the lane has been removed. As I have experienced myself, commuting regularly through the area by both of these routes, many locals practice a stubborn disregard for interloping cyclists.

Controversial DIY urban design interventions are not limited to the efforts of hip and privileged newcomers. Plenty of longtime residents in neighborhoods where I spent time in Brooklyn irritated their neighbors with self-serving activities like parking space spot saving. (Then again, spot saving

‡ In another case of violent anti-bike vigilantism, angry locals in the small suburb of Woodside, a wealthy enclave between San Francisco and Silicon Valley, have been known to lay carpet tacks along popular cycling routes to puncture riders' tires in a conflict that apparently goes back more than a decade (see Nevius 2015).

is also viewed as totally legitimate in some places, and even the efforts of some wealthy Malibu residents to restrict access to public beaches might well be viewed positively by their immediate neighbors.) As noted, the Satmar Hasidim embrace all manner of informal urbanism themselves, sometimes tied in part to a doctrinal commitment to independence from state governance. In fact, about exactly a year before the 2009 bike lane controversy on Bedford Avenue, it was members of the Hasidic community who first brought DIY tactics into play in opposing another bike lane a couple blocks away. They installed an unauthorized, faux-civic "detour route" sign (billboard-sized, in black and construction orange, and complete with detailed directions), advising motorists to take an alternate route to avoid being "inconvenienced" by "the bike lane and parking problem created by NYC department of transportation"; volunteers also passed out leaflet advisories to drivers. Other instances of informal urbanism in the Satmar community include the aforementioned volunteer police force—which has been accused of racism—and DIY signage that marks cultural regulations in the community, some of which, instructing women to step aside for men on public sidewalks and to sit in the back of public buses, has proven quite controversial.§

I also found that DIY improvements made by longtime residents of rapidly gentrifying areas can themselves attract opposition from wealthier newcomers or developers if they appear to conflict with intentions for growing land values. As Pattillo found, even legal activities by some longtime residents in the public spaces of a gentrifying neighborhood may be viewed as undesirable and conflated with vagrancy and lawbreaking. While looking at one of the urban "living rooms" Steve Cancian has helped build with low-income community groups in Los Angeles, which are designed to encourage use of the sidewalks as public gathering spaces, he gave an example of real estate developers fighting the projects on exactly these grounds:

> We've had that experience over and over again, of specific landowners saying to cities, "I can't rent my apartments," or "I can't do this or that, because there's all

§ A private company has paid New York's transit authority since 1973 for the right to operate a public bus route connecting South Williamsburg to another Orthodox neighborhood in Brooklyn. Designed for the use of the Hasidic community, but technically still public and stopping at public bus stops, buses on this route were gender segregated until 2011 when a non-Orthodox woman sitting toward the front of one (and being observed by a reporter) was asked to move to the back (see Chavkin 2011), causing enough public outcry that the Metropolitan Transportation Authority ordered the private operator to desegregate its buses. That same year, another report described unauthorized signage bolted to street trees in the Satmar neighborhood, written in Yiddish, asking women on the sidewalk to please "step aside when a man approaches" (Rosenberg 2011; Short 2011). On the unofficial "detour route" sign, see the article by Calder (2008).

these people hanging out on the street." [One developer] very actively pushed and campaigned to get the city to remove the living room, and told me that as long as the living room is there, the neighborhood can't become, in his words, "Beverly Hills," because the only people that hang out there are drug dealers. And as we sit there—I'm talking to him in front of his hotel—he says, "Like those people, they're drug dealers." I think there was like fifteen people there, moms, kids—mostly people who are distinguished by the fact that they're taking the bus. To work!

This shows the persistent tension between capitalism and urban life, and the limits of tolerance for diversity or creative transgression when it does not match dominant affluent aesthetics or threatens economic growth priorities. Yet it is situations like Deborah's, in which a white do-it-yourselfer's ostensibly harmless and even populist community improvement effort is met with skepticism and a (not unfounded) fear of cultural displacement, that cut to the heart of these uncomfortable aspects of DIY urban design. Especially when the do-it-yourselfers are newer residents of traditionally underserved communities, their perspectives on what needs "improvement" are likely different from the priorities of the longtime residents. A recent arrival may look at their new neighborhood and see the need for a bike lane; a longtime resident may wish for more responsive and just police protection, rapid transit access, or other services. While a DIY intervention may make its creator feel more comfortable in his or her new community, it can be negatively viewed by longtime residents who see the project as illegitimate, unresponsive, or outright offensive to the needs or values of the community. In these cases, the do-it-yourselfers and their actions are perceived as threats to the established character of a community and may be understood as part of a broader trend of cultural change or gentrification in the area. The intended improvements themselves may not in fact be the issue so much as the local perception of the interloper behind them. In some contexts, being a white, middle-class do-it-yourselfer can effectively make gaining acceptance and legitimacy in the eyes of a nonwhite community more difficult.

DIY urban design can also seem condescendingly paternalistic at times, as those with the confidence to intervene effectively assert that they "know better" than other (less technically savvy or less fortunate) members of their communities. As one contributor to LA's Department of DIY put it, while speaking proudly about his effort to improve cycling access to a freeway underpass by softening a square curb with a cement ramp, "I know like the teenage girl riding her dad's bike around, she's not going to think like 'I should cement a curb here' and she probably doesn't have the resources to do it."

Many DIY urban design contributions do require monetary invest-ment: trips to Home Depot for materials came up dozens of times in my interviews, and I learned about project costs ranging from the tens to the hundreds of dollars in many cases.[16] But certainly not all do: another thing that came up all the time in my conversations with do-it-yourselfers was the humble wooden shipping pallet, the main ingredient in DIY interven-tions from Larry's planters and bus stop seating in Oakland to DoTank's Adirondack chairs in Brooklyn to the benches the two young students were building in Pittsburgh when I came across them that night in Friendship Park. And while access to the sorts of educational and professional experi-ences had by most of those discussed in Chapter 4 is undeniably correlated with higher socioeconomic status, the technical know-how employed in creating these projects is not limited to the privileged majority of do-it-yourselfers. Still, members of this group, who do distinguish themselves from the general public in these very terms, suggest that they view them-selves as uniquely endowed with the ability to create positive design inter-ventions in their communities.

## 'I WOULD BE STUPID NOT TO NOTICE'—REFLEXIVITY, AWARENESS, AND CONSCIENTIOUS INTERVENTION

So, for all their familiarity with professional planning concerns and under-standing of urban social science, might do-it-yourselfers also understand these sorts of local cultural politics and their own positionality therein? The answer is that some do and some don't, and among those who do I found fairly different attitudes toward their own responsibility for how they might be perceived. When confronted directly with the prospect of their improvements being insensitive to long-standing communities, most of the do-it-yourselfers I spoke with were sympathetic in principle but ultimately unconvinced that their own actions had any unanticipated implications. Whether as a sensible improvement from which everyone should benefit, a creative way to enliven a blighted area, or something the city "should" be doing anyway, most DIY urban designers argued that their own projects are too subtle, too harmless, or too well-thought-out to have negative conse-quences. And while many of those I spoke to certainly demonstrated sen-sitivity around poverty and neighborhood inequality, many also saw the processes of gentrification as inevitable and unrelated to their efforts.

At one extreme, a do-it-yourselfer in Los Angeles was outright dis-missive of the prospect—not of whether his project of stenciling bicycle sharrows on the streets of his (unquestionably gentrifying) neighborhood could cause something like gentrification, but of gentrification as a problem at all. He offered the following remarks on the subject:

That whole gentrification argument is just so specious to me. [ . . . ] It's just like, what are you going to do, you know? You get your money together and you buy that house and you make sure the stupid property owners stay out, and then invest in it and make it a nice place, right? So yeah, I don't give two shits about it. [ . . . ] I mean, this neighborhood used to "have the gentry." The property owners that own this building we're in now, they used to live here. [ . . . ] The people that own buildings in this neighborhood that live in this neighborhood that I've met, they get it. Like their investment in this community is not just dollars and cents, it's their entire persona and they're going to care more about it. So I mean, there's this whole thing like you're going to push all the poor people out, and it's like, dude, we need these [wealthier] people back here. Those are the people that are going to make it so that your dumb kid will not be isolated with a bunch of other dumb kids with nothing else to look up to and do. And it's okay to live in a mixed income neighborhood and it's okay that some people get pushed out and other people get pushed in.

For this do-it-yourselfer, increasing numbers of affluent, educated property owners means more people who "care" and are invested in the quality of the neighborhood, something he views as a plus and indeed something that DIY urban design is a part of.

On the other hand, some of my interviews revealed do-it-yourselfers thinking critically about the cultural impacts of their interventions and their own positionality in the communities they are working to improve. They are concerned about how they are perceived and the possibility of producing unintended consequences like gentrification. Steve Cancian, as we have seen, is one of those who is explicitly concerned about this. He was not surprised by the reaction that Deborah's guerrilla gardening effort received: "If their process isn't to ensure that local people are the leaders of their efforts, then they're gonna get this kind of result." Of course it is easy to cast stones. But Steve has a point, and his experience working with low-income communities of color has given him insight into these sensitivities: "I think people also have a really good radar—even more in the African American community, but also in the Latino community—of who's a first generation and who's a second generation gentrifier. Like who really wants to be with us, and who doesn't?"

Other interventionists, like Graham in Baltimore or Clint, now in Vancouver, expressed a wish to avoid the appearance of just "parachuting in" to neighborhoods they do not have a close connection to. Like Deborah, Clint frames his DIY park repairs as a gift. But if he is still hopeful that his project is not one of the bad ones, Clint was nonetheless introspective on the question of his improvements being viewed as unwelcome intrusions:

> I mean, nobody's brought it up. But I guess maybe that's kind of . . . I would be stupid not to notice those things. [ . . . ] I don't know if [DIY improvements] are acts of gentrification, but I do see how they can get lumped in there rather quickly. I mean part of it is that I'm hoping that they fall into that category less because I'm spending time here, because this is where the studio is, I didn't take the bus from the nice part of town, this is where I go to school and where I play shows and things like that, so this is the neighborhood that I'm in and these repairs are part of what I'm doing here, and you know they have less of that parachute project mentality. At least I hope.

Others also worried about just the opposite of "parachuting in." Ryan, a Chicagoan who created a series of free public book exchanges out of curbside magazine racks, felt responsible for installing them in places where they might be more "needed" than the hip, gentrifying areas that he lived, worked, and hung out in:

> I should be doing this more in neighborhoods where it's less of a social experiment and more of a resource. [ . . . ] I stopped with Pilsen [a mostly Mexican American neighborhood], but that had me thinking about like Rogers Park or neighborhoods where there'd be kids that maybe would be more interested in getting the free books or whatever. And even parents, because they said in Pilsen that there were parents that were coming and getting children's books out of there with their kids and everything.

Indeed, in the hours I spent observing the sociospatial contexts and everyday uses of Ryan's book exchanges in different parts of Chicago, I saw them used by people of all stripes. In Logan Square, a husband and wife I spoke with told me how they had been using the one on a nearby corner since it first appeared and view it as a real benefit to the neighborhood. The woman, a Latina in her late 20s, even said that she has been able to find popular books that she is looking for: "I couldn't find them in the library, but I found them there! I borrowed them and brought them back," she said. "Then some little girl was looking for them—I was there putting some other books in—and I told her just take them sweetie!" In Pilsen, a young man said he appreciated the book exchange there too, though he did note that "it would be great if it said '*libros gratis*' instead of just 'free books,'" as a nod to the dominant language of many residents. As quirky

A Pilsen resident leaving some books in one of the DIY community book exchanges that a man named Ryan created and placed around Chicago. Photo by the author, 2015.

and interesting as they are, the book exchanges have today largely folded into the fabric of funky, workaday Chicago.

On the other hand, as we saw with Deborah, even the most well-meaning efforts can backfire. Frankly, regardless of the good intentions behind a DIY intervention or the reflexivity of its creator, longtime residents are likely to view privileged newcomers with skepticism. And because of the form of most DIY improvements and the backgrounds of their creators, some do risk appearing more as acts of gentrification than acts of improvement. This connection is not abstract. Something as a simple as a tree can impact property values and other indicators of economic development.[17] Other seemingly neutral features, such as bike lanes, can likewise be tied to economic development and may be viewed in American cities as reflecting white, affluent values.[18] More subtle streetscape improvements, such as signage or seating, are less obviously connected to rising rents or cultural change in and of themselves. But even these, when created as acts of creative transgression by skilled young urbanites in areas experiencing new influxes of development capital, tend to garner attention as part of a hip and authentic cultural trend. In the context of "creative city" development trends, boosters are quite happy to latch on to anything that can be construed as "culture" and promote it as such, just as the "creatives" being promoted to in places with exorbitant housing costs like New York and California are eager for any "sign of life" suggesting the next cool (or just remotely feasible) place to look for an apartment.

Negative responses and unintended consequences can be mitigated. Do-it-yourselfers can increase their awareness of the contexts in which they intervene, involve longtime residents in the process, and try to design and implement interventions that address widely acknowledged common needs. Two hopeful examples come from Baltimore. A mobile community center and a vacant lot farm built there in 2006 and 2007 were, not unlike Deborah's Bed-Stuy Meadow project, intended to enjoin local participation and bring services to areas threatened by neglect and starved of use values. Aware of their outsider status and concerned that these efforts might be viewed as "colonial," however, the members of the Baltimore Development Cooperative communicated a plan from the outset to withdraw after several years, leaving the farm in the hands of longtime community members. "We saw our role more as a kind of catalyst," one of them explained.

Joe Linton and his neighbors at the LA EcoVillage were also careful to proactively engage other members of their neighborhood when they planned to create their own crosswalks and other improvements to their intersection:

> We don't interact enough with the kids and the families in our neighborhood, so it was a good opportunity for us to reach out to the folks living in the buildings here and walking down our street. We fliered in English and Spanish and invited people to come out and paint with us. And there were a lot of kids out there painting.

Sometimes, with little more than a nice thought and coincidence, community involvement in a project can bring itself. When an Oakland man named Dan Stevenson epoxied a small stone Buddha statue to a rock in a planted median strip in 2009, he was just trying to discourage loitering, vandalism, and illegal dumping on the spot. He isn't religious, he was just tired of garbage and signs of criminal activities at the corner near his home. (He had called the city countless times, but the problems had not let up.) He thought perhaps having something else on the spot like the Buddha, which his wife had bought at a hardware store, might discourage some of the trouble. Yet Dan soon had fruit, flowers, and other offerings showing up on his doorstep from grateful neighbors—members of the area's large Vietnamese community.[19]

Worshippers, many of them older women originally from Vietnam, soon began visiting the Buddha every morning, and before long they had constructed a wooden shelter around it and added other features—flowers, flags, and more Buddhas—to complete a sizable shrine on the corner. Trash dumping and other signs of disorder seemed to decrease, according to residents nearby, and statistics show a drop in crime in the area.[20] When the city's Department of Public Works tried to remove it in response to a complaint, the outcry was so strong that the city gave up. Members of the immigrant community and people from all different backgrounds continue to worship at the shrine, and have now built a second one at a similar corner a few blocks away. The Buddha, placed by a non-religious white man, was received by his Vietnamese neighbors as a gift, and even inspired them do more.

Back in LA, I asked Steve Cancian to take Deborah's project as an example and consider how it might have been better implemented to avoid local backlash. His response was to suggest taking a more collective or backseat approach to developing DIY improvements, involving local leaders as he had when working with Hood Builders in Oakland, and the then-leader of the group, a man named Big Will:

> If they had actually developed local leadership who were actually making the decisions and deciding what to do, the local leadership wouldn't prevent her deciding to do that! So it wouldn't have been an issue. Now they could have . . . like Big Will did, in the forebears of Hood Builders: Big Will knew the neighborhood and used whatever I brought to the table and said, Hey we could do this. But without Big Will it wouldn't have been targeted in the right way to actually work and be an improvement without being gentrifying. [ . . . ]

· · ·

This chapter furthers the analysis of DIY urban designers' backgrounds in order to interpret the cultural contexts of their actions. I argued in the previous chapter that the sophisticated knowledge that many do-it-yourselfers possess around the planning and justifications of their interventions produces an imperfect reflexivity on their parts that emboldens them— in most cases they see their work as a perfectly appropriate alternative to more official alterations—without necessarily provoking concern for the feelings of others or the value of the democratic planning process. Here I have shown how their knowledge interacts in complicated ways with the more fundamental position of privilege that most are in as well, raising fundamental dilemmas about the equity of DIY urban design, its potential as an open form of local participatory placemaking, and the prospect of unintended impacts.

Considering that the individuals involved in DIY urbanism are predominantly white and middle class, draw on sophisticated urban planning knowledge, and frequently act in demographically and economically transitioning neighborhoods to which they are relatively recent arrivals, the truth is that many DIY urban design interventions are created from a position of privileged self-entitlement, in which legal repercussions are unlikely and unintended consequences are scarcely acknowledged. The typical do-it-yourselfer has little faith in the system, little faith in bureaucracy, and lots of faith in their own abilities; their privileged position in society gives them little to fear. The result is a great potential for hubris and for insensitive interventions.

City planners and private developers are far from perfect on these counts themselves, but democratic input and equitable benefits are at least theoretically fundamental considerations in the official planning and design of public spaces. These are elements that unauthorized interventions can either embody and expand, or conflict with and undermine. If DIY urban design aims to do better than the status quo, the final cases above offer some hope for taking it in this more democratically minded direction. The fact that many do-it-yourselfers have done their homework at least bodes well for the possibility of functionally valuable contributions. If they can add to this knowledge a greater awareness of their own place in their communities, they might also tread more sensitively, allowing them to be the sort of unauthorized yet positive forces they hope to be.

Getting it right is all the more important because, in spite of the few controversies we have seen, DIY urban designers are also trend-setters. For all the local cultural and interpersonal consequences that they must contend with, at the same time they are part of an evolving discourse of popular urbanism, subjects of news articles and blog posts, and even an influence on professionals in the field. This paradox, and its potentially even more drastic implications for the impact of DIY urban design, is the subject of the next chapter.

# Pop-Up Planning

*From Park(ing) Day to Parklet Dining,*
*DIY Goes Official*

"How can such a small plaza generate so much buzz?" The question, raised in a community news blog from the UC Berkeley Graduate School of Journalism, referred to a recent effort in Oakland, California.[1] Transportation planners had pedestrianized part of one street at its angular intersection with another, creating a triangular park in the city's downtown business district. With its industrial metal-work planter blocking traffic, crafty benches of recycled wood, and simple paint designs on the existing asphalt, all installed quickly, cheaply, and with an eye for easy removal if needed, the transformation of Latham Square fit a pattern. On the one hand, it immediately resembled intersections "reclaimed" in DIY efforts by groups from Portland to Baltimore. On the other, it closely followed the model of similar official pedestrian plazas "popping up" in recent years in cities around the United States, made famous with the dramatic closing of New York's Times Square to traffic in just this way in 2009.

In Oakland, the redesign of Latham Square plaza was a very official effort. Although explicitly a temporary pilot project (with the intent of previewing plans for a permanent plaza that had been approved in principle), the design was shaped by city planners, informed by traffic and design studies, and approved by the city council following public presentations

A promotional poster celebrating the opening of the Latham Square pedestrian plaza from the City of Oakland, 2013.

and council meetings. Official proposals noted that the plaza "strengthens core City goals related to economic development and improved pedestrian friendliness within downtown."[2] With agreement from the local business improvement district to provide maintenance, Latham Plaza was designed and installed for around $200,000 in state grant money.

The trendy craft aesthetic was no accident either. As one local reporter noted, proponents hoped the plaza would "bring a bit of Oakland's vibrant Uptown Arts District closer to the grittier city center."[3] Plans called for using "readily available and temporary materials," even emphasizing that these should be "salvaged from the City and Port of Oakland surplus supplies."[4] A "community design workshop" was held early on to facilitate local input, and community members were invited to help paint the plaza during its installation. What's more, overall design was led by Rebar Art and Design Group, the Berkeley architecture and design grads who started Park(ing) Day as a guerrilla intervention in San Francisco in 2005 and went on to help realize that city's ambitious "pavement to parks" program.

Oaklanders enjoy the wooden planters and seating, painted asphalt, and sign (made from reclaimed street signs and industrial materials) that doubles as a planter and a barricade, in Latham Square shortly after its reopening as a pedestrianized public space in 2013. Photo by Michael Santiago.

In all of these ways, the Latham Plaza redesign was part of an increasingly trendy urban revitalization practice known as "creative placemaking"—the use of public art, eye-catching public seating, and all manner of other funky, silly, artistic, or handmade design elements to enliven or "activate" city streets and public spaces. Embraced by cities and communities around the country and the world, creative placemaking has proven in many cases to be an effective and relatively simple way to transform particular places and attract users while stimulating local businesses and investment.[5] In both implementation and aesthetics, the resulting public spaces often have much in common with some of the more prominent forms of DIY urbanism we have seen (to the extent that some DIY urbanism might well be considered a form of creative placemaking).

Latham Plaza's similarities to more informal streetscaping efforts did not go unnoticed by Oakland do-it-yourselfers like Larry, who said he "went so far as to take one of [the plaza's benches] apart and put it back together. And I'm like, This is the same shit!" Larry didn't know who was responsible, but he felt they were effectively stealing the Hood Builders' design ideas for their own financial benefit and the improvement of a different part of town. "Some other group," he complained, got "$200,000 to do the same thing we do, in Downtown Oakland only though." (At the same time though, to Larry, while it copies his style, the official version is also a little overdone: "They put these awful big huge wood projects out, and it's just like, they have screws where they don't need them!") Although the price tag was far more than the Hood Builders or any other DIY urbanists I spoke with ever came close to spending, to Oakland planners it was still a bargain—a fraction of the $8.6 million that a planned plaza at the site was estimated to cost in 2005.

In the end, road closures for the new public space proved controversial and led to its undoing. Under pressure from motorists and others, the city council reopened part of the area to cars, putting an end to Oakland's first pilot plaza less than six months after it opened. One council member called the whole project a "comedy of errors," as criticism of the planning process piled on: hence the "buzz" noted in the article mentioned at the outset. But the question—"How can such a small plaza generate so much buzz?"—is also a fitting summation of a planning trend in cities across the United States.

Low-cost, quick-build public spaces have taken municipal planning by storm. In New York, the Plaza Program became a signature planning success of Mayor Michael Bloomberg's administration, expanding to dozens of sites across the five boroughs under the mayor and his successor. The familiar painted pavement and cheap, removable street furniture can now be found in Chicago, Los Angeles, Philadelphia, San Francisco, and other cities.

Sunset Triangle Plaza, in the Silver Lake area of Los Angeles, is the first new pedestrian space in the city created by simply closing a street to traffic and installing cheap, temporary barriers, chairs, and other features. Photo by the author, 2012.

The goals, the implementation, and the aesthetics of these plazas are symbolic of an important dynamic in the emergence of DIY urban design: its correspondence with official urban planning and development trends like creative placemaking and pro-pedestrian and pro-cycling street design. If, as I have argued, unauthorized streetscape interventions can be viewed largely as local responses to the inadequacies of late modern urban planning and uneven development conditions, by the second decade of the 21st century these very do-it-yourself interventions had begun to influence official planning and development as well. In cities at the leading edge of urban planning innovation, and now many others as well, the renewed emphasis on creatively designed public spaces and pedestrian- and cycling-oriented streetscapes has often included designing and building these things in ways that reflect the tactics, ideals, and aesthetics of DIY urban design. Approaches such as "tactical urbanism" that in some incarnations effectively bring DIY attitudes to officially sanctioned placemaking are visible in cities from New York and San Francisco to Paris and Melbourne. In other cases, initially unauthorized improvements themselves have been adapted directly into policy.

This chapter departs from the previous focus on the characteristics and justifications of individual do-it-yourself urban designers and their projects. Instead, I examine aspects of DIY urban design that have been co-opted by formal actors in the planning and development process. In so doing, I argue that the significance of DIY urbanism as a cultural trend extends beyond the impacts of its singular, localized, and often very temporary interventions: it has become highly influential on official planning and development. And it has brought with it both its promises and its problems.

I explore DIY urbanism's relationship to formal urban planning and policy on several levels. I begin by discussing professional planners' conflicted views of informal urbanism: sympathetic to its motivations, wary of its implications, and in some ways envious of its potential effectiveness. I then step back to describe the recent shifts in policy in certain major American cities that have emphasized creative placemaking and other planning approaches more closely aligned with the tactics, aesthetics, and values of DIY interventions. I discuss examples of the influence of informality on official planning and cases where cities have adopted specific preexisting DIY projects as well. I then assess the advantages and disadvantages of this new planning trend from a sociological standpoint, an analysis that raises further concerns about the potential for some streetscape design features—formal or informal—to reproduce privilege and inequality in urban space while blurring the distinction between formal and informal in contemporary urbanism. This presents opportunities and dangers for cities and communities.

## THE CONFLICTED PERSPECTIVES OF PROFESSIONAL PLANNERS

"You can't expect me to answer that question while I'm sitting here in my suit!" Andy Wiley-Schwartz protested from behind his desk. I had asked New York City's assistant transportation commissioner for public space whether there are some situations in which it might be acceptable for people to make urban space improvements without official authorization. In the high-rise offices of the Department of Transportation, even during the Bloomberg administration—known for its bike-riding transportation commissioner and some of the most innovative urban planning in a generation—the formality of city bureaucracy was palpable. Even in the office of a man with a background in advocacy who had been appointed to rethink the city's relationship to its streets, the trappings of institutional inertia were heavy in the air. "When you come at it from the perspective of a city official, right, which I am, you realize that there—I mean, certain things need to follow a certain process, right?"

The assistant commissioner offered a long list of reasons to explain why DIY urban design activities are fundamentally problematic, from the practical and technical to the higher callings of government. These were arguments I heard again and again from the professional planners I spoke to. First, for instance, he brought up functional concerns relating to unauthorized installations like benches:

> I mean this is going to sound very bureaucratic, but your bench, are you taking care of it? What happens if it breaks? [ . . . ] I mean, this stuff doesn't go away right? Like so you move and your bench is still there and the next guy moves in, doesn't want to have anything to do with your bench. And that bench deteriorates and the paint peels, somebody spills their ice cream on it. Nobody's cleaning it up. [ . . . ] So the city is like littered with this crap that nobody's taking care of, that may have been put out with the best intention.

He raised similar concerns with guerrilla gardening:

> If you plant a tree, which I think is a great thing to do and we want you to do, you know, Parks should know that that tree is there because ultimately, they're the ones who have to take care of it, right? And it should be a tree that's on their species list, because they know it's not going to—the limbs aren't going to split

in a wind storm or it's not going to drop smelly berries all over your sidewalk or whatever it is. And they have criteria for how they should be planted and the time of year they should be planted so that they'll be healthiest.

And with unauthorized bike lanes as well:

> Streets have many different contexts. You have the transportation context, they have an economic context, they have social context, they have a store context. You have to understand all these different layers and be sensitive to them. Maybe the bike lane isn't appropriate there, maybe there are loading issues or curbside issues that are really critical on that block and that should really be a shared lane instead of a separated lane, or instead of a Class I, it should be a Class III.

I also asked Wiley-Schwartz (who is now a consultant with Bloomberg Associates) what he thought of the homemade "cross traffic does not stop" sign in Pittsburgh, a quintessential and seemingly harmless DIY urban design intervention described at the beginning of Chapter 2:

> I think it's deeply problematic. I mean I think you can go through a process of having the city study your intersection and see what changes might need to happen and we have a safety division here that does that. And signage may or may not actually be your fix, you know? I mean there's a whole basket of tools that officially could be employed to help fix that intersection, short and long term. Taking matters into your own hands and printing up a sign probably isn't going to be that effective, and, you know, I think is the wrong way to go.

Finally, he appealed to the broader implications for democracy in the city:

> You're trying to manage the city and public space and make sure it's equally distributed and people have fair access to it and it's not—I mean you don't want to allow someone to privatize or take over in any way. [ . . . ] You can't just like take it over and decide you're going to tell people how to use it or how it's supposed to be used, you know?

Although the specific examples differed among the planning and design professionals I interviewed in New York and Los Angeles, these sentiments were shared by every one of them. Claire Bowin, a planner in LA's Department of City Planning, made almost identical points. On practical concerns like maintenance: "Street Services doesn't want to be maintaining all these different things. They don't even like it if we try to introduce a different type of paving material." On benches: "What happens if somebody sits on that bench and it collapses, and there's all kinds of lawsuit issues?" On guerrilla gardening: "It's not legal. I mean I have a neighbor [ . . . ] who's done beautiful plantings in the tree well, which I'm sure if Street Services saw it they'd have heartburn, because maintaining it is their job." On bike lanes: "The city's answer would be, We get sued. All the time. Like even if we put in a bicycle lane, if it's five inches too narrow and somebody has an accident in there, we get sued." And she too returned in the end to the fundamental democratic role of planning in smoothing over competing claims on public space with the "highest and best use":

> You know it's fairly hard in the city to find consensus. So you might have one group or community who just kind of on their own goes and puts something in, without talking to everybody else, and pisses somebody else off. And what, do you get another group coming in and erasing it?

All of this sounds pretty insightful in light of the individualistic realities of DIY urbanism that we've seen.

The professionals I spoke with also turned quickly to the importance of official processes and their own expertise, referencing specific regulations and technical terms. There are obvious reasons for these, including basic safety and order. Yet in doing so, the professionals effectively marginalize the non-professionals while perhaps defending their professional turf.[6] When asked directly, the planning officials I spoke with told me that nobody in their field would feel their toes were being stepped on or otherwise professionally threatened by DIY urban design. But there would nonetheless appear to be at least some professional posturing going on beneath the surface (or, perhaps, simply a sort of Weberian commitment to bureaucratic standardization), in addition to a sincere concern for the public good.

That said, the broad rejection of DIY interventions does not mean these same officials are unsympathetic to them. "There's a weird space where like as a professional I probably can't say that it's good," another Los Angeles planner said to me, "but as an anonymous person, as long as you're not hurting anybody . . ." These professionals emphasized that they were working hard to realize the same sorts of improvements that do-it-yourselfers wish for, and many acknowledged frustration or impatience with official processes in their own experiences. LA's Claire Bowin described how, before joining the planning department, she and her neighbors had "wanted to put in some crosswalks, and some street lighting, and some street trees." Even though one participant was a well-connected project manager at a community development agency that was funding these local improvements, "it was still a very long, complicated, frustrating process" that took "several years" to organize. As another official admitted, "I feel like we, the city, we don't provide people with things. [ . . . ] I think we're frustrating communities and forcing them to go kind of guerrilla around these issues."

To this end, some planners also distinguished between DIY interventions that they could never condone and those they felt "don't hurt." A Los Angeles transportation planner, who even had some involvement in community cycling activism before joining city hall, started by emphasizing that DIY bike lanes simply cannot work because they are dangerous: "If someone had used that bike lane, and thought it was a real bike lane, and had gotten in an accident, they could sue the city. And so the city had to paint those over, just had to, just basic professional responsibility." Yet he also argued that a series of unauthorized sharrows (chevron symbols painted on the road denoting that motorists and cyclists must share a traffic lane) were "technically illegal" but "probably didn't bother anybody" and did not "put anybody at risk." He applauded the homemade "4th St. Bicycle Boulevard" signs that some citizens installed, saying they "probably help a community get a sense of itself" and suggesting it might not be a coincidence that 4th Street became "the first bike boulevard that we'll be working on."

A few of the professionals I spoke to were also willing to concede that even DIY actions that could never be officially sanctioned—and might even be dangerous—could nonetheless play an important role in effecting policy change. "Maybe you have to piss people off to get things done sometimes," one Los Angeles planner mused. "I mean that's how we got the LA River moving right? People start cutting holes in the fences and then professionals get directed by the politicians to go back and do it correctly . . . you know, I mean safer." And as we have seen in more than a few instances guerrilla efforts have directly presaged (even inspired) official improvements to come. A planner from a different department in LA concurred:

> When cities aren't doing it themselves, why shouldn't we be encouraging communities to? [ . . . ] And is it provocative, does it raise attention and awareness around something? Absolutely. Yeah. It's a good thing. [ . . . ] That's exactly the kind of controversy and communication and discussion that needs to continue to happen if the city is gonna ultimately have more green spaces or have more public services or put more bike lanes in.

In these ways, while they cannot condone unauthorized alterations to the urban streetscape and may defend the right of professional planners to shape it officially, some officials clearly admire DIY actions. They sympathize with the bureaucratic frustrations and sense of institutional inertia that seem to motivate many do-it-yourselfers. They may even feel stymied by the same basic conditions. The difference is the faith (or security) that they nonetheless find in the value of the regulations and codes that govern official planning and keep the city functioning. This ultimately precludes them from wholeheartedly embracing DIY urbanism.[7]

For this reason, many of the planners I spoke with expressed a desire to figure out ways to recognize and encourage citizen participation in planning through more formal channels. (This of course has been a fundamental goal of progressive planning since its initial reactions to urban renewal and other nefarious acts of top-down planning in the 1960s, if not before.) New York's Andy Wiley-Schwartz told me that as much as he admires what they do, his goal is "for the DIY guys of the world to not have to be around" by making the city itself "easy enough to navigate" with "the right programs to plug into to allow you to create a more livable city without having to do it illegally."

Others expressed an interest in accommodating actual DIY efforts where they could be adequately incorporated into the official process. And this has happened, even with cycling infrastructure. When a group of do-it-yourselfers called the San Francisco Municipal Transformation Authority (SFMTrA) installed their own reflective soft-hit posts (like official ones used elsewhere in the city) to better defend a bike lane in Golden Gate Park from speeding cars, rather than removing them officials acknowledged that they were needed and allowed them to stay; the mayor's office has said it hopes to cooperate with the SFMTrA in the future. Bill Roschen of the Los Angeles Planning Commission agreed with this approach: "If the city could help facilitate a partnership with communities? That's the way I would encourage the guerrilla effort to go." Another Los Angeles planner likewise suggested that a city might "create a process for people who want to do it do-it-yourself, so it's more legitimized, so the city's not gonna come and take it down." He felt that they should "take advantage of the fact that we have a community out here that's very active and I think has tons of ideas and is very creative and has lots of energy. Let's figure out a way where we can be encouraging folks to do it on their own."

Ramon Arevalo, manager of maintenance for Long Beach, California's Parks, Recreation, and Marine Department, deals with more unauthorized planting and landscaping than most, due to the thriving guerrilla gardening scene in this relatively small city. Among others, Scott Bunnel, a postal carrier and lifelong gardener, has been providing the road medians and dusty parkways of Long Beach with beautifully landscaped and drought-tolerant succulent gardens since the 1980s. Arevalo gushed with appreciation for

Scott Bunnell inspects one of the succulent gardens that he has been planting in Long Beach, California, road medians since the mid-1980s. The city has given him a key to the watering spigot. Photo by the author, 2011.

the guerrilla gardeners on his turf, lauding their efforts and calling them "an amazing part of our community." He has done everything within his power to aid their efforts:

> For me, what a guy like Scott provides, it's green and growing, he fits right in with Parks. [ . . . ] This guy did a fabulous thing. Let's support him, let's see what we can do, and let's move from there. [ . . . ] I met Scott, I said hey, what can we do for you? Can we give you a key to this irrigation controller? [ . . . ] This is a city that belongs to the citizens of Long Beach.

Although they noted problems with unauthorized interventions and emphasized the importance of official processes, the professional planners I interviewed seemed to see great promise in finding ways to adopt the tactics of DIY urban design. Many of these professionals have also embraced the language of DIY and in some cases explicitly worked to integrate informal projects into the formal process. In other words, they are eager to walk the line between the efficiency of DIY attitudes and the safety and stability of professional accountability. As it would happen, this very combination of design ethics neatly describes a dominant placemaking trend that has emerged in recent years. A broad shift in contemporary planning priorities and in particular the embrace of so-called tactical urbanism approaches are the subjects of the next section.

## TACTICAL URBANISM AND THE NEW PLANNING LANDSCAPE

American urban policy over the past 50 years has been defined in large part by an emphasis on privatization and pro-growth decision making. (Even early 20th-century planning was heavily guided by private benefactors and civic associations dominated by business interests.) This has had tremendous consequences for the physical streetscape and the everyday lives of citizens. DIY urban design, I have argued, can be seen as emerging in reaction to these conditions. But however much planning practice has been shaped by fiscal policy realities, the progressive ideals of planning have followed their own paths and shaped urban life as well. In many ways, they too have evolved in reaction to the failings of the late-modern city and some of the planning decisions that created it.

A whole discourse of progressive planning theory notwithstanding, I am referring here especially to the socially and environmentally conscious planning for which cities like Portland, Oregon—not to mention a handful of European capitals and American college towns—have been known for decades, and which has recently become more widespread. Indeed, perhaps the most prominent movement in late 20th-century urban design is defined by a focus on earlier urban ideals of community and "human scale" in response to the negative social and spatial consequences of mid-century auto-centric landscapes, architectures, and suburban sprawl.[8] Representative trends include "livable" (pedestrian-friendly) streetscapes, mixed-use and transit-oriented real estate development, and "smart growth" (anti-sprawl) strategies at the metropolitan scale. These ideals, sometimes collected under the umbrella of "New Urbanism," are generally inspired by nostalgia for the walkable "urban villages" or small towns of an earlier America.[9] Bicycle infrastructure and other ecological priorities, from energy-efficient "green" architecture to "sustainable" (and more recently, "resilient") development policies, are also part of the picture.

These ideals can be understood as a central planning component to the much-touted "urban renaissance" that many cities in the United States and elsewhere have been beneficiaries and boosters of since the late 1990s. They can claim many powerful, positive impacts on cities and communities. They also found their way into reality in part through an increasingly accepted calculation that they can be good for business. New real estate development in even a small city's downtown might well be a complex of "luxury lofts" with ground-floor retail; in the most car-centric exurban sprawl, a new shopping mall fashioned in the style of a nostalgic walkable Main Street (or Tuscan village, or Middle Eastern bazaar). And in major cities, bikes, transit, and vibrant street life are the new order of the day for economic development and inter-urban competition.* With them comes the cultivation of something more abstract: an air of cultural dynamism, locally spiced yet globally palatable (and vice versa!), with just enough environmental consciousness to be responsible and just enough edge to be "creative."[10]

It is in this emerging urban policy landscape that a planning trend related to—even inspired by—DIY urban design seems to have found a place. In pursuit of more dynamic and pedestrian-friendly streetscapes, or simply wishing to try something different without the obstruction of conservative stake-holders or their own glacial review and approval processes, planners have lately been turning to strategies that in many ways reflect the rising visibility of DIY urbanism as well as the tension between creativity and capital. This is an increasingly prominent trend, attracting praise from urbanism's chattering classes and many websites, magazines, and other popular forums and being taken up by cities and communities around the United States and beyond. As with urban space interventions and other spatiocultural phenomena discussed in this study, the borders of these novel planning trends are undefined and the nomenclature varies. One term that has gained considerable recent traction, however, is "tactical urbanism."[11]

At its core, tactical urbanism emphasizes more creative, inexpensive, and easy-to-install (and easy to remove) methods than have typically been employed in big city urban planning, with an eye for making local improvements quickly to demonstrate their potential and facilitate more permanent changes. As described by one of its principal advocates, the urbanist Mike Lydon, the guerrilla "chair-bombing" of groups like DoTank (of which

---

* Is this really so new? While there are always firsts and outliers, in the US urban context the answer is basically yes. Although the earliest bike-share programs as such were started in Europe in the 1960s, for instance, the modern citywide initiatives gaining popularity today date only to the mid-'90s (in Copenhagen and Portland). Edmund Bacon's classic *Design of Cities* (revised 1972), makes no mention of bicycle planning or other current planning tropes such as "healthy" or "sustainable" cities even in its sections on "emergent trends" and "looking to the future" (and it gives considerable attention to the automobile). The professional planners I interviewed in New York and Los Angeles made frequent references to a cultural, political, and even "paradigm" "shift" toward bicycle initiatives and pedestrian-oriented planning in only the most recent city administrations, since the early 2000s.

Lydon was a member) provide a tactical solution to the lack of street seating, just as the New York City Department of Transportation's quick work with paint and folding chairs was a tactical way of transforming Times Square into a pedestrian plaza. (As an inexpensive pilot project, while still thoroughly planned, the latter was made with less public discussion or opportunity for legal hang-ups than usual—the official version of acting first and asking for permission later.)

In other words, tactical urbanism can be official or unsanctioned, though a key element is that the projects function as an easier but significant first step in a "phased approach" with an explicit eye on long-term improvement. The term "lighter, quicker, cheaper," coined by British real-estate developer Eric Reynolds and embraced by the New York–based Project for Public Spaces organization, has a similar connotation and describes the basic philosophy behind these initiatives. The concept of "lean urbanism," popularized by the architect Andrés Duany, likewise refers to loosening or removing bureaucratic obstacles to enable cities and communities to more nimbly make simple improvements. And, in addition to straightforward streetscape efforts, tactical urbanism has found great success when applied as a form of creative placemaking.

Tactical urbanism has clear commonalities with DIY urban design; some interventions (DoTank's chair-bombing, for instance) fit in both categories. The important difference is that DIY urban design is by definition unauthorized and homemade despite its civic-minded intentions (so the very official redesign of Times Square does not count), and some examples of DIY urban design are too limited, casual, and ineffective to be what Lydon and others count as "tactical." As Lydon described it to me over a beer in the gentrifying Brooklyn neighborhood we both called home, "We're trying to underscore the importance of intent, and how we should be connecting the short-term to long-term policy and/or physical change. DIY urbanism does not always purport to do this, yet as you know often does." In case after case, however, we can see how one informs the other in terms of methods and aesthetics, not to mention the cultural cache of a hip and "authentic" urban phenomenon.

## FROM THE STREETS TO THE BOARDROOM—THE FORMALIZATION OF DIY URBAN DESIGN

A large number of contemporary streetscape design trends reflect the influence of DIY approaches. Community gardening started as a local and in many cases informal activity before becoming a community-building tool orchestrated by city agencies as a symbol of healthy and sustainable planning. "Open Streets," "Weekend Walks," and "Play Street" initiatives, which temporarily close streets to car traffic, draw from DIY traffic calming and space reclaiming efforts. Popular "cyclovias"—the opening of streets and even large areas of major cities exclusively to cycling and other human-powered transportation for a period of time—take some inspiration from informal events like Critical Mass, Midnight Ridazz, and other clandestine bicycle street takeovers.

Even commercial bike share systems, like New York's CitiBikes (sponsored by CitiBank), have DIY roots. The first bike share, the "White Bicycle" plan launched in 1965 in Amsterdam, was created against police wishes by an anarchist organization as a policy provocation.[12] Usually public-private partnerships, these programs have today become another object of urban one-upmanship, from São Paulo to London and Hoboken to Hangzhou. Some cities have also embraced creative pedestrian infrastructure designed by artists (one of my interviewees was engaged to paint a crosswalk in the style of a hopscotch game in downtown Baltimore) and even aspirational, community-sourced development ideas: Candy Chang's "I wish this was . . ." sticker campaign has become the slick "neighborland.com" project in dozens of cities. And, of course, various "pop-up" style parks and pedestrian plazas, like the Oakland example above, demonstrate the embrace of DIY tactics and aesthetics by city planners around the world.

## "We Need to Change the Way Things Are Done"—Using Informal Techniques to Create New Public Spaces

Bill Roschen, an architect who has been president of the Los Angeles Planning Commission since 2007, effused over the advantages of helping "guerrilla interventions" become more "institutionalized." This is what he feels was accomplished in the creation of Sunset Triangle, his city's first pop-up pedestrian plaza, which opened in 2012 at what had been an awkwardly angled intersection in Silver Lake:

> The key pieces here were to make it temporary, so you could try it out, that would allow it to be about safety, that would also allow the community to embrace it more quickly, because they can always reverse it, you know, nothing's been changed here, just paint. And to sort of explore what it means in terms of

these issues—placemaking, neighborhood identity—and I think for me in Los Angeles, a culture change around taking back pieces of street from the car. [ . . . ] If this was a park, it probably would have cost two to three million dollars to do this. Instead we did it for thirty thousand. And it probably would have taken 10 to 20 years, and instead we did it in four months, from beginning to end. So to me I think this is unbelievably promising. [ . . . ] With a relatively modest investment of time and money we were able to figure out a process that now, citywide, is possible! Now if you really want to recapture pieces of street, you can do it in a way that's got certainty for the motorist that it's gonna be safe, certainty for the community that it's gonna be maintained, right? The guerrilla stuff doesn't have that.

A similar strategy for converting pavement to public space—or, more precisely in this case, converting parking spaces to parks—has found even greater traction and is probably the single best example of a DIY project going mainstream. "Parklets" are created from the transformation of one or more on-street parking spaces into a temporary or semi-permanent seating area—essentially a thoughtfully designed extension of the sidewalk in the street. Adjacent businesses often sponsor the creation and maintenance of these, though occasionally they are outside of residences (sometimes they are even mobile). Parklets have their origins in the DIY "Park(ing) Day" phenomenon first staged in guerrilla fashion in San Francisco by members of Rebar. The group found a curbside parking space, fed the meter, and instead of parking a car they turned heads by turning the space into a temporary park. The effort immediately garnered a great deal of press and copycat efforts in other cities. It took the City of San Francisco all of a year to get behind it, endorse Rebar's idea, and declare the third Friday in September to be Park(ing) Day. Inspired by San Francisco, where Rebar also helped install the first official parklets as part of the Pavement to Parks initiative in 2010, sanctioned parklets are now found in cities around the world.[†]

Some cities have also begun to import the language of informal interventions into official documents and public relations efforts. New York City's

---

† Among cities included in this study, Chicago, Los Angeles, New York, Phoenix, Seattle, Toronto, Vancouver, and all three major cities in the Bay Area have formal parklet initiatives. They can be found in places as varied as Ames, Iowa; Columbia, Missouri; Davis, California; Fort Lauderdale, Florida; Frederick, Maryland; and Montpelier, Vermont, as well as Cincinnati, Milwaukee, Montreal, Philadelphia, and Puebla, Mexico. Most programs have begun since 2012, and new cities seem to be launching them almost monthly. Park(ing) Day, meanwhile, has occurred in every city in the study and well over a hundred more.

A public parklet in San Francisco's Mission District, 2011. Photo by the author.

Department of Transportation, for instance, notes on the website for its plaza program that "outside of parks there are few places to sit, rest, socialize, and to enjoy public life. To improve the quality of life for New Yorkers, DOT creates more public open space by *reclaiming* underutilized street space and *transforming* it into pedestrian plazas" (my emphasis).[13]

Janette Sadik-Khan, the city's transportation commissioner under Michael Bloomberg, has done the same herself. "Up until now city planning was largely ceded to traffic engineering and traffic engineers," she told the CityAge Conference, a well-heeled gathering of executives, academics, policymakers, and other urban elites that I attended in 2013. "We need to change the way things are done." She then noted that one of the best things the New York City Department of Transportation had done on her watch was embrace the idea of "transforming our streets virtually overnight." She continued, using very much the language of DIY urbanism, to explain how she had led the Department of Transportation to take a more tactical approach:

> Rather than waiting on years of planning studies, we use paint and planters to change our streets in real time. [ . . . ] The construction process in New York City, it takes about five years to get a project done. So we'd still be talking about it if we had taken the conventional approach. [ . . . ] It is possible to change the streets of the city in close to real time.

The Fowler Square Pedestrian Plaza in Brooklyn's Fort Greene neighborhood illustrates the approach pioneered by New York City's Department of Transportation in closing off part of an existing street to traffic and creating a plaza with tables, chairs, and planters. Photo by the author, 2014.

Even Sadik-Khan's book on her work as transportation commissioner and as a consultant with the private Bloomberg Associates employs the radical language of DIY urbanism in its title: *Street Fight: Handbook for an Urban Revolution.*

### "And Then the Council Voted It In . . ."—The Official Adoption of Unofficial Improvements

DIY urban design has been more than just influential on planning. In some cases, informal improvements have actually been directly adopted and incorporated into official policy or development efforts. Consider the "Better Block" phenomenon: in 2010, a Dallas software designer named Jason Roberts and some of his friends and neighbors decided to make a single block in their artsy but under-resourced neighborhood of Oak Cliff a little more welcoming to pedestrians, families, and businesses. The local city councilmember gave the project tacit approval and permits were acquired where possible, but many of the added streetscape design elements—from planters and seating to overhead Christmas lights, hand-painted crosswalks and bike lanes, and dozens of potted shrubs creating a median down the center of the street—knowingly and provocatively violated city codes.

The success of this DIY intervention, which Jason and his friend Andrew Howard, a transportation planner, named Better Block, led Dallas to alter ordinances and approve a number of permanent improvements in Oak Cliff. Jason's ideas for a hypothetical streetcar to the neighborhood, which began as a related aspirational urbanism provocation, even became reality in 2015. Better Block has now become a highly regarded neighborhood development model implemented in more than 150 communities and, via a for-profit consultancy, a full-time job for Jason, Andrew, and others.

Similarly, Matt Tomasulo's DIY "Walk Raleigh" intervention, described earlier, in which he placed pedestrian wayfinding signs throughout that city to encourage walking, not only became official policy there but has since evolved into a program that can be contracted by other cities and communities (so far, more than 30). Matt described the process by which his guerrilla signage, installed by hand one night in January 2012, began making headlines online almost immediately, at first prompting removal by the city, but ultimately leading to widespread approval:

> One citizen in particular saw [the signs], and responded to an Atlantic Cities article. [ . . . ] [The editor] loved it so much she put it up on the front page of Atlantic Cities. [ . . . ] And the BBC followed up that day about it and then came to town the following week. And that's when I tweeted at [Raleigh's then-planning chief, Mitchell Silver] saying, Hey do you want to talk to the BBC tomorrow? He happened to be the American Planning Association president at the time and was having to leave town the next morning but he canceled that flight to talk to the BBC. It aired on the BBC, it was one of the top three videos on the BBC that week globally, and that kind of opened the floodgates. But it also forced the signs to come down because media were contacting the city, and the city said, No we did not install them. Then why are they up? That constituted a formal complaint, and the city had to take them down. But there was such an uproar in Raleigh about it, in the papers and et cetera and elsewhere, that [Silver] and his staff had to figure out how they could actually have them reinstalled.

The following week, Silver proposed to the city council that Matt's signs were in fact aligned with the Raleigh Comprehensive 2030 Plan on "everything from health and welfare to safety and awareness and access to information, and when it comes to pedestrian and bike and people wayfinding." Matt collected more than 1,000 signatures to restore the signs and the council unanimously approved the effort as a pilot educational program. The city reinstalled the signs over the next three months ("I actually had to donate them, they didn't pay me at all," Matt laughed). In January 2013, Walk Raleigh was adopted into the Comprehensive Plan itself.

Matt's project had gone from guerrilla action to city policy in the space of a single year. He has since parlayed his success into the "Walk [Your City]" program as well as an interactive website and mobile app through which anyone can design and order pedestrian wayfinding signs to put up in their own neighborhoods. "It's now evolved into a much larger platform that could actually be purchased by cities and can bridge not only into the physical world as real wayfinding signs but also bridge-out to the mobile," he explained. Walk [Your City] has now been contracted by more than a dozen cities and communities.

This formalization came at the expense of the literally hands-on, do-it-yourself experience that made Walk Raleigh so attention-getting in the first place: "Given liability reasons, [unauthorized] people can't actually hang the signs," Matt said. But he is happy with the opportunity to broaden his impact and welcomes any help he can get in promoting walkability and livability in the cities he works with: "This is part of the process of changing the culture of the way that things are done in the built environment." And, he added, "things like Better Block and parklets are doing the same—all of these are kind of part of this iterative process of testing and resolving opportunities and solutions on the ground."

The impact of the initial project in Raleigh can be ascribed to several factors, especially a combination of significant and positive media coverage and a rapid groundswell of public support (both of which essentially forced the city's hand). The spotlight that Walk Raleigh received online, Matt noted, was in large part a lucky break, although positive press is not at all uncommon among the DIY urban design projects I studied. But the media attention and the community support suggest the project hit a nerve.

It is also worth noting that Matt conceived the project to address the very sorts of urban policy and planning concerns that are hot on the minds of young planners (like Matt). He was frustrated with the lack of attention being given to walkable, "livable" streets by policymakers in Raleigh, even as they worked to make the city competitive and attractive to the much-sought-after creative class. He actually timed the initial installation of his DIY signage in part to contribute to this discussion:

It was the day before this big innovation summit that was being held in Raleigh, and it was my hope to get attention from them, because I was kind of frustrated with the conversations that they were having about how to make Raleigh more attractive to "talent," as they called it. [ . . . ] I knew from my friends in San

Francisco and New York and Austin that, it's like, our generation cares a lot more about place. [ . . . ]

I was just so frustrated that no one was realizing that, hey, if we just make sure that we start shaping downtown for people and start actually locating the assets and amenities that you are all talking about close together, then you'll have the "spontaneous collisions" and you'll have the "network solutions" and, you know, the "cooperations" that [attendees at the conference were] talking about!

If the project did not quite communicate all this to the summit's attendees ("I didn't realize that [the summit] was held a little bit outside of down-town," Matt laughed), the connection to these ideas and its general appeal from a progressive planning perspective help explain the support it quickly received from planners and politicians, and the enthusiasm it has found in other cities since.

Another example illustrates well the complexity and uncertainty inher-ent to the transition from the unauthorized to the formalized. Gil Lopez, a Mississippi transplant in his 30s and a professional landscaper and "green roof" installer in Queens, is the lead organizer of a unique urban place known as Smiling Hogshead Ranch. In 2011, Gil and some friends from a master composter certificate course at a nearby botanic garden founded this urban farm without permission on an out-of-use railroad easement just

Two farmers stand amid the vegetables at Smiling Hogshead Ranch, a squatted farm in Queens, New York. Photo by the author, 2011.

outside of the bustling Sunnyside rail yards. I interviewed Gil at the end of their first season at Smiling Hogshead Ranch, and in time, having some background as I do in urban gardening, I was invited to join the dozen or so farmers and play a small part in the place's remarkable transformation over the following years. (In addition to planting and tending the crops there— everything from tomatoes and herbs to corn, potatoes, and a wide variety of greens—I volunteered to help out with some of the legal and administrative maneuvering that was required once the actual landowners got in touch.)‡

Although the founding members had done some research on who owned the land—which appeared entirely abandoned except for a large billboard on one corner—their efforts had only revealed two layers of a complex real-estate puzzle: a land management company and its lessee, the outdoor advertising firm responsible for the billboard. One day in August 2012, late in the farm's second season, Gil received a phone call out of the blue from a representative of the Metropolitan Transportation Authority's Division of Real Estate, the real owners of the land. Gil recounted the ensuing conversation in an email to other farmers:

> I was wondering exactly how he got my phone number. He had a somber and interrogatory tone. I was very nervous. He asked if I was involved with [the farm]. I concurred. He stated that this property belongs to MTA and he doesn't have a record of MTA permitting any other uses on this parcel. I noted that there is no fence and no posted signs proclaiming no trespassing. [ . . . ] I also tried countering with our position of doing something good now and asking permission later, after we have built capacity and community around the project. He asked if we were a nonprofit? I explained that we were just a group of proactive citizens. [ . . . ]
>
> Finally the inquisition ended, he seemed to lighten his tone and took on a more conversational approach. [ . : . ] He went on to say that it is serendipitous that we are using this property for urban agriculture because the MTA is considering options for the land and urban ag. is a major consideration. [ . . . ] He believes the MTA will be open to granting us full permission to use the property for a minimal rent ($1/year) provided we secure insurance for our activities.

The process wound up being more complicated than it sounded (due in part to some difficulties for our inexperienced group with incorporation and insurance), but the Transportation Agency made good on its word. For the slightly

---

‡ The other regular members were all aware of my research interest in the project, and my involvement continued to take this perspective even as it became a personal passion as well. See Appendix 2 for more on this and other questions of ethnographic entanglement.

higher but nonetheless reasonable sum of $125 per year, Smiling Hogshead Ranch entered into an agreement to continue farming on the site entirely above board. What began with a few friends squatting (and quite illegally upending) an old railroad embankment had by the spring of 2014 become a registered non-profit farm, hosting school groups and corporate volunteer workdays, collaborating with other organizations, and winning grants and public accolades.

In many ways, the sanctioning and formalization of this squatted farm in Queens can be described as mutually beneficial. Despite the hassles of incorporation and some additional costs, the farmers gained legal legitimacy, the ability to collect donations and win grants as a nonprofit, and a sense of relative permanence on the land. The MTA—and by extension the state of New York and the structures of authority in general—achieved a policy priority and a public relations coup in activating their underutilized land with a "green" use, potentially increasing the value of the real estate in the long term, and in being seen as accommodating community participation. They also diffused what was technically an anarchic and potentially dangerous situation from their perspective, limiting their liability while reinforcing their authority.

There were those among the farm's founding members who would have preferred to remain off the books. These individuals did not oppose the decision to sign a garden license agreement with the MTA—once Gil had been contacted, it was clear that continuing to operate without permission was not an option—but they expressed wariness around the increasing organizational encumbrances. Some felt that formalization conflicted with ideals they held for the place; most felt it simply distracted from their interest in "just growing stuff." In the end, though they emphasized they were happy that the farm could continue to exist and even grow, a few of these people left the group and stopped coming to the farm. But many more have since joined. And I have watched, standing amid the rows of crops, as Hogshead has grown into a quirky but established institution, its members speaking out on local development issues, and in 2016 I walked the property's still-wild periphery with MTA representatives discussing even bigger plans for the future along a decommissioned railroad spur called the Montauk Cutoff. It is remarkable to see that something like this can still happen in a city like New York, both the audacity of its informal beginnings and the scale of its continuing success under greater recognition.§

§ The area around the Montauk Cutoff, the Newtown Creek, and the wider surrounding districts of Long Island City and Sunnyside, long predominantly industrial, are today experiencing a flurry of new activities, from "secret" pop-up events to condominium developments. In late 2015 the MTA asked for public input on "reuse concepts" for the cutoff itself. See, for instance, an atmospheric piece of reporting by Anne Correal (2015).

The formalization of unauthorized improvement efforts can be seen as compromising an inherent value that some do-it-yourselfers see in the informal process. Others might argue that formalization can allow DIY projects to last longer, grow bigger, or have more powerful impacts. Certainly the very strategy for a city or other authority willing to formalize these informal activities is to harness their material benefits and creative spirit while neutralizing the uncertainty and liability of unsanctioned activities. This again is a matter of different concepts of legitimacy in different contexts. However, perhaps the more important question at this juncture is what implications the formalization of DIY urbanism can have for cities and local residents, especially in underserved communities where quality public spaces and streetscape improvements are most needed. This is the subject of the next section.

## SOCIAL AND ECONOMIC IMPACTS OF MAINSTREAM TACTICAL URBANISM

Many official planning interventions inspired by DIY urbanism are popular with residents, and some result in valuable social, ecological, and economic benefits. In Oakland, for instance, in arguing for "focusing more on the pedestrian aspects of the design" at Latham Plaza, city planners noted "increased public interest in less auto-oriented public space" (in addition to the economic rationales cited above). They called the pilot project there "consistent with emerging community desires for vibrant urban space." Indeed, many community members I spoke with in California, Chicago, and New York professed support for these sorts of changes, at least in principle.

Janette Sadik-Khan's overhaul of Times Square went against the concerns of many businesses and provoked significant controversy in its effort to create a safer and more welcoming public space. As if inspired by DoTank's chairbombing and the bus stop bench interventions described in Chapter 3, her department also launched the "CityBench" initiative to install 1,000 new benches. Funded by a federal grant, the project prioritized "bus stops without shelters"; the benches have no advertising, and an online system even makes it easy for community members to request one where they think it is needed. Andy Wiley-Schwartz, then Sadik-Khan's deputy commissioner, explained the advantages of the program:

> These are the small accumulated interventions in the city that make it more livable and that let citizens, people, property owners, business owners, sort of

plug in to a way to make the city more livable at a very low threshold. So before, you wanted to put a bench out and you get this 20-page form and all these fees you have to pay and all the rest of it. And now if you want a bench, you can fill out, you know, three lines on an online form and submit it and somebody might come and install that bench, you know? [ . . . ] It's a very quiet way of developing these sort of standard materials that can really create some powerful public spaces.

A similar process in New York allows citizens to request trash cans— something that Derek in Seattle, who removed an entire bus stop in his frustration with the city's failure to provide a trash can there, would probably appreciate. As Wiley-Schwartz put it, "All that creativity that's going in to trying to get around the system can now go in to plugging into the system, because there's actually a system to plug in to." Numerous other "smart city" interfaces promise similar potential for crowd-sourced input on problems and possibilities that can make cities more responsive, while civic open data initiatives make it possible for any citizens with the technological know-how to find answers for themselves and build powerful digital tools for others. (For instance, a constellation of data-based projects and activist websites in the Bay Area and New York provide easy access to otherwise hard to find housing regulations and rent affordability information to help at-risk renters understand their rights and organize against displacement.) It is not hard to imagine a platform that, rather than obviating the need for DIY projects, instead collects and incorporates data on them to make them less chaotic and bureaucratically threatening.

The formalization of some DIY urban design activities, if done right, could also present especially hopeful opportunities for low-income communities and communities of color. Knowing that local government tends to be less responsive to the concerns of these citizens and that race can influence the allocation of community-improvement funding to local groups in these neighborhoods,[14] DIY urban design might offer an effective alternative for making locally preferred improvements happen. But we also know that members of these groups tend to systemically be less willing or able to engage in unauthorized activities. So the official acceptance of these activities in a way that encourages do-it-yourself contributions and brings them "above ground" could enable residents of resource-poor communities to make improvements themselves.

Matt feels the formalization of his Walk [Your City] project is a good thing for society and for the local governments in question, in particular because of what he described as the "iterative process" that more tactical,

DIY-inspired approaches can offer for cities and communities with limited resources:

> Actually a lot of the communities that are loving our platform are smaller communities, communities where the mayor, or the city manager or city planner are contacting us and they're saying, Hey we want to do this, we don't really care what the rules are, we haven't been able to provide wayfinding for our citizens ever, and we can do this in a collaborative matter, in a matter of weeks, for a couple thousand bucks!

Matt feels this can be especially beneficial for places that have seen limited investment or responsiveness from authorities: "You know, the fact that it's so inexpensive, communities can actually implement it." He conceded that this may be "kind of idealistic," but emphasized that in principle these sorts of approaches are far more accessible than traditional, top-down planning. As for the specific goals of his own initiative, when it comes to increasing walkability, wayfinding, and community engagement, official support is to his mind an "absolute bonus."

In other cases, cities co-opt DIY tactics and aesthetics to operationalize their value for economic purposes. It is not for nothing, for instance, that New York rents out the newly pedestrianized Times Square for corporate events that bring in big money; the pedestrianization itself was followed by a massive spike in retail rents in the area.[15] And, as Sadik-Khan noted regarding the new pedestrian plazas, "the business community has been asking for this for years." Near one such project in Brooklyn's trendy DUMBO neighborhood, she added, "Retail sales for businesses adjacent to the plaza have increased 172 percent." She touted the Times Square numbers too. In its pitches for Latham Plaza, the City of Oakland likewise emphasized that the park would be a boon to local merchants and even cited the same impressive sales figures surrounding the DUMBO plaza that I heard from Sadik-Khan.[16] (Of course, more charitably, one could grant that boosters of creative placemaking for socially progressive reasons might well sell them on their potential economic upsides just to get them approved.)

In monetizing the value of the new spaces themselves in these ways, cities, businesses, and property owners also typically monetize their cultural value as well. DIY urban design and tactical urbanism are popular trends and aesthetics that, like other signs of unique character and cultural "vibrancy," can be instrumentalized for economic development and branding at local and even inter-urban scales.[17] As Cathleen McGuigan, editor-in-chief of the magazine *Architectural Record*, put it bluntly at the CityAge Conference I attended, "The creative class, as Richard Florida has coined the term, has a preference about the sort of city they want to live in—a well-designed city." At the same time, the quirky cultural activities of the creative class themselves are broadly beloved as signs of local vibrancy and thus of economic development appeal.[18] DIY urban design projects, at least when harmless and "design-y" enough, can easily walk this line.

The widespread popularity of parklets is a powerful example of the use of a new, DIY-inspired planning strategy for creating dynamic urban cultural experiences that foster economic development. Proposals for new parklet programs that I reviewed, like the usually gushing news reports that often accompany their launch, typically feature the unauthorized, spontaneous origins of the trend in Rebar's original Park(ing) Day intervention. But the same proposals and reports also consistently emphasize parklets as a boon to local businesses. Although parklets are generally understood as public spaces, in many cities, they are authorized explicitly as economic development tools, granted directly to restaurants or other businesses to provide additional seating. The new prominence of dining parklets on trendy commercial streets from Montreal to San José to Washington DC suggests the allure they can have. Some businesses fronting parklets have reported substantial increases in sales, and "parklet dining" has been described in the press as an exciting new trend.[19]

A parklet in downtown San José, opened in 2015, as part of the campaign to brand the SoFA (South First Area) corridor as an arts district. Photo by the author.

These examples demonstrate how the formalization of DIY urban design interventions and the rise of new urban planning trends that build on the aesthetics and tactics of DIY urbanism can have social, civic, and economic benefits. Homespun design ideas can rise above bureaucratic inertia and provide citizen-driven solutions to problems, while "lighter, quicker, cheaper" approaches allow politicians and planners to try out innovative or politically difficult projects. Culturally astute planning and development policies that embrace hip aesthetics and progressive design trends yield desirable public spaces that benefit local residents and businesses. Yet there are problems inherent to both formal planning and DIY interventions that appear amplified by the combination of the two. As popular improvements with economic benefits that also embody trendy design thinking, these new public spaces can be exclusionary and risk displacing the very communities they aim to serve.

### "Public Spaces as Affluent White Spaces"—Creative Placemaking or Creative Placetaking?

In principle, a parklet is a public space. In many cities they are signposted as such. (In a few cities, including Long Beach, California, nonpublic parklets have also been allowed as literal extensions of businesses.) As described in the 2013 "San Francisco Parklet Manual":

> A parklet repurposes part of the street into a public space for people. They are intended as aesthetic enhancements to the streetscape, providing an economical solution to the need for increased public open space. Parklets provide amenities like seating, planting, bike parking, and art. While parklets are funded and maintained by neighboring businesses, residents, and community organizations, they are publicly accessible and open to all.

But how public is a space designed to look and in many cases function exactly like the outdoor seating of a sidewalk café? No matter how many signs denote their public-ness (and these are not always especially prominent), parklets may not appear at all welcoming or accessible to those who are unwilling or unable to buy something or who do not feel comfortable sitting in what feels like part of a fashionable business. And the social coding of these places does not stop with their design and location—they are also commonly and prominently populated by white, affluent bodies, furthering the implication that they are spaces of privileged access.

In other words, knowing what we do about who creates DIY urban design and how these DIY-inspired spaces are typically used, we might consider whether the embrace of DIY urban design aesthetics in professional planning perpetuates sociospatial privilege. Design itself is reflective of who produces it. Now, following this logic, one might well argue that almost all architecture and urban design reflects the white, male, and educated middle-class backgrounds of most of its creators, and that urban spaces tend by default to privilege a dominant culture of affluent white consumerism wherever they do not work explicitly to do something else. This may well be the case.[20] But there is something especially (and ironically) problematic about the dominant aesthetic of an artistically inspired and culturally trend-setting sidewalk seating extension as public space.

Seemingly benign or even broadly positive elemental additions to public space, from street trees to bike lanes to farmers' markets, can in fact code areas as spaces of affluence and privilege. As Alison Alkon and Christie McCullen found in their 2011 study of California farmers' markets, trendy public spaces like these can perpetuate the normalizing and privileging of affluent, white values, not only in the spaces themselves through the cultural associations of how and for whom they are designed, but in claiming such uses as the norm for public space in general.[21] This would seem to be all the more a danger with pedestrian plazas and parklets that, although emphatically public, often look more like extensions of the business that sponsor them and can likewise be understood as effectively affluent-coded, with full access a matter of privilege. How welcoming are these public spaces to someone who cannot afford to buy anything or does not look like a typical consumer? Pedestrian plazas like New York's are also more explicitly controlled and regulated than standard streets and sidewalks, with things like smoking, skateboarding, and lying down restricted.[22]

What's more, improvements that are coded as spaces of privilege impact urban processes beyond the immediate spaces themselves. Although creative placemaking is unquestionably needed and beneficial in many cities, especially those that have not experienced the economic and cultural revitalizations of their coastal cousins in recent years, most of these projects, like DIY urban design actions, appear to be most common in newly hip and gentrifying urban neighborhoods. The benefits they do provide are unlikely to be felt where they are most needed. Instead, the potentially negative impacts of such improvements are especially damaging in the very socioeconomically transitioning neighborhoods where they are most common.

San Francisco's hotly contested and rapidly gentrifying Mission District, for instance, is also home to its highest concentration of parklets. Simply by boosting sales at local businesses (as they are often explicitly intended to do), parklets and plazas may contribute to higher property values and rents in neighborhoods like this, further displacing poorer residents or business owners. By attracting hip consumers and adoring coverage from tastemakers in the press, these amenities can begin to rebrand whole neighborhoods.[23]

This is not to say there are no improvements in underprivileged areas. One of New York's new pedestrian plazas was built in the Brooklyn neighborhood of East New York, among the city's poorest; a parklet on the Lower East Side attracts a diverse and far from affluent crowd. But my analysis of plaza locations in New York City and parklet locations in San Francisco, as well as anecdotal observations of similar new public spaces in Los Angeles, Chicago, Philadelphia, San José, and several other cities, revealed a clear predominance of these places in trendy or otherwise relatively affluent parts of these cities. The application, funding, and ongoing maintenance expectations for these spaces in all of these cities would also seem to make their successful realization more likely in areas with greater economic strength, organizational density, and political capital.

In New York, one of the most controversial of the city's pedestrian plazas was created at the request of the local business alliance in a rapidly gentrifying part of Brooklyn, producing a backlash from other longtime residents. As Wiley-Schwartz remembered,

> I mean we had a lot of support from the businesses, the property owners, et cetera. But there was some resistance and the resistance mostly came in the form of, "We've lived in this neighborhood for 30 years, nobody asked us and this is all a plot by the [business improvement district] to control the neighborhood." And it's very [ . . . ] residents versus businesses, right? "This neighborhood is changing, I've been here for a long time, I'm not a part of these changes, I don't identify with these changes, I don't think this is going to work, maybe this is all for yuppies."

For community members I spoke to, the simple matter of the way the plaza was supposed to look—a reproduction of every other apparently trendy "Bloomberg plaza" they had seen in other parts of town—was a real part of the concern and alienation they felt with the project.

Bicycle infrastructure is another planning ideal that many DIY urban design efforts have focused on that can also be associated with gentrification. Research shows that policymakers are increasingly using bicycle infrastructure to appeal to young "creatives" and promote economic development. Reports also suggest bike lanes have come to be seen as white, affluent planning priorities and are associated with gentrification fears in some neighborhoods.[24] The installation of a city bicycle parking corral (in a former parking space) out front of a café in Crown Heights, Brooklyn, in 2012 raised the ire of some longtime neighborhood residents who associated it with gentrification and planning imposed from outside.[25] A recent *New York Times* real estate report emphasized that access to well-planned bike lanes is viewed by some apartment hunters as a selling point comparable to subway access, thus potentially raising rents and property values.[26]

In these ways, however cynical it may sound, the official embrace of the cultural values behind many DIY urban design activities must be viewed as more than a happy opportunity for collaboration. It can be symbolic of an effort to reproduce trendy and exclusive values at the expense of existing communities. Planning and development policies aimed at attracting the creative class, including the promotion of amenities like public art and sidewalk cafés, have been used in explicit strategies of urban renewal.[27] Such cultural changes can distort the underlying character of a place, displacing longtime residents economically and culturally.

Geographers John Paul Catungal, Deborah Leslie, and Yvonne Hii (2009) have argued that even the most authentic actualizations of "creative city" placemaking walk a thin line with regard to causing gentrification. Melissa Checker (2011) has suggested the same thing about well-meaning efforts at sustainability planning and urban "greening." These sorts of initiatives can be successful at enlivening long-neglected neighborhoods, promoting healthy and environmentally sustainable practices, and facilitating investment and renewal in places where they are badly needed. But they often fail to address the byproducts: inequality, displacement, and exclusion. So too with tactical urbanism and other creative placemaking efforts. The very connections to informal methods and aesthetics that make these approaches so appealing and successful can spell negative consequences that run counter to their principles.

Tactical urbanism and related trends in urban streetscape planning represent a highly effective tool for making real improvements to the urban landscape. Proponents like Mike Lydon are thoughtful and progressive planners deeply committed to creating better, healthier, and more responsive cities. The experiences of New York and dozens of other cities prove that these approaches can produce valuable, well-designed, and locally beloved public spaces and other amenities, which can in turn influence policy and do permanent good. Some cities and communities desperately need such things.

We must nonetheless maintain a critical eye on the social qualities of the spaces we are building, on who benefits and who is excluded. Along these lines, there might also be concern that the formalization of some projects or types of projects that best fit with white and affluent values could risk crowding out or further marginalizing ideas, uses, and design sensibilities that do not match mainstream, market-based ideals. (How might these sorts of interventions differ if created primarily by people of color? If they were more about immigrants' rights or Black Lives than urban development and consumption?) The problem isn't that these spaces are being created by educated, privileged people; it's that the opportunity to influence the character of one's community in this way is not open to all.

In her research on farmers' markets, McCullen (2008) asserts that trendy and artistically designed public gathering spaces are not doomed to perpetuate privilege: if designers and policymakers stop assuming that potentially exclusive spaces are "culturally neutral" by default, they can be programmed in ways that code them as inclusive instead. This outlook parallels the approach advocated by Steve Cancian, members of the Baltimore Development Cooperative, and other do-it-yourselfers who, conscious of their potentially problematic status as privileged outsiders, have made certain to involve more longtime community members in their projects. Doing this, at the formal or informal level, requires intentional effort and may mean looking for models beyond the most successful and white-coded examples. Unfortunately, although many officials who embrace tactical approaches—like many unauthorized do-it-yourselfers—frame their efforts as responses to a lumbering city bureaucracy that they are quick to critique, it is a smaller number who turn their creativity to explicitly confronting deeper socioeconomic ills.

· · ·

The embrace of the tactics and aesthetics of DIY urban design by formal planning and placemaking authorities continues at a fever pitch. As a *Cincinnati Magazine* post recently put it, "Parklets are a thing now."[28] There may be no better example than the City of Los Angeles's "People Street" initiative. Since 2014, the city's Department of Transportation has officially encouraged citizens to apply for and make use of approved "kits" to create parklets, pedestrian plazas, and bike corrals. The goal, as described on the official peoplest.lacity.org website, is to "transform underused areas of LA's largest public asset—our 7,500 miles of city streets—into active, vibrant, and accessible public space."

The City of Angels has fully embraced the language and the aesthetic of DIY and combined it with a standardized process (plus a little cross-promotion from sponsors thrown in for good measure). As one local planning blog summarized:

> The goal of the program is to improve the quality of life of Angelenos by providing a toolkit of cost-efficient design elements that can be quickly installed

to help the city come alive with minimalist wood and steel planter boxes full of succulents, sleek picnic tables, and even GameTime exercise equipment. [ . . . ] Each kit contains packaged, required configurations for Plazas, Parklets, and Bike Corrals to choose from. Specifications provided in these documents simplify and automate the process, efficiently eliminating the need to reinvent the wheel for each project and streamlining the workflow with thoughtfully pre-approved design kits.[29]

As with many instances of the formal appropriation of DIY urban design discussed in this chapter, there is much of value here. This Los Angeles effort certainly responds to a need, not only for more public space and bicycle infrastructure at the expense of cars, but also among citizens to make positive changes themselves. Many of my interviewees, including several in Los Angeles, told me quite explicitly that they "wish the city would do it" so that they would not have to. As one do-it-yourselfer opined in Chapter 4, "if there's a place where we can do it [ . . . ] up to spec and everything, we should be able to put it in ourselves." Planners echoed similar sentiments. And this is exactly what the Los Angeles Department of Transportation is hoping for with People Street.

Yet, as I have argued here, there are reasons to keep a critical eye on these efforts. Not least is that, rather than explicitly building upon LA's influential and promising homegrown "Latino urbanism" and other more organic cultures of local placemaking, the aesthetics of the People Street program largely just replicate San Francisco and New York models.[30] The opportunity to participate in the program is still largely limited to those with the familiarity and the finances (not to mention the free time) to take advantage of it. And although these interventions are touted as ways of expanding a city's public space, the way the application and approval process is structured and the basic realities of contemporary urban economics can lead them to wind up as little more than cute extensions of adjacent businesses. For better or worse, People Street projects may have a bigger impact as economic development tools than as community resources. For now, the initiative does at least seem to indicate a broadly positive and refreshing step among city officials and planners there, one that does justice to what LA mayor Eric Garcetti (2014) has called the "fundamental shift in how we make our city streets safer and more enjoyable." This is something to applaud. It entails all the dangers and contradictions inherent in the making of urban space, but also great promise.

All in all, the formalization of DIY approaches and aesthetics is an uneven process. We can see prominent examples of especially effective or popular DIY efforts being co-opted by open-minded planners and savvy policymakers, but this remains uncommon. And despite the rising popularity of official planning efforts that take some cues from unauthorized models, DIY urban design itself remains (by definition) unsanctioned and frequently illegal. No matter how mainstream a planning priority bicycle infrastructure has become, guerrilla bike lanes on city streets are highly problematic for practical reasons: they can be dangerous and place cities at great risk of being held liable for deaths or injuries. Regardless of the personal admiration they won from some transportation planners I spoke to—one literally whispered "good for them" before hastily emphasizing that was not an official position—all of these city workers said there was simply no way their agencies could do anything other than quickly remove DIY bike lanes, much less give them even symbolic approval. Yet unauthorized signage, traffic cones, and defensive posts installed along *existing* bike lanes have found some approval. And the symbolic power of even these most illegal DIY urban design efforts on the formal planning process—simply by being visible and challenging to it—still gives them extended influence.

The majority of unauthorized streetscape improvements I found in my research are not trendy public spaces: homemade traffic signs, vacant lot gardens, and improvised places to sit do not conform to the popular design aesthetic I have focused on here, beyond their association with the phenomenon of DIY urbanism in general. But it is this association itself that is the point. The often singular and low-impact unauthorized efforts become part of a larger shift in urbanism that is having a significant impact on the planning field. It is a fitting complement to the "trickle down" of professional and scholarly knowledge to inform do-it-yourselfers that we see this simultaneous—and equally conflicted—trickle up of the tactics and aesthetics of unauthorized efforts to professional planners. In capturing the minds of those responsible for official policy, do-it-yourselfers influence contemporary placemaking far beyond their individual actions, resulting in mainstream acceptance and support for creating the types of urban spaces that they value.

Then again, there is also a possibility, unmentioned by the do-it-yourselfers I spoke to but implied by several of the professionals, that a more adaptive and responsive city could obviate the need for DIY activities altogether. (In fact this seemed to be an important part of Larry's concern about Oakland's official but DIY-style Lapham Plaza.) Andy Wiley-Schwartz believes that the improvements New York City made during the Bloomberg administration have essentially done as much:

> It's fascinating, this whole mentality of changing a city that was not getting anything that it wanted, so it operated on this big sort of outlaw mentality, painting

your own bike lanes and whatever else you're doing. You know, now you have a supportive administration, so how do you change to become a partner from becoming, you know, an outsider? [ . . . ] I think that's really important and it always irritates me because these people still want to be outlaws, they want to be outside a system that they don't have to be outside of anymore.**

Joe, for his part, has a relatively moderate and nuanced take on the roles of both the formal and informal in urban placemaking. In one of our conversations, sitting in the sun outside the EcoVillage and looking out at their "reclaimed" central Los Angeles intersection (similar in so many ways to the official pedestrian plazas that have since appeared in New York and even just up the street in LA), he explained:

> I mean I have a lot of critique of how the city does things, but I think sanitation and roads are probably something we're gonna do together and not village by village, block by block. [ . . . ] But I think a lot of the quality of life, neighborhood things can be done. [ . . . ] I think when we sort of say, "Oh good, government's got a handle on it" then we go down the wrong path, and when we sort of say total DIY, I think we end up with temporary things that get overwritten in some ways. And so I think that there are healthy spaces that have chunks of all of those.

The difference here, between the eventual systematization of all informal efforts that New York's deputy transportation commissioner envisioned and the distinction that Joe sees between the city's job and the community's job, reflects the contrasting perspectives of two men with remarkably similar goals for public space in their communities. They further challenge any black and white notion of formality and informality in urban placemaking, where any such line can be meaningfully drawn, and what value these terms really have in the contemporary city where the more important question ought to be whether our streets are being made better for everyone.

---

** Of course, as I have shown, most do-it-yourselfers are not especially interested in being "outlaws" or being "outside a system" anyway; they see their efforts as valuable and important contributions that they happen to be in a good position to make, and do so because they feel it is helpful and fun. Plenty of them are quite pleased with official efforts like New York's, if sometimes wary of how they are implemented. And even those who will surely continue to view their interventions as needed in spite of any increasing systematization are, with the possible exception of one or two cases, hardly devout anarchists.

7

# Conclusions

*Inequality, Legitimacy, and the Momentary*
*Potential of Participation*

The design of cities, of urban landscapes and built environments, is a deeply human thing. Throughout history, our alteration of the surrounding environment (urban or otherwise) "without permission" has been an everyday occurrence, and we continue to physically shape our surroundings in countless ways. The coordination and rationalization of urban planning, and ultimately the professional formalization of design and placemaking work, has been a long and uneven process. Cities have over time remained unfathomably chaotic places, and workaday organic places, and dynamic, unpredictable places. The city, as Henri Lefebvre told us, is an *oeuvre*—a work or opus, our collective work of art. It is also the place where what he called the far order and the near order, the top-down and the bottom-up, come together.

A banal yet wonderful example: Nearly every day for many years, commuting by bike from my home in Brooklyn to work or other engagements in Manhattan, I cycled up an oval-shaped incline allowing me and thousands of other cyclists to climb from street level onto the Manhattan Bridge bike path and on over the bridge. Every day I observed changes to this piece of transportation infrastructure. I don't mean the multitudes of endless and overlapping graffiti that I read in glimpses, nor the constant work being done to the roadway and subway tracks and steel trusses and everything else that make up this centenarian workhorse of a suspension bridge. I mean the "desire path"—the worn dirt track that legions of renegade cyclists (and frequent wayward pedestrians) have formed by taking a shortcut from a high point on the bicycle ramp straight through the grassy middle of the sloping oval down to the bottom, and vice versa.

Desire paths (also known as desire lines, cow paths, or social trails) are a favorite landscape feature of mine, and of anyone else who likes going the most direct route across a field. They're also a favorite subject of discussion and instruction for landscape architects because they demonstrate incredibly clearly how different a conceptual design is from everyday user experience, undoing all the artful planning and paving of intended walkways with a simple shortcut. The one on the Manhattan Bridge bike path approach not only provides a shortcut but also opens up the whole green slope to being more than just scenery. Cyclists and others stop to hang out, some people use it as a place to sleep, various street art pieces have been installed, and a guy named Trevor spontaneously turns up about once a year with a wagon full of free beer (and a sign saying as much) urging people to stop and join him in an annual "social experiment."

I don't tend to take the desire path on the Manhattan Bridge bike approach myself (it's a bit bumpy and pretty steep, and I enjoy whirring around the turn on the pavement), but I watched with fascination in the autumn of 2014 as the city's Department of Transportation attempted to put an end to it. Workers extended an existing fence so that it cut off the path at the top. It seemed a surprising show of force to me, the city's attempt to rein in this minor bit of organic urban redesign with a heavy metal barrier installed by a sizable work crew. (Most desire paths are left alone or even ultimately accepted and paved; to be fair, maybe this one was viewed as a dangerous liability, like many informal pieces of bike infrastructure are.) With far less surprise and much amusement, I watched as within weeks another desire path appeared just beyond the extent of the new fence.*

Things are not the same in other contexts of course, even elsewhere in the United States. In some places local government is so strapped, and private investment so rare, that do-it-yourself interventions are the least of anyone's concern. In New Orleans, DIY urbanism is everywhere. Residents of the Central City neighborhood, predominantly African American and very low income, have built lot-sized gardens and installed all manner of

---

* Studies have shown that as few as 15 traversals along the same line can be enough to begin making a visible path in the underlying vegetation (for a review, see Hampton & Cole 1988).

New York City Department of Transportation contractors install a fence to block off an informal "desire path" on the Brooklyn approach to the Manhattan Bridge in 2014. A new path was quickly created by cyclists just beyond the fence. Photo by the author.

street signs on their streets, which are off the beaten path of most affluent New Orleanians or visitors despite their central location. Just outside of the city limits, in Jefferson Parish, I visited an entire informal community of stilt houses along the Mississippi River batture that has existed for many decades on the wrong side of the levee, and thus outside official recognition. In the Bywater, a scrappy but artsy area on the opposite side of town, situated along the same industrial canal that overflowed to deluge the Lower Ninth Ward during Hurricane Katrina, I saw DIY installations of everything from bike lanes and speed limit postings to neighborhood welcome signs and public seating. Candy Chang's "I wish this was . . ." stickers started here, and another local woman has been known to plant trees in broken pavement. (Street art, a different sort of informal improvement, is also prevalent, from the work of local artists to renowned ones like Swoon.)

These guerrilla interventions exist in a very different context. For one thing, the whole of the built environment in New Orleans, both formal and informal, is in struggle with the natural environment as well. I was told by one of the many kind locals who took time to show me around their neighborhoods that an invasive species of flowering vine called cat's claw— visible digging into the walls and roofs of many a Central City shotgun

A homemade speed limit sign and, several blocks away, a DIY table built around a fire hydrant, both created by community members in the Bywater neighborhood of New Orleans. Photos by the author, 2012.

house—was responsible for the destruction of more homes in the Big Easy than Katrina. The folks down on the batture contend with erratic water levels and erosion along the Mississippi, as sea levels rise against the levees. The city is being made and unmade in different ways on a daily basis. And of course it is changing socially as well. Among other things, an influx of architects and urbanists from all over the country since 2005—even as many longtime residents who left the city as refugees from the hurricane have not returned—has reshaped the demographics, the culture, and the streetscape of New Orleans dramatically. Central City is changing too: a recent story about the neighborhood in a local newspaper featured a couple of white do-it-yourselfers with an urban farm built on two vacant lots there, on which they "grow crops, tend bees and herd goats for local restaurant members and host a series of dinners with live music."[1] (With fencing, raised beds, and an extensive irrigation system, they have now invested tens of thousands of dollars in the space and grown it into a business.)

In truth, the urban environment has always been a place of both structure and informality, evolving and fluctuating over time and across contexts. There is a nearly universal constant, however: whether dominated by a centralized or dictatorial state, vestiges of feudalism, or more free-wheeling urban mercantilism, while the masses lived the everyday streetscape of the historical city, its planning and design have always been directed by elites. And whether dutifully in the public interest (ordering, sanitizing, providing, beautifying) or more unabashedly capitalistic (facilitating growth, development, or trade), the planning goals of these elites have largely, ultimately been motivated by power and wealth. Today's big city administrations and their surrounding "pro-growth" coalitions are no different. (Those who might feel untouched by dominant organizing forces are rarely better for it, notwithstanding the remarkable informal adaptations they might make to improve their conditions. In most cases, apparent depravity from capitalist development or government services and order is only more evidence of the degree to which the situation really *is* determined by structural and political-economic forces outside the control of the least privileged.) A question central to this study—to modern society, really—is just how problematic this elite ordering of things is for the average person. Another is what any of us can do about it. This concluding chapter takes up these questions in the context of my findings about do-it-yourself urban design in the help-yourself cities of today.

The most powerful social science builds from the observed microphenomena it takes as its subjects to inform our understanding of more universal causal mechanisms and macro social processes. It is my hope that this study of a discrete spatiocultural practice provides insight into such grander processes and to the theoretical questions that continue to drive social research. Defining DIY urban design sociologically provided an opportunity to examine illegal urban space interventions more generally and to question our assumptions about who creates them and why. Placing DIY urban design in the context of the economic restructuring and market-driven urban policy and planning processes that have defined urban space over the last half century helped to show how people experience these in everyday life and demonstrated that cultural practices cannot be separated from structural contexts.[2] We have also seen how design reflects the cultural values of its creators, coding personal preferences as well as exclusivities into the places that result. The formal appropriation of some of DIY urban design's tactics and aesthetics reveals aspects of dominant policy ideologies in a growing number of cities today, including the ways that creative city policy agendas materially impact urban neighborhoods.

In the remainder of this concluding chapter, I aim to expand upon four more overarching contributions raised by these findings and alluded to in the questions above. First are the implications that the contradictions and dilemmas of DIY urban design seem to have for social equity in civic participation, demonstrating the limitations of participatory citizenship even in an ostensibly popular grassroots practice. The second is the rethinking of the formality-informality binary in urbanism that my findings demand. There is in fact considerable interplay between the formal and the informal in contemporary urban placemaking, and these categories are so socially and culturally contingent that their usefulness in describing social practices is limited. Third, I argue instead that a concept of socially constructed and locally contingent legitimacy offers a more helpful interpretive framework for explaining why boundaries between sanctioned and unsanctioned urban interventions are effectively eliminated in some cases and built up in others. Status-based mainstream legitimacy can explain the relative acceptance and "successes" of some do-it-yourselfers and DIY interventions over others. But legitimacy can also be operationalized to expand opportunities for participation, allowing more democratic and locally sensitive interventions while staying true to their spirit and intention in ways that outright formalization cannot. Finally, I return to the radical optimism with which my interest in DIY urban design began. I argue in the end for the persistent potential of the practice in terms of the critical value of transgression as well as the more practical benefits that some interventions do provide and which official actors are simply not well positioned to make. When done right, DIY urban design can offer a hopeful model for positive, locally relevant direct action that does not have to perpetuate unequal access, uneven development, or displacement.

## URBAN CITIZENSHIP AND CIVIC PARTICIPATION

Cities are places of profound inequality. The world over, they are concentrations of extreme poverty, but also citadels of the elite. Considerable attention in social science, public policy, and popular media has long—and quite rightly—been given to the persistent and expanding gap between rich and poor in urban areas and the drastic differences in living conditions and life outcomes across neighborhoods. Less discussed is the irony that the city—the *polis*, the cradle of democracy—is a place of profoundly uneven forms of citizenship as well.

Much has lately been made of the great dynamism of cities, as centers of bottom-up innovation, creativity, and production, and human capital more generally.[3] But participation in this dynamism—much less enjoyment of its benefits—is not equally accessible. Participation, access, influence, the basic ability to have a say in the building of healthy, exciting, and "livable" places and communities—these things vary widely across numerous variables of social status. Urban planning itself, while easy for some to overlook as a rote bureaucratic task or professional creative endeavor performed above the common concerns of the street, is a fundamental form of democratic governance. Yet despite years of vocal concern about participatory planning and budgeting and serious intentions toward community engagement in policymaking, in most circumstances a small number of prominent voices—whether public officials, institutions, or development interests—still hold most of the power in shaping urban policies and places.

Some of these powerful actors are well-meaning elected representatives and others are public servants doing their level best to work for the "highest and best use." Many of those I spoke to told me earnestly about listening to the opinions of community members, giving examples of ways that people writing letters or making a stand at a public forum could have a real impact. It is also true, as the professional planners were quick to remind me, that it wouldn't do to turn over control of the design and use of a great city's streets and other public spaces to just anyone with a pet project in mind. But it is tempting to say that this is exactly what we have done: not by ceding planning power to lay community members but by ceding it to private development interests. Several planners I spoke to, after emphasizing the time they spend at community meetings, conceded that at the end of the day, word coming down from on high was that economic development was still the priority.

I have argued in this book that the policy ideologies prevalent in American cities since the 1970s produce an uneven and undependable urban development environment that has been conducive to unauthorized local improvement efforts, despite the professionalization of urban placemaking in the decades prior. Informal urbanism is a natural, even logical way of taking action in the help-yourself city. Some unauthorized urban space interventions of the sort described in Chapter 2, whether minor vandalism or major political public space occupations, implicitly or explicitly challenge the status quo. They do little to rattle its underlying foundations, however, or to meaningfully improve conditions in needy communities. Do-it-yourself urban design presents another alternative: not a personal, radical, or particularly deviant form of expression, but a form of active, direct, and ostensibly positive participation in improving urban streetscapes. The practice clearly has the potential to be a democratizing force as a medium for active participatory citizenship. Certainly it is celebrated as such by its practitioners, in popular media, and to some extent even in planning and design discourse.

Unfortunately, in many ways the phenomenon serves as much to highlight the limits to citizenship along lines of social inequality as it does to expand participation. Especially worrying is its limited accessibility to people in the underserved communities who might benefit from DIY urban design the most. Certain do-it-yourselfers, certain projects and types of projects are viewed differently than others by society and authorities due to underlying inequalities and biases as well as blunt priorities and aesthetic tastes. The result, in practice, is no more equitable or democratic than a deep-pocketed developer having his way (even if many of us, myself included, do prefer a whimsical guerrilla intervention to, say, a high-priced condominium tower or sports arena).

DIY urban design can thus essentially propagate the very uneven development it often hopes to resist. And the celebration of the practice among urbanists, politicians, and others for the civic participation it supposedly enjoins can in fact reinforce unequal, undemocratic social and spatial conditions. The same goes for more officially sanctioned tactical urbanism and creative placemaking. In this way, my findings contribute to the rather discouraging but essential task laid out recently by Edward Walker, Michael McQuarrie, and Caroline Lee (2015), and by Gianpaolo Baiocchi and Ernesto Ganuza (2017), to explore the limits and indeed failures of the recent political emphasis on expanding local participation, which they argue has not been accompanied by a real expansion of popular democracy.[4]

All the more troubling is the idea of politicians, developers, and other elite interests attempting to mobilize and exploit grassroots popular participation like DIY urban design in their favor, whether to claim community support and credibility or harness the cool factor of a trendy aesthetic. This is analogous to what Walker (2015) found in his study of the limited (and cynical) participatory campaigns of American corporations. This sort of engagement may sound like a democratic innovation, but is ultimately shallow and shaped by social inequalities, offering little real empowerment. The embrace of public participation by elites coincides fittingly with the era of neoliberal policymaking. And as this book has shown, DIY urban design itself can be, despite its populist potential, a quintessentially neoliberal act, frequently carried out by privileged and entitled individuals with no government oversight.

Perhaps this last point ought to be our deeper concern. With the intentional manipulation of participation by elite interests, at least the cause of the problem is apparent. The prospect that even relatively unhindered, innocent, organic—and, to many, counternormative and transgressive—popular participation is *still* limited due to fundamental inequities drives home just how stubborn the persistence of inequality in urban space is. In short, all this participation is not so empowering. It is fragmented, individualistic, and still frequently elitist, in many ways not equally open to all. This raises the question of whether the more accessible medium of democratic voice and participation in urban placemaking is the opportunity to "do-it-yourself," or the opportunity to be represented, however ploddingly, by a formal process that is at least theoretically concerned with public input and social equity.

All of this also makes further apparent how little the difference between any two projects' success, benefits, or acceptability in a particular context actually has to do with issues of informality and formality. What I have called creative transgression is viewed very differently when perpetrated by individuals in a position of social privilege and in forms that fit with mainstream "creative" aesthetics and values than when it is not. The question of who has the ability or willingness to participate in DIY urban design and what projects find social and official acceptance has far more to do with a complex of competing notions of legitimacy than a simple binary of formal and informal.

## PROBLEMATIZING FORMALITY AND INFORMALITY

Without a doubt, we have certain normative assumptions about how our shared urban spaces are officially or unofficially designed, built, and altered in the cities of the United States and other advanced economies. In particular, we have understandings—laws and regulations even—about who is supposed to do this work. Urban planners and policymakers, property owners and developers, architects and engineers, and a variety of government employees and contracted workers are all familiar actors on our streets. Their actions, if not universally loved, are governed by established codes and ordinances, land use agreements, and the planning process. At the same time, we may think of graffiti artists, mobile vendors, tent city dwellers, radical occupiers, and a handful of other unsanctioned actors who physically shape the built environment. Their activities, if sometimes celebrated for the character, authenticity, and "life" that they bring to city streets, are viewed as chaotic and potentially threatening. These opposing forces—archetypically perhaps the planning bureaucrat and the graffiti vandal—personify the distinction between the sanctioned and the unsanctioned in urban placemaking.

This formality-informality binary is prominent in urban studies. Indeed it is central to my definition of DIY urban design. Yet my findings call it out as overly simplistic; they color and complicate it. We have seen throughout this study the complex and highly interrelated connection between DIY urban design activities and the formal planning and development process. In Chapter 3, I demonstrated how many DIY interventions are direct responses to the perceived failures of the official process while others work like vigilante efforts to enforce laws that are not being enforced, for social good and ill. In Chapter 4, I showed how knowledge of the official planning process, from professional tools to academic theory, directly informs much

DIY urbanism. Chapter 5 complicated the backgrounds and impacts of do-it-yourselfers further through a critical analysis of the role that inequality and privilege play in the uneven interpretations of creative transgression in different contexts. And, as discussed in Chapter 6, although planners and policymakers express wariness of DIY efforts for practical and professional reasons, they recognize that do-it-yourselfers produce ideas, methods, and results that people want and which cities have begun to adopt in turn. In several cases, initially unauthorized DIY interventions have ultimately found official approval. The do-it-yourself urban designer stands in between the archetypes of the planner and the vandal.

It is worth stating then that this study makes abundantly clear that potentially constructive forms of informality are at work in the physical shaping of cities in the global North. This is a finding that in and of itself runs in some contrast to those perspectives (which at their worst amount to a sort of racist neocolonial attitude) that seem to assume urban informality is a distinguishing feature of the developing world. The truth is that the making and remaking even of something as regulated as a New York City street is still the result of a web of formal and informal practices: city officials acting both within and around bureaucratic constraints, real estate developers under varying degrees of regulatory scrutiny, elected representatives and community groups, and everyday citizens with all manner of motivations and no particular authority.[5]

My findings also bring into question the premise of a formal-informal binary in urbanism to begin with. I have demonstrated instead a considerable flow of ideas, techniques, and theories between the formal and the informal that a strong bifurcation between the two would belie. While the principal distinction of DIY urbanism from official urban planning and placemaking is that it is unauthorized, what distinguishes it from other forms of unauthorized urban intervention is actually just how many formal elements it includes. These formalities of informal improvement are a defining feature of DIY urban design.

Charles Horton Cooley, writing in the early days of 20th-century modernism, argued that formalism essentially turns the creative and beautiful into cheap repetition, leaving individuals at the "prey of apathy, self-complacency, sensuality and the lower nature in general."[6] For systems and institutions, too much formalism stymies innovation. Whether Cooley's assessment of these dangers of bureaucratic standardization serves as a call for professional planners to embrace DIY urban design or a caution for do-it-yourselfers to avoid appropriation is a matter of perspective. Interestingly, however, for Cooley, while the "apparent opposite" of formalism may be disorganization—a sort of reactive individualism of the type we saw in the worst sorts of antisocial do-it-yourself alterations—the "real opposite" of both formalism and disorganization is "that wholesome relation between individuality and the institution in which each supports the other, the latter contributing a stable basis for the vitality and variation of the former."[7]

This degree of intermingling between the formal and the informal in urban design would then seem to be a positive thing. And the conditions I observed imply some chance of productive mutual acceptance, even cooperation, where the regulatory environment is flexible enough to accommodate it. For planners and city agencies, embracing what Judith Innes, Sarah Connick, and David Booher (2007) have called "informality as a planning strategy" can introduce innovative ideas and perhaps a more dynamic and responsive institutional culture. Janette Sadik-Khan's ability to make enormous changes to New York City's streets relatively unencumbered by the bureaucratic processes faced by her predecessors was a boon to the city and its residents. (On some level, official urban development and governance itself has condoned a great deal of "informality" with the privatization of everything from trash pickup to healthcare and transit services in some cities.)

For do-it-yourselfers, formal recognition or approval of their tactics can enable the scaling of DIY projects to previously inconceivable levels of impact. This is ultimately the point of tactical urbanism. Cities might, as some of the planners I spoke to even suggested, find ways to "set the stage" for the public to more freely engage in making local improvements themselves, as new policies in Los Angeles and elsewhere have tried to do. Further integration of the formal and the informal might ideally result in a more fluid understanding of planning responsibility across these parties and, as Innes and her colleagues (2007: 207) put it, a redistribution of power and authority to being "co-located with key knowledge and with the nodes of the network that can take action."

The problem is how manifestly uneven the exchange can be and how socially determined the categories of formal and informal actually are. The distinction is essentially made by those with political or economic power. In his work on identity and neighborhood change in Venice, California, Andrew Deener (2012) demonstrated how perceptions of formal and informal (in this case, economic activities) are effectively set by those in positions of authority, especially local stakeholders and the police, based on subjective cultural impressions of "order and disorder." He recounts the story of wealthy newer residents and city officials recasting the beach's informal "free speech zone," a well-known bohemian tourist attraction, as a "stigmatized problem." These conditions mean that some informal activities that might be locally accepted or welcomed can be nonetheless criminalized while a proposal that only benefits outside interests can still receive official approval despite opposition from a community that has little recourse to object. And the types of informal interventions that city officials are willing to embrace are likewise those that meet their priorities or fit with mainstream ideas of what creative placemaking for economic development should look like. In these cases, the important question becomes less whether something is formal or informal, but whether it is deemed acceptable and appropriate, where, and why.

A better term to describe what is actually happening when we talk about who has the right or the ability to alter urban streets and public spaces, and a more meaningful concept with which to assess a project's "success," is a sort of multifaceted sense of legitimacy. The condition of an actor or intervention being accepted as appropriate and valid in a particular cultural context is what I refer to here as legitimacy. Throughout this book, as we have seen the formality-informality binary exploded and broken down, we have seen legitimacy at work. In particular, the conferral of legitimacy based on mainstream cultural norms, status expectations, or political or economic rationales tends to perpetuate existing power dynamics and helps explain the unequal acceptance of DIY urban design and unequal participation in its creation. By turning our attention to legitimacy, rather than just questions of legality or formality, we can more clearly interrogate the dynamics at work and think about ways to address these inequalities.

## OPERATIONALIZING LEGITIMACY FOR COMMUNITY PLACEMAKING

Legitimacy has long been a central preoccupation of political philosophy, with theorists striving to understand what allows one group of people to make decisions on behalf of others in a democracy. In the context of urban placemaking, interventions are or are not given local legitimacy based on the positionality and status of their creators and the way they are perceived by those arbiters in the position to confer acceptance. When planning professionals and policymakers look favorably on DIY urban design, they tend to embrace those interventions and aesthetics that match mainstream ("creative city") ideals of vibrancy, sustainability, and economic development. Interventions that signal the priorities of low-income groups, transgressive ideas, or less fashionable aesthetics are less likely to be granted official or normative legitimacy. And we know that even in the anarchic environment of unauthorized streetscape interventions, those with social privilege feel more comfortable acting because they risk less in transgressing authority and have confidence in their efforts. Extrapolating from research that has repeatedly demonstrated the influence of status characteristics in determining expectations in social interaction, do-it-yourselfers of higher socioeconomic status may be more likely viewed as legitimate actors as well—regardless of their actual qualifications.[8] In all these ways, legitimacy is both a function and arbiter of privilege in DIY urbanism. And the selective embrace of certain efforts by government agencies or business interests can be useful to them in proving the legitimacy of their own authority as well. Laying bare these power relationships of placemaking through the lens of legitimacy opens them up to critique. Keeping these dynamics in mind is essential to the task of improving and developing our cities more equitably.

Focusing on legitimacy is more than just a useful critical analytical move, however. It can suggest ways of actually addressing the inequalities that it helps us to see. Economic development priorities and the aesthetic expectations of dominant cultural elites set some standards of legitimacy, but in ways that reproduce inequality. State actors, laws, and regulations confer legitimacy too, but we have seen that the line between formality and informality can be arbitrary and again reflects, in many cases, underlying biases. Beginning to see and think about urbanism through the lens of legitimacy invites, even demands, us to put the concept to work for communities.

We can operationalize legitimacy in two ways that can help encourage more equitable, democratic, locally preferred placemaking. On the one hand, we might prioritize the cultural legitimacy conferred upon a project by community members rather than official or moneyed interests. At the same time, we can think of ways to confer greater legitimacy on structurally illegitimated actors so that they can feel freer to make improvements themselves.

If our concern is to identify DIY urban design interventions that are truly positive and welcomed contributions to their communities, the opinions of community members themselves must be a factor. This community-based social legitimacy is messy, inherently site-specific, and culturally contingent. It is not a quality that can be determined by an architect, validated by a budget analysis, or settled in court. But it is powerful because it cuts across other categories and draws our attention so crucially, simple as it may sound, to what people actually want and find acceptable on a case-by-case basis. All of a sudden the impacts of an intervention on the community in which it is made become the priority, rather than the background or qualifications of the do-it-yourselfer, or the political or economic selling points of the project. Looking to residents for legitimacy, even if only in principle, gives authority back to the community at a substantively demo-cratic level in which its own values and needs actually matter.

The qualities that longtime community members look for could well be different from those that city planners or property developers consider when conferring legitimacy. In addition to specific local needs, residents might value historical relevance and authenticity, broad community benefits, or their own culturally attuned assessment of value or appro-priateness. Although some of New York's "Bloomberg Plazas" and other creative placemaking interventions have made community members (and some planners and designers) wary of their cookie-cutter similari-ties or perceived inauthentic outsider aesthetics, others have been suc-cessful in reflecting local cultural character. The redesign of Corona Plaza in Queens, for instance, was done with extensive input and involvement from the immigrant communities living around it. It won design acco-lades while being representative of local identity rather than a threat to it.[9] And a more antisocial or undemocratic intervention, such as remov-ing a bus stop, would not likely find reception in many corners as legit-imate. (That said, efforts by Malibu homeowners to limit public beach access, while illegal and opposed by many, may actually be in keeping with the values of their neighbors in that famously exclusive "quiet little beach community"!)

Crucially, by making social and cultural legitimacy a priority, the bur-den of finding such local acceptance falls on those who would shape urban space, forcing them to think about inclusivity, authenticity, and local needs and desires. Do-it-yourselfers without long-standing ties to a community they hope to improve, who thus risk being perceived as unwarranted, insen-sitive, and unwelcome, could work to gain cultural legitimacy at the neigh-borhood scale—through engaging longtime residents in the planning and implementation of their projects and creating modest improvements that are widely seen as beneficial. Steve Cancian's perspective, honed over years of working with low-income communities of color to make local improve-ments, could serve as an ethos for more contextually conscientious DIY urban design:

> We could mostly sit at the table, but we don't have to be in the lead. If people who live in the neighborhood and look like, earn like, the majority in the neigh-borhood aren't in the lead of what you're doing, then you should stop. Just stop. Because it can't, you know, it's somebody else's place! And it doesn't mean that we don't have a role as designers and architects. To me I think that's a cop-out when people say, Oh well then what's my role? I mean there's plenty for us to do. But the moral is we shouldn't be, we *can't be* making the decisions.

This model extends beyond DIY urbanism. Urban planners and scholars also need to fundamentally rethink the way we assess the social value and validity of projects that impact the use and meanings of streets, public spaces, and surrounding communities. Progressive planning, whether for environmental sustainability, social or physical resilience, public health, or simply the ideal of more walkable, livable streets and communities, should take the question of whether it is viewed as locally legitimate in inception, form, and function as at least one of its measures of viability, value, and success. Legitimacy provides the framework for a community-based, substantively democratic metric for assessing the acceptableness of any planning intervention or development project. In terms of placemaking, one hopes, the result might be more truly positive, restorative place-enhancing interventions and fewer exploitative or individualistic place-taking ones.

Of course, the real ideal behind DIY urbanism is people improving their *own* communities. As I have argued, from discreet signage or street seating in under-resourced neighborhoods to the EcoVillage or the Astoria Scum River Bridge, these tend to be the most uncontroversial and in some ways most successful interventions. With this in mind, perhaps the most tangible value that can come from focusing on legitimacy in urban placemaking is that these lessons can be brought back to the level of official authority and inform the operationalizing of legitimacy as a delicate policy tool for making practices like DIY urban design themselves more democratic, equitable, and ultimately beneficial—not just by guiding more locally sensitive interventions among those who already participate freely, but by encouraging expanded participation among groups whose participation is constrained by the biases of authority or development priorities.

If wielded responsibly, the intentional but subtle granting of normative legitimacy to would-be do-it-yourselfers who worry about participating visibly could be a more eloquent move than outright legal formalization or appropriation. For instance, the right DIY urban design interventions can be especially valuable in underprivileged communities where city services are known to be less responsive to local needs, but residents of these communities tend to be less willing to engage in unauthorized activities. Outsider interventions or top-down formalization of DIY efforts in these places could risk silencing local voices further and limiting the value of local participation (or, worse, coopting local initiatives as tools of gentrification). The best models here are those like Union de Vecinos's DIY public plazas throughout East LA, created by longtime community members. Or perhaps the streetside Buddha in Oakland, which, although placed on the corner by a non-religious white man, was welcomed by many in the surrounding Vietnamese community and set the stage for them to expand the shrine and even build a second one nearby. Though it would admittedly require a more limber policy environment than may be realistic in many cities, finding additional subtle ways to give such a sense of legitimacy to the grassroots efforts of willing local actors could encourage and enable more local placemaking that might then be viewed as legitimate and welcome across the board.

All DIY urban design efforts, no matter how well-meaning and civic-minded their creators' intentions for them, are articulations of the particular concerns and values of a group or individual enacted upon public space. Too few do-it-yourselfers I spoke to recognized that local acceptance and appropriateness of fit should be a central ingredient in creating effective DIY improvements. And yet, with the exception of some downright antisocial interventions (to which the formalities of the democratic planning process, however burdensome, are clearly preferable), there is value in the local relevance, efficiency, and even the almost magical spontaneity of DIY interventions that outright formalization by the often heavy-handed state risks destroying. Again the search for local legitimacy, however messy, would seem a more effective approach that assures an appropriate and beneficial improvement without sacrificing the spontaneous, creative informality that makes DIY urbanism so exciting and potentially valuable.

## VALUING THE UNAUTHORIZED

This discussion raises, finally, a question that has dogged this study from its outset. Is there some inherent value to the act of unsanctioned improvement itself, in its unsanctionedness? To be sure, as long as the actions are essentially individualistic ones, celebrating DIY urbanism risks further dismissing the importance of democratic oversight and bolstering a culture of privatized development and service provision that already so problematically characterizes our cities. But there are many hopeful aspects of the spirit of critical awareness, personal initiative, and creative transgression in DIY urban design as well. It would be an enormous loss—and simply misguided—to fail to recognize that despite all of its contradictions, DIY urban design does reveal, enable, even promote a promising fluidity and consciousness in the structures of urban placemaking. The task is to identify and nurture this potential while understanding the imperfections.

Clint Sleeper, the reader will recall, is a young white man who has been making repairs and improvements to playgrounds and other public spaces in Reno, Vancouver, and a handful of other cities since 2011. Though his are among the smallest and seemingly least provocative types of interventions I encountered in my research, Clint offered some of the most thoughtful assessment of the deeper meaning and transformative potential of DIY urban design work. I asked him, as I did everyone I spoke to, if he would prefer the state to be fully responsive and provide all of these repairs, so that there would be no need for people like him, or if he found some added value in doing it himself? He admitted there was not an easy answer, but said:

> I lean toward that idea that it is better that we do this ourselves. And maybe it's like the beginning of thinking about a lot of things that we can do ourselves. And um, I'm just trying to get over a lot of the political problems that come along with trusting state organizations to help us out when they don't. [ . . . ] So it's not just that it's necessary that we do it, because I guess it *is* necessary, but it's a little bit of that it has hints towards utopia, right? Like it is, however lofty or absurd that that is. [ . . . ] We know that it's absurd but we also still want it, you know?

Clint, who was in art school in Vancouver at the time that I interviewed him, connected these ideas to the artist and scholar Ted Purves, whose writing on gifts and generosity has influenced his thinking:

> I think it's really powerful too, even small gestures that are—Ted Purves calls these generous gestures "blows against the empire." Maybe they're not that serious. But if you call it public space, then we take it as public space and like take ownership of this thing. And I think maybe that's—although it's a little bit more lofty than anything I've gotten at yet—I think that's maybe the ultimate thing that I would like [DIY urbanism] to hint at or to suggest or to work towards, is more ownership of these public spaces.

And he noted that San Francisco's Rebar connects with Purves as well: "When they talk about their Park(ing) Day where they turned parking spaces into parks, is that these kind of small generous gestures fly in the face of the empire."[10] This is bold language, reflecting not only Clint's exposure to critical social theory, but the claim, essentially, that DIY placemaking can in some way challenge the global political-economic order, the dominant hegemony of the ruling classes, what many of us more colloquially call "the system."[11]

Is the willingness to take the shaping of our surroundings into our own hands, to briefly ignore the laws and standards and norms of urban space, to think for a moment about what could be changed for the better, the first step in a more transformative praxis? Does doing so open doors to a more engaged and active democratic citizenship? Or is it the limited, tragic response of people who can muster only a momentary act of resistance?

Perhaps it is simply a cheap thrill, a creative flourish, a solitary provocation, or a completely counterproductive bit of public nuisance that costs someone money.

I asked Clint bluntly whether he felt his actions have a transformative value as critiques of the system.

> I do. Right? I absolutely do, but I'm hesitant to define it that way [ . . . ] Maybe because that wasn't what I was thinking when I started doing the project and therefore I'm a little bit hesitant to say like this is a bold, kind of loud political action when that wasn't the initial intent. [ . . . ] But I do think that there's something necessarily political, because it is public space.

Clint is one of the many do-it-yourselfers I spoke to who made these sorts of connections, if not always as eloquently. These are, of course, by and large the idealistic thoughts of young, college-educated members of the creative class. But the premise is worth considering; it invites us to ponder the implications for grander theories of personal agency and consciousness in two of the more popular settings for interpreting them: everyday life and urban space.

The social theorist Henri Lefebvre is probably best known in urban studies for originating the call to "the right to the city" in 1968. Essentially the idea that everyone should be able not only to exist and participate freely in the city but to make and remake their surroundings their own, reclaiming the city from the state and from capitalism, the right to the city has found considerable popularity and is relatable in obvious ways to DIY urban design.[12] Lefebvre saw the city as a crucial site in the negotiation of systemic power and individual freedom, the place where everyday life could confront the "far order" of overarching sociostructural conditions. But the right to the city was for Lefebvre a justification and an ideal; it was not a means to an end. Later in his life, Lefebvre concluded: " 'To change life,' 'to change society,' these phrases mean nothing if there is no production of an appropriated space."[13] Certainly many acts of DIY urbanism do the latter. But do they do the former?

For Lefebvre, the possibility of societal transformation begins with subjective, critical awareness in the individual as a means for breaking free of the alienation of everyday life. Although Lefebvre was a more optimistic Marxian cultural critic than many of his contemporaries, he still wavered between optimism and cynicism for the real revolutionary possibility of this. What he returned to frequently over a long career, however, was the liberating and potentially transformative power of tiny *moments* of subjective consciousness—what he called "partial totalities" like love, play, struggle, and creative activity that provide opportunities for consciousness and agency.† At his most romantic, Lefebvre suggested that pursuing simple pleasures and restoring a more humane or organic sort of beauty to one's everyday life and everyday surroundings could lead people to begin to live differently and realize grander possibilities. And with the concept of *autogestion* (loosely, worker self-management), he suggested that instances of grassroots self-determination inherently challenge state order and capitalist production. At scale—and to Lefebvre autogestion is pregnant with the possibility of its spread and radicalization—it could mean a disalienated populace in confrontation with state authority, a "practical way" toward the foundation of a more democratic society.[14]

Are DIY urban design interventions, for all their flaws, examples of such Lefebvrian moments of critical awareness and transformative potential? Perhaps. Could they, despite their largely innocuous appearances, their questionable physical impacts, their inequities and limitations, and the claims of many of their creators to be anything but radical or revolutionary, constitute a different way of thinking about self-determination and the right to the city that might actually lead to something better? I'd like to hope so. Yet whether there is real critical value here, or not, comes down essentially to how high a bar we have set—for even at best these acts are clearly not "revolutionary" in and of themselves.

This question essentially confronts the wall against which Marxist and critical theory has been banging its head since Marx and Gramsci through Adorno and Horkheimer to Harvey and Purcell: there may be "cracks" in the system, moments of hope, but to exploit them requires revolutionary efforts of herculean proportion. Acts of DIY urbanism do not "fly in the face of empire." Painting a bike lane, planting a garden, removing an

---

† Lefebvre's moments are strenuously ambiguous when variously and vaguely mentioned across his writings. They are first discussed at length in his 1959 autobiographical work *La Somme et le reste*, as a concept that Lefebvre says he has long struggled with (since prior to his affiliation with Marxism), but are crucially tied for him to the formation of individual subjective consciousness and agency. As something like subunits of consciousness, he calls them here "terms of presence" and opportunities for subjective understanding, using the examples of "partial totalities" that are moments of play, work, struggle, love, rest, and, crucially, the creative activity of art and the production of creative work (1989 [1959]: 234–37; my translation). Two years later, Lefebvre offered a "theory of moments" in which a moment is defined as "the attempt to achieve the total realization of a possibility" (2008b [1961]: 348). Two decades after that, he added that some moments "are seeking to shatter the everydayness trapped in generalized exchange" (2008c [1981]: 57). A somewhat clearer formulation of the idea is given by Andy Merrifield (2006: 29): "Just as alienation reflected an *absence*, a dead moment empty of critical content, the Lefebvrian moment signified a *presence*, a fullness, alive and connected."

advertisement—to the political-economic structures of late capitalism, in all their productive glories and inhuman depravities, these are a flash in the pan, a stress relieving tremor along a fault line, even a small and welcome contribution through the ongoing commodification of creative transgression. And if, as David Harvey (2007: 42) argues, it is the "profoundly anti-democratic nature of neoliberalism" that must be the main focus of critical struggle, then I have shown that on the whole DIY urbanism is no better than the status quo; it embraces individualism and can be flatly undemocratic. From this perspective, these DIY interventions, which have the potential to be what Lefebvre would call everyday moments of transformation, often become in fact everyday moments of collaboration in the march of uneven development.

Whether positive or negative, the long-term impact of DIY urban design, whether on individual streets, local communities, or urban governance as a whole, cannot yet be judged. And it will always be hard to separate out from other trends, policies, and processes. I asked Clint if he could be more specific as to what impact repairs like his could have, even at some slightly larger scale, on how cities are governed. "I still really hold on to those more ideal or those more optimistic versions of democracy, where you really hope that policymakers are watching," he laughed. But he did get more specific:

> So then if it's lofty, or if it's not lofty, let's say that it is 10 or 12 people in a city that are really actively doing these repairs, then it just, it calls the attention of policymakers and it calls the attention of people in neighborhoods, and maybe there's a little bit of pride, and maybe a little bit of policy shift. I don't know.

Perhaps it is enough that the connection to a better form of citizenship can be drawn, and that this connection is at least meaningful to the creators of DIY urban design themselves. We might also consider the act of participation aside from its more common civil society context, as something more like an act of individual critical practice that has its own value simply for the participants.

What I hope to emphasize most in conclusion, building from Clint's comments, and Steve's ethos, and the simple creative insights of that traffic sign in Pittsburgh and the Astoria Scum River Bridge, is the constructive hopefulness embedded in all acts of DIY urban design. I have noted that the individualistic nature of DIY urbanism is fundamentally no more democratic than the existing planning process where money and power dominate, but we have seen how interventions inspired by the most local of concerns may capture some elements of local sentiment and cultural character in ways that top-down development may not. I have connected the professional backgrounds and other technical and academic knowledge of do-it-yourselfers with hubris, but connecting relevant skills to DIY improvements and doing the research intended to make them effective is surely better than not doing so. The space of privilege that most do-it-yourselfers operate from should give us pause but should not cause us to dismiss the value of their contributions outright. To fully realize its intended "civic-minded" potential, DIY urban design must engender more equitable access to participation and a more socially conscious intentionality behind it. Yet for all the value of people helping themselves, we must be careful not to scoff at the value of those with privilege helping those who are less fortunate, provided they do so sensitively.

At its best, DIY urban design can reflect a hopeful critical consciousness of urban conditions and inspiring energy for engagement in the city. It can be a powerful medium for direct participation in the shaping of community spaces. And while there are countless urban challenges far beyond its capacity to address, DIY urbanism can provide real, functional, and broadly beneficial improvements to the streetscape. I have noted many of the best examples, to my mind. They are some of the simplest and in many ways least obviously radical or political, like a homemade bench at a bus stop or an official-looking sign intended to improve safety at an intersection.

To return to the data a final time, I offer another humble and yet provocative example. The Mad Housers, of Atlanta, show how DIY urban design can provide a real social good, at a scale nearly that of a government agency, which formal actors are not only failing to provide but essentially could not provide with anywhere close to the same effectiveness or creativity. The Mad Housers build small huts for the chronically homeless and other people in need of shelter. They do so in existing camps that they identify—usually on private land in discrete areas, with or without permission—and in close collaboration with the people for whom they are providing homes, cultivating greater legitimacy. They teach the recipients engineering and carpentry skills in the process and emphasize that they are being given the huts with the understanding that must take care of them, further perpetuating the do-it-yourself attitude. As their website notes, "Usually, the client will then make additions and improvements according to their own ideas; in fact, many of the best design improvements have come from the clients themselves." Nick Hess, a longtime member and current president of the Mad Housers, elaborated:

> You know folks take it to heart. And some folks run very neat shelters and improve the campsite. Usually actually one of my favorite things is coming back a couple weeks after the build, because they're so neat and tidy. They've picked

up their area, you can tell that they're sleeping better. [ . . . ] It's really cool to see. They'll look like three to five years younger.

The Mad Housers are unambiguously providing a service for the least privileged. By only aiding people in existing campsites, their efforts simply make an existing situation more livable for the most unfortunate and pass on material improvements and useful skills to those who can use them most. At the same time, Nick recognizes the limitations of their work:

> It is ultimately a policy problem. I do not, after all these years of doing this, I do not feel like, Oh if only we had enough Mad Housers we could solve homelessness. That's flat-out ridiculous on the face of it. We *could* be the first step of outreach for the most difficult homeless, and that's something that we try to do. [ . . . ] But that's not, you know, it's not as easy and certainly not as glamorous as, OK we're going to take this radical step of building you a shelter and giving it to you and putting it down wherever you happen to be.

Regardless, he is certain about why he does what he does.

> It's wonderful to know that something I've done has had such a profound improving effect on somebody else's lives. It's a really powerful feeling that keeps me coming back, through all the frustrations that doing this bring me. [ . . . ] It's amazing to be able to do something so profound, without it being just, you know, it's sort of a one-time intervention. We try to keep working with folks but for the most part we can just say I have done this and it has helped this person. And that's just an amazing feeling.

• • •

I have tried with this book to at once introduce the phenomenon of DIY urban design, explore its culture and its contexts, and appraise it from the perspectives of sociology and urban political economy. I have connected it to other phenomena of different scales, from the urban planning trends of tactical urbanism and creative placemaking to the broader social problem of widening inequality despite ostensibly growing civic participation. This has been a fairly critical appraisal, describing DIY urban design as individualistic and potentially undemocratic, as the hubristic acts of a privileged and entitled creative class, as reinforcing elite values and certain dominant aesthetics in urban space. These are real concerns for a rising trend that has received considerable praise and precious little criticism.

Yet DIY urbanism would not have attracted the attention it has— especially from planners, designers, policymakers, and other urbanists, myself included—if it did not hold so much promise. For each problematic finding about DIY urban design, we have seen its clear potential: as a generally sincere and civic-minded approach to fixing problems that the system has failed to address; as the thoughtful product of skilled, knowledgeable, and engaged citizen urbanists; as a creative spark influencing the creation of socially and environmentally beneficial planning ideals. The design flaw is that access to this promising medium of participatory citizenship is less than full.

The liability in too quickly celebrating DIY urban design for its promise is failing to recognize the tendency that it shares with all urban space production to be dominated by the values of a bold few (often privileged or powerful) at the expense of those whose participation is more limited for a number of reasons. Even as many DIY urban design interventions can be viewed as clear responses to the deficiencies of market-driven planning, they are themselves rather perfect embodiments of the uneven redistribution of responsibilities from the state to private or individual actors, with little concern for regulation or democratic accountability.

In other words, DIY urban design, and the exciting but imperfect ethic of more open civic participation that it entails, are fundamental features of the help-yourself city. And they offer a mixed bag for cities and communities. Whether the phenomenon ultimately represents a further erosion of democratic planning, a flurry of organic, locally determined placemaking, or perhaps the possibility of a dynamic, collaborative middle ground, has yet to be seen. This need not lessen the positive potential inherent in the fact that people are interested in and willing to make these sorts of contributions to their communities. Rather, it emphasizes the need to better understand them, to view them with a critical eye, and to consider them as one would any other intervention in urban space—formal or informal—as having the ability to do good or do harm with greater or lesser cultural legitimacy. Uncritical urbanism limits the questions we can ask, the demands we can make, and the futures we can dream.

The rise of DIY urban design may indicate a shift in how people in the United States and elsewhere relate to the physical and policy environment of the contemporary city: a willingness to act without permission to make what they believe to be improvements to a place, taking their ideals for urban space into their own hands, and in a sense doing professional urban planners' work for them. This shift implies changes to how we conceive of the boundaries between personal, public, and private property, of who is entitled to alter urban space, of the authority and responsibility of local government, of urban use value, and yes, of creative, critical, personal agency. And of course, to the degree that these actions are an indication of what some people actually want out of their streets, we can learn a great deal about how to design our urban spaces more responsively in the first place.

A Buddhist shrine, installed on a street corner in Oakland by a resident in 2014, gets daily use from members of the local Vietnamese community and others and has attracted attention from national media. Photo by the author, 2017.

# APPENDIX 1

# List of All Projects in the Study for Which Interviews Were Conducted

The table below presents a list of all DIY urban design projects in the study for which interviews were conducted, arranged by the typological categories described in Chapter 2 (Spontaneous Streetscaping, Renegade Renewal, Aspirational Urbanism), and denoting the location (city) and year of each project, type of physical intervention, an approximation of the perceived negative conditions responded to (including those that exploit an opportunity rather than addressing a specific problem), the aesthetic style of the project and attitude behind it, and the name of associated interviewee(s) where given.

Interviews with 69 do-it-yourselfers provided information on 80 projects in 17 cities. Some interviewees provided information on more than one intervention, while some interventions were described by multiple interviewees. Because some interventions were recreated more or less identically in multiple locations, I consider all such multisite "campaigns" in a single city to be one intervention, but count them again when they occur in very different contexts or multiple cities.

| Project Name | City | Year | Category | Type of Intervention | Responding To | Style | Attitude | Interview |
|---|---|---|---|---|---|---|---|---|
| 110 Fwy. Guerrilla Public Service | Los Angeles | 2002 | Streetscape | Traffic signage | Poor signage | Official-looking | Practical | Richard |
| 20-is-Plenty signage | New York City | 2013+ | Streetscape | Traffic signage | Policy, Unsafe streets | Handmade | Critical, Political | Keegan, Hilda |
| 4th St. Bicycle Blvd. signage | Los Angeles | 2007+ | Streetscape | Traffic signage | Lack of bike infrastructure | Handmade | Practical | Anon. |
| 6th Ave. bike lane extension | New York City | 2013 | Streetscape | Road marking, Bike infrastructure | Lack of bike infrastructure | Official-looking | Practical, Critical | Keegan |
| Astoria Scum River Bridge | New York City | 2009 | Streetscape | Pedestrian infrastructure | Failing infrastructure | Utilitarian | Practical | Jason |
| Baltimore Devel. Cooperative Participation Park | Baltimore | 2007+ | Renewal | Guerrilla gardening, Urban agriculture | Poverty, Lack of investment (social services) | Utilitarian | Social, Critical, Political | Scott |
| Bedford Ave. bike lane restriping | New York City | 2009 | Streetscape | Repair, Road marking, Bike infrastructure | Policy, Removal of bike infrastructure | Official-looking | Critical, Political | Anon. |
| BedStuy Meadow seed-bombing | New York City | 2009 | Renewal | Guerrilla gardening | Lack of investment (aesthetic), Local history | Utilitarian | Social | Deborah |
| Being Pedestrian | Los Angeles | 2009 | Aspirational | Event, Traffic signage, Informational publication, Public space, Uniform | Overdevelopment, Lack of pedestrian infrastructure | Official-looking | Critical | Sara |
| Better Block | Dallas | 2010 | Streetscape | Street furniture, Road marking, Bike infrastructure, Guerrilla gardening, Public space | Lack of investment (development), Lack of bike infrastructure | Official-looking | Social, Political | Jason |

| Project Name | City | Year | Category | Type of Intervention | Responding To | Style | Attitude | Interview |
|---|---|---|---|---|---|---|---|---|
| **Bridgeport Streetscaping Society** | Chicago | 2014 | Streetscape | Street furniture, Guerrilla gardening, Public space | Lack of investment (development, aesthetic), opportunity | Handmade | Social | Ed |
| **Bunchy Carter Park for the People** | Los Angeles | 2009 | Aspirational | Development proposal signage | Overdevelopment, Lack of public space | Official-looking | Critical, Political | Anon. |
| **Bus stop removal** | Seattle | 2012 | Streetscape | Transit sign removal | Lack of investment (services) | Utilitarian, Destructive | Practical, Critical | Derek |
| **CampBaltimore mobile community center** | Baltimore | 2006 | Aspirational | Mobile trailer, Publications, Service | Poverty, Lack of investment (social services), Gentrification | Handmade, Artistic | Social, Critical, Political | Scott |
| **Community Book Exchanges** | Chicago | 2006 | Renewal | Functional conversion, Service | Lack of investment (social services), (opportunity) | Handmade, Artistic | Social | Ryan |
| **Dept. of DIY Fletcher Bridge bike lane** | Los Angeles | 2008 | Streetscape | Traffic signage, Road marking, Bike infrastructure | Lack of bike infrastructure | Official-looking | Practical | Anon. |
| **Dept. of DIY tunnel bike ramp curb** | Los Angeles | 2009 | Streetscape | Curb alteration | Lack of bike infrastructure | Utilitarian | Practical | Anon. |
| **Dept. of DIY Sunset Blvd. lane extension** | Los Angeles | 2009 | Streetscape | Road marking | Poor signage, Unsafe streets, Lack of bike infrastructure | Official-looking | Practical | Anon. |
| **DIY DPW cross traffic sign** | Pittsburgh | 2010 | Streetscape | Traffic signage | Poor signage | Official-looking | Practical | Anon. |

| Project Name | City | Year | Category | Type of Intervention | Responding To | Style | Attitude | Interview |
|---|---|---|---|---|---|---|---|---|
| **DIY maintenance** | Reno | 2011 | Renewal | Repair | Lack of investment (parks), Failing infrastructure | Utilitarian | Practical | Clint |
| **DIY maintenance** | Vancouver | 2012 | Renewal | Repair | Lack of investment (parks), Failing infrastructure | Utilitarian | Practical | Clint |
| **DoTank chairbombing** | New York City | 2011 | Streetscape | Street furniture | Lack of pedestrian infrastructure | Handmade | Practical | Ted, Aurash |
| **DoTank BYO at the BQE** | New York City | 2011 | Aspirational | Temporary conversion, Event, Street furniture, Public space | Lack of public space | Handmade | Social, Critical | Ted, Aurash |
| **DoTank Digital Community Message Board** | New York City | 2011 | Streetscape | Informational signage | (opportunity) | Handmade, Artistic | Social | Ted |
| **East LA alleyway plazas** | Los Angeles | 2012 | Streetscape | Road marking, Street furniture, Public space | Unsafe streets, Lack of public space, Lack of investment (aesthetic) | Handmade, Artistic | Social | Steve, Anon. |
| **East Vancouver yarn bombing** | Vancouver | 2009+ | Renewal | Yarn ornamentation | Lack of investment (aesthetic), (opportunity) | Handmade, Artistic | Fun | Anon. |
| **EcoVillage Intersection Repar** | Los Angeles | 2009 | Streetscape | Road marking, Guerrilla gardening, Street furniture | Lack of pedestrian infrastructure | Handmade, Artistic | Social, Critical, Political | Joe |

| Project Name | City | Year | Category | Type of Intervention | Responding To | Style | Attitude | Interview |
|---|---|---|---|---|---|---|---|---|
| **ER Granville Island performance space** | Vancouver | 2007+ | Aspirational | Temporary conversion, Event, Public space | Law, Lack of community space | Utilitarian | Social, Critical, Political | Ryan |
| **Fallen Fruit Project** | Los Angeles | 2006+ | Aspirational | Event, Temporary conversion, Publication | Poverty, Surplus, Lack of investment (food) | Utilitarian | Practical | David |
| **Figueroa Blvd. yarn bombing** | Los Angeles | 2010 | Renewal | Yarn ornamentation | Lack of investment (aesthetic), (opportunity) | Handmade, Artistic | Fun | Anon. |
| **Gentrification the Game** | Toronto | 2010+ | Aspirational | Event, Temporary conversion | Overdevelopment, Gentrification | Handmade, Artistic | Social, Fun | Kate, David |
| **Graffiti Guerrilla graffiti removal** | Los Angeles | 1992+ | Renewal | Repair, Graffiti removal | Vandalism, Lack of investment (aesthetic) | Utilitarian | Practical, Political | Joe |
| **Guerrilla Garden Memorial Signs** | Chicago | 2008 | Renewal | Informational signage | Lack of investment (aesthetic) | Handmade | Social, Practical | Andy |
| **Guerrilla gardening** | Chicago | 2007+ | Renewal | Guerrilla gardening | Lack of investment (aesthetic) | Utilitarian | Social, Practical | Anon. |
| **Guerrilla gardening** | Los Angeles | 1994+ | Renewal | Guerrilla gardening | Lack of investment (aesthetic) | Official-looking | Social, Practical | Scott |
| **Guerrilla gardening** | Los Angeles | 2008+ | Renewal | Guerrilla gardening | Lack of investment (aesthetic) | Utilitarian | Social, Practical | Anon. |
| **Guerrilla gardening** | London | 2004+ | Renewal | Guerrilla gardening | Lack of investment (aesthetic) | Official-looking | Social, Practical, Critical | Richard |
| **Guerrilla park bench** | Pittsburgh | 2012 | Streetscape | Street furniture | Lack of investment (parks), Lack of pedestrian infrastructure | Handmade | Social, Practical | Anon. |

| Project Name | City | Year | Category | Type of Intervention | Responding To | Style | Attitude | Interview |
|---|---|---|---|---|---|---|---|---|
| **Guerrilla Preservation** | New York City | 2008+ | Aspirational | Repair, Informational publication | Lack of investment (preservation), Local history | Utilitarian | Social, Critical | Anon. |
| **Guerrilla sharrows** | Los Angeles | 2010 | Streetscape | Road marking, Bike infrastructure | Lack of bike infrastructure, Poor signage | Official-looking | Practical, Critical | Anon. |
| **Haz Ciudad bike lane** | Mexico City | 2011+ | Streetscape | Road marking, Bike infrastructure | Lack of bike infrastructure, Poor signage | Official-looking | Practical, Critical | Anon. |
| **Haz Ciudad bridge walkway** | Mexico City | 2011 | Streetscape | Road marking, Pedestrian infrastructure | Lack of pedestrian infrastructure | Utilitarian | Practical, Critical | Anon. |
| **Haz Ciudad crosswalk** | Mexico City | 2011 | Streetscape | Road marking, Pedestrian infrastructure | Lack of pedestrian infrastructure | Artistic, Official-looking | Practical, Critical | Anon. |
| **Highland Park Book Booth** | Los Angeles | 2010 | Renewal | Functional conversion, Service | Lack of investment (social services), (opportunity) | Handmade, Artistic | Social | Amy, Stu |
| **Holly Whyte Way/ Sixth 1/2 Ave.** | New York City | 2011 | Streetscape | Traffic signage, Informational signage | Overdevelopment, Lack of public space | Official-looking | Social, Critical | Graham |
| **Howling Mob 10 Historical Markers** | Pittsburgh | 2007 | Streetscape | Informational signage | Local history, (opportunity) | Official-looking | Critical | Anon. |
| **Hoyt St. block** | New York City | 2008+ | Renewal | Street furniture, Guerrilla gardening | Lack of investment (aesthetic) | Handmade, Artistic | Social | Hendricks |
| **Hypothetical Development Organization** | New Orleans | 2010 | Aspirational | Development proposal signage, Informational publication | Lack of investment (development) | Official-looking | Critical | Carey |

| Project Name | City | Year | Category | Type of Intervention | Responding To | Style | Attitude | Interview |
|---|---|---|---|---|---|---|---|---|
| **I Wish This Was** | New Orleans | 2010 | Aspirational | Community aspiration signage, Development proposal signage | Lack of investment (development) | Handmade | Social, Critical | Candy |
| **Islands of LA National Park** | Los Angeles | 2007+ | Streetscape | Informational signage, Public space | Lack of pedestrian infrastructure, Lack of public space | Official-looking | Critical | Ari |
| **LA Urban Rangers beach access campaign** | Los Angeles | 2004+ | Aspirational | Informational publication, Event, Temporary conversion, Street furniture, Public Space, Uniform | Overdevelopment, Enclosure, Lack of public space | Official-looking | Critical, Political | Sara |
| **Mad Housers shelters** | Atlanta | 1987+ | Renewal | Structure | Poverty, Homelessness, Lack of investment (services) | Utilitarian | Social, Critical | Nick |
| **New Public Sites** | Baltimore | 2007+ | Aspirational | Informational publication, Event, Street furniture, Public Space, Uniform | Lack of investment (development) | Official-looking, Artistic | Critical | Graham |
| **New York Street Advertising Takeover (NYSAT)** | New York City | 2009 | Renewal | Advertising removal | Commodification, Policy | Utilitarian, Destructive, Artistic | Critical, Political | Jordan |
| **Park(ing) Day LA** | Los Angeles | 2006+ | Aspirational | Event, Temporary conversion, Street furniture, Public Space | Lack of public space | Handmade, Designy | Social, Critical, Political | Stephen |

| Project Name | City | Year | Category | Type of Intervention | Responding To | Style | Attitude | Interview |
|---|---|---|---|---|---|---|---|---|
| **Park(ing) Day NYC** | New York City | 2006+ | Aspirational | Event, Temporary conversion, Street furniture, Public Space | Lack of public space | Handmade, Designy | Social, Critical, Political | Ian |
| **Park(ing) Day PHX, vacant lot parties** | Phoenix | 2011 | Aspirational | Event, Temporary conversion, Street furniture, Public Space | Lack of public space | Handmade, Designy | Social, Critical, Political | Stacey |
| **Pass with Care signs** | Los Angeles | 2010 | Streetscape | Traffic signage | Lack of bicycle infrastructure, Poor signage | Utilitarian | Practical, Critical | Anon. |
| **Phoenix Chalkboard** | Phoenix | 2011 | Aspirational | Community aspiration signage, Development proposal signage | Lack of investment (development) | Utilitarian | Social, Critical | Stacey |
| **planter boxes** | Toronto | 2011 | Renewal | Repair, Functional conversion, Guerrilla gardening | Lack of investment (aesthetic) | Utilitarian, Artistic | Social | Sean |
| **Pop-Up Lunch** | New York City | 2009 | Streetscape | Street furniture | Lack of pedestrian infrastructure | Designy | Practical | Ali |
| **Poster Pocket Plants** | Toronto | 2009 | Renewal | Functional conversion, Advertising removal, Guerrilla gardening | Commodification | Handmade | Practical, Critical | Sean |
| **Public Ad Campaign** | New York City | 2000+ | Renewal | Advertising removal | Commodification, Policy | Utilitarian, Destructive, Artistic | Critical, Political | Jordan |

| Project Name | City | Year | Category | Type of Intervention | Responding To | Style | Attitude | Interview |
|---|---|---|---|---|---|---|---|---|
| **Reuben Kincaid Realty/For Squat signs** | Chicago | 2010 | Aspirational | Development signage | Poverty, Lack of investment (housing) | Official-looking | Critical | Ed |
| **Seed Bomb Vending Machines** | Los Angeles | 2010+ | Renewal | Functional conversion, Street furniture, Guerrilla gardening | Lack of investment (aesthetic), (opportunity) | Designy | Fun | Daniel and Kim |
| **SignChair, SignBench** | Los Angeles | 2009 | Streetscape | Street furniture | Lack of pedestrian infrastructure | Designy | Practical | Ken, Jenny |
| **Smiling Hogshead Ranch** | New York City | 2011 | Renewal | Urban agriculture, services, Public space | Lack of investment (services, development), (opportunity) | Handmade, Utilitarian | Social, Practical | Gil |
| **street opening** | Los Angeles | 2010 | Aspirational | Event, Temporary conversion, Public space | Overdevelopment, Lack of public space | Utilitarian | Social, Critical | Stephen |
| **Take a Seat** | New York City | 2007+ | Streetscape | Street furniture | Lack of pedestrian infrastructure | Utilitarian | Practical | Jason |
| **TENT Life-like Living shelters** | Toronto | 2009 | Aspirational | Temporary conversion, Development proposal structure, Informational signage | Poverty, Homelessness, Overdevelopment, Lack of investment (housing) | Artistic | Critical, Political | Sean |
| **Toronto Street Advertising Takeover (TOSAT)** | Toronto | 2010 | Renewal | Advertising removal | Commodification, Policy | Functional, Destructive, Artistic | Critical, Political | Jordan |
| **Tourist Lane** | New York City | 2010 | Aspirational | Event, Temporary conversion, Road marking | Overdevelopment, Commodification | Handmade | Critical, Fun | Jason |

| Project Name | City | Year | Category | Type of Intervention | Responding To | Style | Attitude | Interview |
|---|---|---|---|---|---|---|---|---|
| **Urban Living Rooms (DTLA)** | Los Angeles | 2010+ | Streetscape | Street furniture, Public space | Lack of public space, Lack of pedestrian infrastructure | Handmade | Social | Steve |
| **Urban Living Rooms (Oakland)** | Oakland | 2002+ | Streetscape | Street furniture, Public space | Lack of public space, Lack of pedestrian infrastructure | Handmade | Social | Steve, Larry |
| **Urban Living Rooms (South LA)** | Los Angeles | 2008 | Streetscape | Infrastructure (street furniture) | Lack of Infrastructure (pedestrian) | Handmade | Social | Father David |
| **Urban Repair Squad bike lanes** | Toronto | 2006+ | Streetscape | Traffic signage, Road marking, Bike infrastructure | Lack of bike infrastructure | Official-looking | Practical | Martin |
| **Urban Repair Squad TTC bikes allowed stickers** | Toronto | 2010+ | Streetscape | Informational signage | Poor signage | Official-looking | Practical | Martin |
| **Urban Repair Squad Pothole Onomotopeia** | Toronto | 2009 | Aspirational | Road marking | Lack of investment (roads), Failing infrastructure | Handmade | Critical, Fun | Martin |
| **Version Fest placemaking interventions** | Chicago | 2001+ | Aspirational | Events, Temporary conversion, Street furniture, Informational signage, Public space | Lack of public space, (opportunity) | Artistic | Critical, Fun | Ed |
| **Walk Raleigh signs** | Raleigh | 2012 | Streetscape | Informational signage | Lack of pedestrian infrastructure | Official-looking | Practical | Matt |

# Research Design and Methodology

The observations, thoughts, and findings reported in this book are based on more than five years of research. The study employed a mixture of qualitative research methods constituting a deep investigative immersion into the phenomenon of DIY urban design in the United States and beyond. My approach was inductive, my research design evolving. I set out to describe and understand a curious and under-studied sociospatial practice, essentially chasing every lead that could offer new information or provoke new questions and theoretical premises. As such, my methodology evolved over time in response to findings and in consultation with colleagues. This approach is fitting with the sequential interviewing and analysis methodology described here as well. The following discussion of my research design and methods describes the three phases in which I collected my data, the logic by which I selected my cases and my field sites, and then takes a moment to offer some thoughts on the value of the photograph and the bicycle as tools in ethnographic research.

## THREE PHASES OF RESEARCH

This research project can be understood as having had three main parts or phases: a pilot study on unauthorized urban space interventions in three cities; a main phase of interviews, participant observation, and background research on DIY urban design in 17 cities; and a final period of interviews with urban planning and design professionals, mainly in two cities.

### Phase One: Pilot Study

In the pilot study, begun in early 2010, I aimed to assess the scope of unauthorized urban space interventions broadly defined. Building out of an earlier interest of mine in the networks formed by street artists who work in multiple cities (see Douglas 2005), I was motivated to investigate all manner of practices by which individuals or informal groups challenge normative uses of urban space through unauthorized direct action. I hoped to test initial hypotheses about the motivations and impacts of these actions and define a more precise subject of research.

In this preliminary phase, I conducted in-depth interviews in New York, Los Angeles, and London with 18 individuals who were involved in a wide variety of practices, from politically motivated squatting and anarchistic occupations of public space to classic graffiti and street art, as well as a range of other seemingly related activities that would come to stand out as distinct. The interviews were semi-structured, aimed at assessing why the subjects created unauthorized alterations, how they learned or otherwise came to do so, and what they hoped to accomplish.

I also looked to the substantial body of popular discourse on all these various individual phenomena, including histories and surveys from respected art and design publishers (especially of street art, e.g., Chalfant & Prigoff 1987; Ganz 2004; Manco 2004; but also of interventionist art more generally, some examples of which do have critical academic authors, such as Lacy 1995 and Seno et al. 2010), radical or independent press accounts of particular interventionist actions (e.g., Wilson & Weinberg 1999; Bloom & Bromberg 2004), "manifestos" and other publications by interventionists themselves (e.g., Fairey 1990; Reynolds 2008; Moore & Prain 2009), and the copious features, photos, interviews, and criticism to be found in both specialty and general interest magazines, newspapers, zines, websites, and blogs.

As my interviews progressed along with my exploration of these other source materials, it became clear that some of the practices I was learning about did not fit with existing interpretations of urban space interventions in the social science literature: they were more intentionally functional than art or vandalism, and while goal-oriented they were still far more subtle and limited in focus than the tactics of broader political activism. (I discuss this distinction at length in Chapter 2.) I began to seek out these more liminal activities, which I came to understand as do-it-yourself urban design, in the second phase that became the core of my research.


**Phase Two: Main Data Collection**

Between 2011 and 2015, I interviewed 61 more individuals specifically engaged in DIY urban design activities. These in-depth interviews were long-form and semi-structured in nature, exploring topics ranging from the participants' personal backgrounds to the details of their interventions to their perspectives on the state of the contemporary city. I always began by asking people how they describe themselves and "what they do" in casual conversation when they meet someone for the first time. I asked what first inspired them to make unauthorized improvements, how they learned to do so, and what impacts they hoped to have. We frequently spoke about the policy context and social, cultural, and economic contexts of their actions.

In addition to interviews, the research included site visits with extensive photographic documentation, participant observation during the creation and installation of some DIY urban design contributions, background research on participants and sites, informal conversations with community members and other observers or users of interventions when possible, and altogether an extended ethnographic immersion into the cultures surrounding these activities. This fieldwork was conducted primarily in New York and the Los Angeles area but also included visits to 10 secondary cities selected for diversity of historical, physical, and policy contexts among cities where DIY urbanism was known to be occurring: Baltimore, Chicago, London, Mexico City, New Orleans, Phoenix, Pittsburgh, Toronto, Vancouver, and California's Bay Area (San Francisco, San José, and, especially, Oakland). Interviews and supporting information were also gathered without site visits for do-it-yourselfers and their projects in Atlanta, Dallas, Raleigh, Reno, and Seattle (though I did visit most of these cities as well during the course of the research). Sixty-nine do-it-yourselfers were interviewed in total (this includes eight in the pilot phase), representing 80 different DIY urban design projects (see Appendix 1). Just over half of these interviews (38) and projects (43) were in Los Angeles and New York, with the others (31 interviews; 37 projects) coming from the other 15 cities. By design, the majority of both interviews (55) and projects (65) were in the United States.

During the main data collection phase, individual project/interviewee selection was based on a logic of sequential replication (see Yin 2002), following a multiple-case-style "sequential interviewing" method as described by Mario Small (2009a, 2009b). This means that each interview (and its accompanying project, observations, etc.) was understood as one in a sequence of cases in which questions were applied repeatedly but analyzed sequentially to support or challenge initial propositions; these propositions and questions were simultaneously revised as the research proceeded to fit what I was learning. Beginning with instances uncovered during initial research and other highly visible cases in New York and Los Angeles, the study then relied on "snowball" referrals and further investigation to yield additional participants who seemed especially unique or indicative of different aspects of DIY urbanism. All individuals who fit the criteria and allowed for constructive "literal" or "theoretical" replication—in terms of type of intervention, location, and other characteristics, as well as unique cases—were asked to participate, up to a point of saturation. I felt I had reached saturation once it became abundantly clear (and was even still reconfirmed several times beyond) that little substantively new information was to be gained from successive interviews within study parameters. (To be clear, the goal at this point was not to collect data on all sorts of unauthorized urban intervention, even all sorts of informal improvement—of which, again, there are countless varieties—though I did make an effort to conduct some interviews along the admittedly hazy line of what does or doesn't count as DIY urban design in order to push my thinking about the definition.)

Due to the potentially sensitive nature of the activities that do-it-yourself urban designers are involved in, I took precautions in talking to participants in my study and carried out the research under guidance from the Institutional Review Board of the Social and Behavioral Sciences at the University of Chicago. All interviewees were offered anonymity and strict protection of their identities from the first point of contact forward, and my interview protocol included verbal statements of informed consent to participate. A majority of my participants explicitly waived this right to anonymity, often explaining that they always conduct their activities in the public eye and asking that their names be used in association with their projects, a request I have tried to honor.

### Phase Three: Professionals

A third and final phase of data collection featured interviews with select urban planning, design, and architecture professionals in Los Angeles and New York to provide an alternative perspective on DIY urban design from the "official" side of the aisle. Participants included members of the departments of transportation and city planning in both cities (as well as the president of the LA Planning Commission), and landscape architects with experience in streetscape and public space design. I also spoke to designers and city staffers knowledgeable about particular issues relevant to the study such as parks and street trees or signage and outdoor advertising. In the course of the research I wound up talking to influential planning professionals in the Bay Area, Chicago, New Orleans, and Pittsburgh as well. All told, I formally interviewed 25 such professionals and spoke more casually to dozens more.

These interviewees were recruited as key informants through my own contacts, and thus represent a limited "convenience sample" (see Weiss 1994; Babbie 2001). I actually found somewhat more difficulty in successfully recruiting these professional participants than I did do-it-yourselfers. Many of them were wary about whether they were allowed to discuss these issues, and one in particular (a policymaker whose work concerned the enforcement of graffiti and vandalism laws in New York City) ultimately refused to speak with me after considerable back and forth. Many more of those who did speak to me were concerned about their anonymity and were careful to emphasize what statements were on or off the record. These small issues are not surprising given the range of difficulties that researchers have identified in gaining access to and interviewing elites (e.g., Dexter 1970; Marshal 1984; Ostrander 1993).

The second and third phases were not chronologically discrete. In keeping with the research design, I continued to investigate every relevant "phase two" lead with regard to the do-it-yourselfers themselves—conducting follow-ups, gathering basic data on dozens of projects, and recruiting more interviews with do-it-yourselfers whom I learned about later in the study and judged to be important for adding further depth to my understanding of the phenomenon—even as I focused on interviews with professionals.

### Additional Data

Throughout the project, I also relied heavily on coverage by websites, magazines, and other popular media as well as publicly available policy and planning documents. I used these sources for identifying and learning initial information about particular DIY urban design activities as well as understanding the scope of the phenomenon and gaining perspective on how it was being perceived. As part of this wider view, I also collected basic information on more than 400 projects beyond those represented in the interviews as I came across them—a process that continued up to the point of publication.

In 2012, I took the opportunity to join the curatorial team for an architecture and design exhibition called *Spontaneous Interventions: Design Actions for the Common Good*, the American Pavilion at the Venice International Architecture Biennale that year. By helping lead the effort to identify, review, and curate hundreds of submitted or recruited projects for the show, I gained access to a large secondary dataset of related actions in the United States and also gained a valuable "in" with many in the architecture and urban design community. The exhibition's criteria for inclusion were different from those of my study, and not all of the projects submitted to or included in the exhibition qualify as DIY urban design by my definition, but having awareness of all of these projects only increased my understanding of the trends in the air. This secondary cache of cases cannot be interpreted or accounted for in anywhere near the same depth as the ethnographic and interview-based research. It nonetheless provided additional perspective on the scale of the phenomenon, and I used the basic descriptive features that I had (location and type of project, often information on the creators as well) to check some of my general claims about DIY urbanism.

All told, while my findings cannot be said to describe everyone in the amorphous and ultimately unknowable population of DIY urban designers (any "random sample" was out of the question), I gathered data on every case I found that met my definition within these parameters until the point of saturation, and collected basic information on a great many more beyond that as well. I am confident that this strategy left me with a comprehensive understanding of DIY urban design in the United States and the necessary familiarity with other cases to effectively analyze it in a wider context as well.

## SITE SELECTION AND THE GEOGRAPHY OF DIY URBAN DESIGN

The initial three cities in the pilot study, New York, Los Angeles, and London, were chosen as not only major urban hubs of cultural innovation but also for being visible centers of street art, guerrilla gardening, and the other types of unauthorized urban intervention of interest to me at the outset of the research and, thus, places where large numbers of potential participants were likely to be found. As the phenomenon of DIY urban design began to stand out and demand attention as a specific object of study, these three cities remained clearly relevant centers of these activities as well. For practical reasons, I decided not to conduct additional fieldwork in London beyond the pilot phase and to focus the study on North American cities going forward.

My data collection remained centered in New York and Los Angeles as primary field sites. Again these are major cities where I knew from my pilot study that time in the field would be well spent. Moreover, due to their size, global importance, and famously contrasting urban morphologies, these cities are often looked to as the two pillars of mainstream American urbanism, including urban planning. In order to gain an understanding of DIY urban design in and across different contexts, I also pursued cases from other cities with various historical, demographic, and urban policy conditions that, as media coverage and my ongoing research suggested, contained valuable cases for understanding the phenomenon. For instance, research revealed Toronto as another thriving center of DIY urbanism early in the second phase, and I went there to conduct fieldwork in June of 2011. Chicago, ever a popular place for urban research, was fortunately a convenient one for me. And when I learned quite late in the process about some unique-sounding projects in Atlanta and Reno, I leaped to include them for the new information they could provide about both the range of DIY projects and the different contexts in which they occur. I lived in New York throughout the study, also spending a total of more than three months in Los Angeles and making shorter research visits—ranging from several days to two weeks at a time—to the remaining field sites throughout 2012 and 2013. I conducted follow-up research, including site visits and interviews, while writing this book from 2014 to 2016. I visited almost all of the cities multiple times.

Despite the large number of cities studied, my site selection unquestionably introduces some bias. Los Angeles and New York are highly developed, technologically advanced, and (relatively) responsibly governed cities, and the two largest cities in the United States. They are and have been planned, designed, and built by the top professionals in their fields. The other cities reflect varying degrees of state and private capital investment and somewhat differing ecological, legal, civic, and planning traditions. But DIY urban design is at once visible enough to be findable yet uncommon enough to be noteworthy in all of them, with the qualified exception of Mexico City. (Like many cities in so-called developing or less developed regions of the global South, unregulated construction and unplanned infrastructure improvements—not to mention informal services and economic activity—are more commonplace in Mexico City than they are in the United States, Canada, or Britain. However, while I visited and spoke to residents in unplanned settlements in remote hillside edges of this megacity, my research in DF was primarily focused on those unauthorized streetscape design changes in the more regulated center of the city occurring in forms, by individuals, and for reasons typical of DIY urbanism in the other cities I studied.)

This focus is intentional. There is a wealth of academic research on informal urbanism in the global South. (And others have studied the myriad informal improvement efforts of poor communities in the United States as well.) My interest is the particular forms of civic-minded improvement that I call DIY urban design in their complex interplay with the professionalized and standardized planning processes and development models that dominate cities of the advanced economies of the global North. The cities and the respondents I spoke to yield unique findings and provoke important questions for understanding the contemporary American city.

## PHOTO ETHNOGRAPHY AND BICYCLE ETHNOGRAPHY

In addition to traditional ethnographic and interview-based research approaches, two less common research tools were integral to my methodology and warrant some brief discussion here: the camera and the bicycle. I conducted the vast majority of the interviews for the study in person and in the neighborhoods where the do-it-yourselfers I was speaking to lived and/or worked, often in coffee shops or bars, sometimes in their homes or offices, sometimes out on the street. (Fourteen interviews were conducted by phone.) Wherever possible I walked, cycled, or rode in their cars with them on local streets to view or even participate in the installation of their interventions.

I was never without my camera on these excursions and I extensively photographed every DIY project that I could. When I could not participate in or observe a DIY urban design intervention in person—for instance, if I learned about the project after it had been removed or I was unable to visit the site for practical reasons—I pored over photos provided by the creator(s) or from coverage in the media, and I even viewed them in context on Google's "street view" feature. (It's surprising how many unauthorized streetscape interventions one can see this way!)

The collection of photographic data was essential to the research, recording the visual qualities of the projects I was studying and the physical contexts in which they were created. Capturing this information not only provided for its later analysis to inform my conclusions but also enabled its inclusion in written research products, including this book, to help communicate the nature of the phenomenon under study. I couldn't agree more with Parkin and Coomber (2009: 21) who have argued (after Becker 1998) that "the collection of visual data becomes almost obligatory during ethnographic fieldwork." The camera was thus in many ways as important a tool for conducting research as my digital voice recorder and my fieldnote journal.

The prospect of using photos in cultural research seems to have been around nearly as long as the photographic medium itself (Jacob Riis's groundbreaking exploration of New York City's 19th-century tenement slums, *How the Other Half Lives*, dates to 1890) and, as Howard Becker (1974: 3) once noted, "Photography and sociology have approximately the same birth date."* The medium has continued to play a valuable role in more recent well-known ethnographic works (e.g., Duneier 1999; Grazian 2003; Lloyd 2006; Snyder 2009). Scholars identifying with the disciplines of visual sociology and visual anthropology continue to refine and codify some best practices in the use of photography as a research method (e.g., Becker 1998; Prosser 1998; Pink 2004; Parker & Coomber 2009).

I found the bicycle to be another especially crucial ethnographic tool. The concept of bicycle ethnography is not a gimmick. A bike is ideal for covering real ground without losing the perspective of human scale, something essential to the study of urban space. In Los Angeles, for example, with the help of a five-speed gray road bike kindly lent by a friend in Echo Park, I was able to ride from an interview in Mid-City to another in South Los Angeles and all the way up to Highland Park, observing changes in land use and local character and arriving in some ways already familiar with a place, having ridden in. Cycling across New Orleans on a borrowed green cruiser—complete with a basket, bells, fake crawling ivy, and of course

Community members install a DIY speed limit sign in Brooklyn's Prospect Heights neighborhood in 2014. Photo by the author.

* That is, Becker calculated, "if you count sociology's birth as the publication of Comte's work which gave it its name, and photography's birth as the date in 1839 when Daguerre made public his method for fixing an image on a metal plate" (1974: 3).

purple and emerald beads—I stumbled upon several casual instances of DIY urban improvement that I would never have seen or known about had I not been exploring by bike.

More practically, time after time having a bicycle allowed me to connect with, gain access to, and literally keep up with my respondents during participant observation in ways that would have been impossible without. When first arriving in Toronto for research, I was met by an interviewee at the subway station and immediately put on a rented "Bixi Bike" for a whirlwind tour of the Urban Repair Squad's guerrilla interventions that yielded other interview opportunities. In New York, I rode my own bike between Park(ing) Day parks and along with community members installing DIY "20 Is Plenty" speed limit signs in several Brooklyn neighborhoods, experiencing the streets as they did.

The use of a bicycle for the research was a natural, efficient, and effective choice for me. But it was not an original one. An emerging cadre of bicycle scholars have embraced the bike as a research tool. Recent studies by Jeffrey Kidder (2006, 2009) and Adonia Lugo (2012a, 2013), for instance, were conducted in no small part by bike and provide compelling examples of the value of this human-powered workhorse both for gaining access to particular populations and simply for "ethnographic flânerie" (Lugo 2012a; see also Lugo 2012b). I am glad to count myself among them.

# NOTES

## CHAPTER 1

1. See Henry Petroski's *Engineers of Dreams* (1995) for a lively history of this and other great bridges.
2. See Hooke (2000, also 1994) on the history and staggering scale of human earthmoving since Paleolithic times and up to the modern era.
3. For instance, Angela (2009) describes labyrinthine networks of streets in all different sizes, walkways jumbled with casual commercial uses, and the urinal jars that industrial launderers would leave on corners as public toilets (they collected urine for use in cleaning). Streets and building facades were covered in creeping homegrown plant life, drying laundry, and voluminous graffiti. Unauthorized construction, even of enormous residential buildings, was common. And these *insulae* themselves were more like informally organized vertical villages than today's apartment blocks, complete with ad hoc architectural additions, underground economies, and local systems of authority, order, and service provision. Attempts at organized urban design—such as Nero's "new urban plan" to widen streets and improve access for emergency personnel, in an effort to improve fire safety—would be quickly undone, "re-infested with unplanned development" (Angela 2009: 107).
4. See Lee, McQuarrie, and Walker (2015), and especially the introduction to that edited volume, for a critical review of this paradox of increasing participation and declining democracy in modern civic life.

## CHAPTER 2

1. See, for example, the classic article by Wilson and Kelling (1982), as well as influential sociological studies such as Sampson and Raudenbush (1999), and more recent work such as that by Keizer, Lindenberg, and Steg (2008).
2. Examples range from works of public art theory, such as Kwon (2002), to sociological studies of the subcultures themselves, such as Snyder (2009). An especially popular premise for the study of graffiti has been its textual analysis for sexual and cultural significance when scrawled on bathroom walls, as has been done by everyone from biologists (Kinsey et al. 1953; Farr & Gordon 1975) to English professors (Bartholome & Snyder 2004).
3. For instance, research by Vivoni (2009) and Kidder (2011), among others.
4. See, for instance, work by St. John (2004), Pickerill and Chatterton (2006), and Lambert-Beatty (2010).
5. For a study documenting the former, see Keizer, Lindenberg, and Steg (2008); for persuasive evidence of the latter, see work by Phillips (e.g., 1999).

6. Especially notable examples include Jeffrey Hou's edited volume, *Insurgent Public Space* (2010), Mike Lydon and Anthony Garcia's handbooks on so-called tactical urbanism (e.g., Lydon 2011, 2012; Lydon & Garcia 2015), and graphical coffee table books like Klanten, Ehmann, and Hubner's *Urban Interventions* (2010). Early reports in online publications include my own (Douglas 2011) as well as others (e.g., Veloz 2011), and whole websites devoted to the phenomena (e.g., Burnham 2012; Partizaning 2012).

7. In addition to the exhibition itself (Ho 2012), see the published catalogue (Ho & Douglas 2012) and the website www.spontaneousinterventions.org.

8. The quote is from Visconti et al. (2010), p. 514.

9. For instance, after giving my first talks on the subject in 2011 and 2012, I found myself in touch with Donovan Finn, Kurt Iveson, and others presenting new research on similar themes, work that evolved not only into articles (Iveson 2013; Douglas 2014, 2016; Finn 2014) but also stimulating conversation and collaboration. Two special issues of the *Journal of Urbanism* in 2014 and 2016 focused on the topic, and the small but exciting multidisciplinary group of scholars working on and discussing similar issues continues to grow. Their work can be found in contexts ranging from law journals (e.g., Pagano 2013; Schindler 2014) to planning scholarship (e.g., Corsín Jimenez 2014; Talen 2015) to cultural studies (e.g., Deslandes 2013; Shepard 2014) to undergraduate thesis projects (e.g., Simpson 2015). A forthcoming edited volume from Mahyar Arefi and Conrad Kickert collects research on a variety of "bottom-up" urbanisms from across urban studies perspectives. Much of the work on DIY urbanism focuses on hard physical installations and alterations to the built environment, as this book does (see also Deslandes 2013; Pagano 2013; Finn 2014). Others also include more ephemeral acts like "flash mobs" and public space occupations (Iveson 2013; Shepard 2014). Some have discussed digital DIY interventions into urban space and planning as well (e.g., Caldwell & Foth 2014; Sawhney, de Kler, & Malhotra 2015).

10. On graffiti and street art as urban intervention, see Ferrell (1995) and (Rahn 2002), among others.

11. See, for instance, Roy and AlSayyad (2004), Lindell (2010), Gaffikin and Perry (2012), Rockefeller Foundation (2013).

12. On the wide range of economic and everyday informalities in American cities, see Venkatesh (2009) and Mukhija and Loukaitou-Sideris (2014). As for physical interventions, besides the other studies on DIY urbanism cited earlier in this chapter (see especially note 8), see also research on urban occupation and squatting by Massey and Snyder (2012), Hammond (2013), Squatting Europe Kollective (2013), and Gonick (2015).

13. E.g., Hou and Kinoshita (2007) and Innis, Connick, and Booher (2007).

14. As McFarlane (2012: 103) writes, "The relationship between informality and formality can shift over time, in a way that is complex, multiple and contingent." And, on informality and formality as existing on a spectrum rather than as two binary nodes, see Cobb, King, and Rodriguez (2009); also Loftus-Farren (2011).

## CHAPTER 3

1. See the quarterly reports of the American Public Transit Association (e.g., American Public Transit Association 2016).

2. Indeed, transportation researchers have found that transit users find waiting time far more onerous than time spent on buses or trains (see Iseki & Taylor 2010; Iseki et al. 2012).

3. Many cities and transit agencies employ benches and other potential seating explicitly designed to discourage sleeping and other unwanted uses. On these intentionally uncomfortable seats and other "sadistic street environments," see Mike Davis (1990), and also Main and Hannah (2009). On the avoiding and removal of seating in public spaces altogether, see Davis (1990) and also Sorkin (1992) and Molotch and McClain (2003).

4. The term neoliberalism is often used as an alternative or complement to the similarly broad and carelessly bandied about concept of economic globalization. Kingfisher and Maskovsky (2008: 116) have described this relationship: "If globalization describes a new form of production that creates new relations of markets and states in an international arena, the concept of neoliberalism is often invoked to make reference to the specific market-triumphalist manner in which capitalist globalization has been shaped and reproduced in recent decades. Since its inception, it has been as social and political as it has been economic." In other words, while globalization is a label for the structural economic and geopolitical rescaling of the past fifty years, neoliberalization is the changes in socioeconomic ideology and policy that have accompanied it in much of the world (see also Castells 1996; Purcell 2008). On the concept of "neoliberalization" in cities, see Brenner and Theodore (2002), Brenner, Peck and Theodore (2010), and Fairbanks and Lloyd (2011), among others.

5. On-the-ground realities in any city today are of course more complex than these ideal-typical descriptions allow (cf. Small 2008), and there is a significant lack of appropriately nuanced research on "actually existing" conditions of economic restructuring or neoliberal policy ideologies (Fairbanks & Lloyd 2011).

6. On neoliberal policymaking as actively working to support private business and the "free market," see especially Kingfisher and Maskovsky (2008). On the unique extremes of this paradox in urban governments as facilitators of private development, see Fairbanks and Lloyd (2011); see also the modern parable of the publicly financed or incentivized urban sports stadium.

7. See the article by Egan (1995).

8. Beginning in the 1960s and '70s in France and the United Kingdom, this practice has become increasingly common throughout Europe and North America since the 1980s (France 2002; Moran 2005; JCDecaux 2013). Other cities in the United States that contract their bus stop infrastructure to advertising firms include Annapolis, Atlanta, Boston, Dallas, San Francisco, Seattle, and Tampa, to name a diverse handful, though the degree to which the specific placement of benches and shelters is determined by the advertising company or the municipality varies. For details on this practice in Los Angeles, which dates to a poorly implemented 2001 contract with CBS Decaux, see Orlov (2012), LA Bureau of Street Services (2013), and McCarty and Mendelson (2016).

9. See a *Los Angeles Times* report by Linthicum (2011).

10. On the privatization of public open spaces and the commercial character of pedestrian malls in Southern California, see Loukaitou-Sideris (1993), Loukaitou-Sideris and Banerjee (1993), Pojani (2008), and Schmidt (2010); see also Hoyt (2005) on the role of business improvement districts in community planning.

11. Detailed breakdowns are difficult to extract for both MTA operating costs or CBS advertising revenues, but, for instance, in 2010 (the year of substantial subway service cuts and station agent layoffs to which Jordan was referring) the transit agency was attempting to close a nearly $800 million budget shortfall for the

year (Grossman 2010; Namako 2010); meanwhile, financial analysts valued CBS Outdoor at greater than $4 billion in late 2012, and reported profits averaging over $150 million per month in the first three quarters of 2012 (see Steel & Edgecliffe-Johnson 2013). Service and infrastructural decay across the subway system was in such a state by 2017 that Mayor Bill De Blasio proposed a tax on the city's wealthiest residents to pay for improvements and New York Governor Andrew Cuomo declared a "state of emergency," committing an additional $1 billion in state funds. Of course, these specifics are largely irrelevant to Jordan's point.

12. In his 2011 documentary film *Vigilante Vigilante*, Good explores the lives of these neighborhood anti-graffiti activists who, in their aggressive efforts to remove graffiti from their communities, have too turned to illegally painting on other people's property.

13. See, for instance, Whyte's classic *Social Life of Small Urban Spaces* (1980), and more recent work by Henderson (2011), Fenton (2012), and Yen and Anderson (2012). And see Elet (2002) for a historical argument on the importance of "the outdoor benches of early modern Florence."

14. Both private interests and public agencies take these sorts of measures, often explicitly to discourage "antisocial or illegal behavior" (Gans 2011; see also Molotch & McClain 2003; Perl 2010; Martens 2012).

15. The practice, known as "spot saving" or "the dibs system" is widespread and more or less normalized in the cities of Boston, Chicago, and Pittsburgh, among others. It has even been condoned by politicians and made legal in some cities (Epstein 2002; Silbey 2010).

16. Somewhat similarly, if on stronger legal ground, sociologist Andrew Deener (2012) found instances of property owners in the Venice Beach section of Los Angeles attempting to "take back" private property that had been established customarily as open to public use. For more on the enclosure of public spaces by private interests, see especially Low (2006).

17. See coverage by Walker (2014).

18. This claim was made by the likes of Joseph Stiglitz (2008), Immanuel Wallerstein (2008), and Elmar Altvater (2009), among others. See also Harvey (2007) and Brenner, Peck, and Theodore (2010). For a thorough retrospective accounting of how this did not happen, see Mirowski (2013).

19. See the article by Davey (2013).

20. Efforts at mapping these services have produced remarkable diagrams in the recognizable style of official transit maps (e.g., Reiss 2014; Stamen Design 2015) demonstrating entire "shadow transit" networks operating alongside state-run ones.

21. General Motors, Firestone Tires, and several petroleum companies have been implicated in promoting and funding the replacement of trolleys with buses in cities throughout the United States, including quite famously in Los Angeles, from the 1930s through 1950s (Slater 1997; Snell 1974). Whether this actually caused a decline in trolleys or an emphasis on automobile usage that would not have happened anyway is disputed (see Slater 1997).

### CHAPTER 4

1. See for instance Paul Davidoff's influential call to pluralism and advocacy in planning in 1965; Robert Goodman's 1971 manifesto, *After the Planners*; and sweeping trends toward participatory planning and budgeting in many cities

and communities or even more recent calls for "co-creation" or "co-design" in planning.

2. For an eye-opening analysis of "ancient urban planning," see the award-winning piece of planning history by Michael Smith (2007).

3. This is evident in accounts by Argan (1969), Shane (1979, 2013), Sutcliffe (1980, 1981), Fishman (2000), Keller (2009), and Levy (2011). The very term "urbanization," from the Roman *urbs*, was introduced by the prolific Catalan planner of Barcelona, Ildefons Cerdà, in his 1867 *Teoría General de la Urbanización* (cf. Pallares-Barbera, Badia, & Duch 2011). I am especially indebted throughout this section to the work of Anthony Sutcliffe (1981).

4. See Sutcliffe (1981).

5. For more on Richard Ankrom's work, see Ankrom (2009) and Stephens (2009).

6. Although a 2014 decision by the Coastal Commission and the State Lands Commission did hand a limited victory to public beachgoers, forcing one private company to stop charging access fees, unlock a gate, and remove its anti-surfing signage (Groves 2014).

7. On the role of businesses, professional groups, and economic institutions in community development, see, for instance, research by Taub, Taylor, and Dunham (1984), Taub (1988), and Suttles (1990). On advocacy and equity planning, see classic works by Davidoff (1965) and Goodman (1971), among others.

## CHAPTER 5

1. Among the overwhelming number of studies finding disproportionate and discriminatory policing among people of color, see Harris (1999, 2003), Huo and Tyler (2000), Lundman and Kaufman (2003), the Center for Constitutional Rights (2009), and the New York Civil Liberties Union (2013). On the disproportionate use of "gang loitering" laws to persecute young men of color, see, for instance, Rosenthal (2000).

2. On the psychological impacts of living with prejudice in everyday life, see Franklin and Boyd-Franklin (2000), Michelson (2003), Brunson (2007), and Franklin, Boyd-Franklin, and Kelly (2006), among others. In addition to those, see Anderson (1999), Weitzer and Tuch (2002), Menjívar and Bejerano (2004), Brunson (2007), Dottolo and Steward (2008), Gabbidon and Taylor-Greene (2009), and Correia (2010) on the attitudes of African Americans and Latinos toward the police.

3. On the last point, see studies by Menjívar and Bejerano (2004) and Michelson (2007). On the social disengagement and skepticism toward authorities that can result from concerns over legal insecurity and deportation within Latino and other immigrant communities, see Asch, Leake, and Gelberg (1994) and Correia (2010) among others, as well as reporting on the fear induced in particular by reactionary Trump administration policies in 2017 from Galofaro and Linderman (2017), Santia (2017), Yee (2017), and many others.

4. See, for instance, research by Weitzer and Tuch (1999, 2002).

5. In addition to McIntosh (1989), see work by Ostrander (1984) and Wildman (1996).

6. Pattillo (2007: 262) writes of wealthier residents' concerns: "When the worry is not about disorganization's links to serious crime, it is about the effects that indecorous acts may have on property values."

7. What Richard Lloyd (2006; also Lloyd & Clark 2001) labeled "grit as glamor" is indeed a fundamental ideological driver of the gentrification process in many places. *See also* Edwards (2009), Zukin and Braslow (2011), and Douglas (2012b).

8. *See* Schumaker and Getter (1977) on the accountability and "responsiveness bias" of government officials and service providers in American cities; also Cavill and Sohail (2003) and Hajnal and Trounstine (2014). Logan and Schneider (1981) found that high-status communities are more successful in efforts to resist unfavorable development, and Hajnal and Trounstine (2014: 67) found that wealthy, white residents are more likely to "feel well represented in the local democratic arena" as well.

9. *See* the website of St. Elmo Village, Inc., the non-profit arts center based in the community, at www.stelmovillage.org.

10. During a similar heat wave in 2011, nearly 2,000 hydrants in the city of Chicago had to be shut down by water management authorities, who required a police escort for their safety (CBS2 Chicago 2011). Some other cities have adopted procedures by which hydrants can be opened legally.

11. In comparison to the rest of New York City, at the census block group level Bedford-Stuyvesant does have a higher than average proportion of vacant lots, if not the highest even in Brooklyn (*see* Kremer, Hamstead, & McPhearson 2013; NYC Dept. of Planning 2013).

12. The article is by Anne Correal (2009).

13. *See* the report by Mitter (2009).

14. Urban sociology has focused considerable attention on the links between place and identity, including classic studies of neighborhood identity by Suttles (1972) and Hunter (1974), and more recent notable work such as Small (2005) and Ghaziani (2014). On the particular importance of authenticity and community cultural expectations for place attachment, see, for instance, Brown and Perkins (1992), Fried (2000), Brown-Saracino (2009), Ocejo (2011), Douglas (2012a), and Tissot (2015).

15. The phenomenon of the so-called hipster is itself a problematic term to tangle with, and has been so widely applied in recent years that it has lost much of its original meaning (Leland 2004). But do see Greif (2010) for a very thoughtful analysis, as well as Lloyd (2006), Douglas (2012b), and Sæter, Aure and Bergaust (2012) for relevant sociological discussion. When I use the term here, I mean to describe an aesthetic- and lifestyle-based cultural identity that is frequently attributed to predominantly white and middle-class adults, usually a little older than the stereotypical "millennial," living in certain trendy (or pre-trendy) urban neighborhoods and defined by an "ahead-of-the-trend" attention to music, fashion, and lifestyle fads. There are countless examples, but the culture is tied to an appreciation of perceived authenticity and cultural capital, and the aesthetic itself is characterized by a quasi-ironic appropriation of the styles of prior generations (often those initially defined by African American youth or the white working class), in addition to components commonly associated with contemporary music or progressive activist subcultures (Douglas 2012b: 3591–92).

16. At an extreme, the notorious Mexican drug lord "El Chapo" Guzman spent some of his considerable wealth funding the construction of roads and other needed services in the remote mountains of Sinaloa dominated by his cartel.

17. For instance, studies by the US Forest Service and others have found that urban street trees and the amount of "urban tree cover" can increase property values

and reduce the amount of time-on-market for homes for sale over sizable areas, among other economic benefits (Sander, Polasky & Haight 2008; Donovan & Butry 2010; Wells 2010). Trees and other vegetation in a neighborhood also appear to be positively correlated with lower crime, less fear, and fewer "incivilities" in the area (Kuo & Sullivan 2001; Donovan & Prestemon 2012) and have a calculable "real value" themselves (Randall 2007). In a study of downtown Athens, Georgia, Wolf (2004) found that consumers also prefer retail areas with more trees.

18. I discuss this proposition in detail in Chapter 6. But see studies by Walljasper (2013), Hoffman and Lugo (2014), Hoffman (2015, 2016), and Hyra (2017) for analyses of the links between bicycle planning/infrastructure and race and class.

19. Details here come from media coverage by Chip Johnson (2014) and Judy Silber (2014). I first visited the shrine in 2016 at the encouragment of my friend and colleague Dean Walt Jacobs of San José State University. My family and I actually moved to the neighborhood, quite coincidentally, a year later and walk past the shrine—now some ten feet tall—and its faithful worshippers nearly every day.

20. According to police crime statistics cited in Johnson (2014), reported crime in the one-block radius around the corner with the shrine showed an overal decline of 82 percent in the year after regular daily worship began at the site, and reports of narcotics and prostitution dropped from three to zero in both cases.

## CHAPTER 6

1. See Nicol (2014).

2. The quote here is from City of Oakland (2013), p. 3. I reviewed a number of official planning documents on the plaza and the designs for its redevelopment, including the one cited here prepared for the city by the director of the Oakland Department of Public Works.

3. See the report by Artz (2013).

4. City of Oakland (2013), p. 1.

5. The report prepared for the National Endowment for the Arts' Mayor's Institute for City Design by Markusen and Gadwa (2010) offers the mainstream take. Though (like most urbanists I've spoken with) I use the term specifically in reference to physical changes to particular spaces, most broadly creative placemaking might include wider initiatives to socially and economically revitalize whole districts or whole cities through a wide array of cultural activities, from streetscape alterations to performances and street festivals to culture-oriented tax and development incentives. A variety of planning departments, business improvement districts, and other local stakeholders in cities throughout the United States have articulated neighborhood revitalization, branding, and economic development efforts quite explicitly in these terms (often receiving external funding from the NEA and other institutions).

6. Urban planning has been a formally professionalized vocation since at least the mid-20th century, in some senses much longer. The rise of DIY urban design poses at least a theoretical and conceptual challenge to this, much as a broader "do-it-yourself culture" and various technological populisms have posed to journalism, music, and other creative professions (Lewis 2012; see also Deuze 2006, 2008). This would seem to put even innovative, open-minded planners in the position of defending their professional jurisdiction.

7. In these ways, professional urban planners and designers are in a situation analogous to the "tension between professional control and open participation" experienced by journalists in the 21st-century media landscape (Lewis 2012). They see value in a more dynamic and populist planning process, but nonetheless see the codes and processes that they work under as vital to the responsible ordering of the city.

8. Fishman (2000: 1) provides an eloquent synopsis of this history: "The last half-century has seen a radical transformation in American cities and regions, but paradoxically, this transformation has stimulated our interest in the older forms of cities and increased our respect for the planning tradition that created them. For example, the tidal wave of single-family suburban tract development after World War II has led to a new understanding of older residential areas where a pedestrian scale and a dense, complex mixture of housing types and other land uses seemed to lead to better opportunities for community. The revolutionary decentralization in retailing and the rise of 'Mallopolis' on every major highway has made the surviving older Main Streets a focus for civic pride and redevelopment."

9. Peter Calthorpe's (1993) *New American Metropolis* and Peter Katz's (1994) *The New Urbanism* are the foundational texts for this philosophy, which now forms the basis for an international nonprofit organization (the Congress for the New Urbanism) boasting some 2,600 members, several of my interviewees among them.

10. An enormous amount of ink has been spilled espousing (and criticizing) the so-called creative city and the role of any number of tangible and intangible cultural amenities in promoting urban economic success. In the social sciences, see, for instance, Florida (2002), Peck (2005), Currid (2007), Greenberg (2008), Brash (2011), and Zukin (2012), among many others. As to whether the combination of growth- and market-driven policy and development ideologies with neo-traditional (and ecological and "creative") urban planning ideals amounts to a distinct urban governance trend in its own right, this is a question for another study. Again, professional planners I interviewed repeatedly identified a recent "shift" in the planning priorities of their cities (see note on page 141), and the dominant policies of these places appear to draw from and fit at a sort of crux of these development-driven but socially and culturally oriented sensibilities.

11. The term itself is generally attributed to the public space planner Mike Lydon and his colleagues (e.g., Lydon 2011; Klayko 2012; Lydon & Garcia 2015). Tactical urbanism was named one of the "top planning trends of 2011–2012" (Nettler 2012).

12. Zack Furness (2010) provides a detailed account of the "Provo" and their White Bicycle movement.

13. See NYC Dept. of Transportation (2014).

14. On disparities in community development funding along race lines, see Bonds (2004). See also footnote 8 in Chapter 5.

15. According to several calculations, including from Janette Sadik-Khan herself, retail rents in the pedestrianized area of Times Square went up by "71 percent" between the pedestrian intervention and the months ending 2010, which Sadik-Khan called "the largest increase in the city's history" (quoted in Goodyear, 2010). See also *The Real Deal* (2009), Pristin (2010), Tadeo (2010), and Moss (2016).

16. See City of Oakland (2013).

17. Studies have shown how idealized conceptions of "authentic," "edgy," even "gritty" urban character become cultural commodities that are used to define and sell whole neighborhoods and cities to tourists, new residents, and real estate speculators (Lloyd 2006; Greenberg 2008; Douglas 2012b; Krivý 2013; Zukin 2012; Rius Ulldemolins 2014) and to engage in this arena of inter-city cultural-economic competition (Currid 2008; Brash 2012). Catungal, Leslie, and Hii (2009: 1098) write: "Following the same logic as entrepreneurial initiatives, creative city policies view the city as a space of consumption and creativity, and have set out as their objective an interurban competitive strategy based on the marketing of their locales as distinctive destinations for work and play."

18. On the priority that cities place, rightly or wrongly, on attracting members of Richard Florida's so-called creative class for their value in local growth and economic development, see work by Peck (2005), Lloyd (2006), Zimmerman (2008), Krivý (2013), and of course Florida (2003, 2005, 2017).

19. For instance, one business in Columbia, Missouri, claimed a 139 percent increase in sales "just by having the parklets outside" (Cho 2013). On the "growing trend" of parklet dining, see Tepper (2012).

20. Some critical scholars have essentially argued as much. See Harvey (1997); Low, Taplin and Scheld (2005); Vasquez (2009); Agyeman and Erickson (2012); and Agyeman (2013).

21. In McCullen's (2008: 81) words: "Insofar as farmers markets are now being touted as excellent ways to boost public space use, the affluent white coding of many farmers markets can spatially reproduce white and class privilege by more broadly claiming public spaces as affluent white spaces."

22. As Jeremiah Moss (2016) has noted about the regulations posted on a new pedestrian plaza at Manhattan's Astor Place, "Prohibited activities include the 'unreasonable obstruction' of sitting areas and pedestrians, along with camping, storing personal belongings, and lying down. This language clearly refers to the presence of homeless people and presumably will be used to harass them out of the new plaza. They can also be used to stop political protest and spontaneous, unregulated art performances. Skateboarding is also not allowed, though it's been an unofficial Astor Place tradition for decades."

23. Public art projects have been similarly implicated in "regeneration schemes" as a "tool to reaestheticize areas within a city" and bring social and economic benefits (Sharp, Pollock, & Paddison 2005: 1012–13).

24. Research on bike lanes as gentrification tools comprises a young but growing discourse. Correlations between the two are strongly suggested, and to some extent assumed, in the literature, if not unequivocally demonstrated. The assumed connections between the two are powerful enough for plenty of communities to be wary, however. See studies by Lubitow and Miller (2013), Hoffman and Lugo (2014), Hoffman (2016), and Hyra (2017), as well as local news articles by Goodyear (2011), Maus (2011), Tavernise (2011), Walljasper (2013), and Stein (2015). As Hoffman and Lugo (2014) point out, bicycle infrastructure may also thus be considered an example of what Checker (2011) calls "environmental gentrification."

25. See local coverage by Clark (2013).

26. The article is by Higgins (2014).

27. See Smith (1996), Peck (2005), Granzow and Dean (2007), and Rius Ulldemolins (2014).

28. The online piece by Rose (2016) reviews five of them in the hip Cincinnati suburb of Covington, Kentucky.
29. See Young (2014).
30. To be fair, some planners and politicians in Los Angeles may finally be recognizing the qualities of streets that have already been shaped by the city's Latino populations, as reflected in redesigns for a stretch of Broadway (already vibrant and predominantly Latino, if threatened by gentrification) through Downtown LA (see Hawthorne 2014). On Latino urbanism in general, see especially work by Rojas (1991, 2010), Davis (2001), and Rios (2010).

## CHAPTER 7
1. See the local news article by Bruno (2016).
2. In these ways, the findings continue the project advocated by Fairbanks and Lloyd (2011), among others, to bring ethnographic analysis to the understanding of "actually existing neoliberalism" and other physical consequences of urban policy.
3. Prominent examples include Florida (2002, 2005), Glaeser (2011), and Montgomery (2013). Of course, these and others are not without their criticisms, nor are they entirely in agreement with one another.
4. As Lee, McQuarrie, and Walker (2015: 9) write, "Celebratory accounts are uplifting, but they do not meet the needs of this moment when expanding participation has occurred alongside the greatest expansion of socioeconomic inequality since the Gilded Age." Baiocchi and Ganuza (2017) articulate the problem as a paradox in which the focus is more on the formation of public opinion than any actual expansion of decision-making power or enfranchisement. The official embrace of DIY urbanism and tactical urbanism risks amounting to the sort of elite manipulation of popular participation that these researchers chronicle as well.
5. As Tonkiss (2013: 98–99) notes, in addition to informality as "urbanization from below," "processes and practices of informality are a systemic feature of rich and poor world cities, and numerous spatial claims and formal outcomes are the effects of powerful modes of informality 'from above.'"
6. The quote comes from Cooley (1909), p. 343.
7. Cooley (1909), p. 350.
8. See, for instance, the work of Berger, Cohen, and Zeldich (1972), Blau (1977), Ridgeway (1991, 2001), and Foschi (2000). This sort of status-based social dominance is essentially self-perpetuating in disorganized contexts, as Berger, Cohen, and Zeldich and others have argued, with higher status individuals more willing to take the initiative, and more socially expected to take it, and so thus more likely to be given it, which in turn gives them the first opportunity to demonstrate leadership and thus to gain further credibility as qualified actors. (Testing the application of the so-called expectation states theory to activities in public space could be a productive avenue for future research.)
9. The 2012–15 community-driven redesign of Corona Plaza was led by architect Quilian Riano, urban planner Aurash Khawarzad (a former member of DoTank), and their design studio, DSGN AGNC, in collaboration with countless community members. For more on the plaza project and its experimental blending of heavy local participation, design expertise, and official support, see Riano (2014).

10. Rather ironically, research has shown that gift-giving generates status hierarchies and can lead to the sorts of status-based performance expectations discussed above (see Bienenstock & Bianchi 2004). In other words, the cynic insists, even if the generosity of DIY urban design actions presents a critical challenge to "empire," it simultaneously reinforces the privileged position of do-it-yourselfers over other members of their communities.

11. In their influential book called *Empire*, Hardt and Negri (2000) use this term to describe the overarching political-economic social structure dominant in our globalized era. Analogues can be found in the critical theory of Marx, Gramsci, the Frankfurt School, and elsewhere.

12. On the right to the city, in addition to the foundation laid by Lefebvre (1968), see the important treatise of the same name by Harvey (2008), and thoughtful assessments of the concept by Purcell (2002) and Marcuse (2014). See also the employment of the term in everything from anti-gentrification housing activism (e.g., Right to the City Alliance 2017) or women's security (Whitzman et al. 2012) to a United Nations charter (UN Habitat 2004) and a formal city policy (Ciudad de México 2010).

13. See Lefebvre (2009b), p. 186 (originally published in 1979).

14. *Autogestion* is essentially an idea of people taking control (of work, life, society) away from the state and capitalist modes of production by organizing their work for themselves. As Lefebvre translators and interpreters Neil Brenner and Stuart Elden (2009: 14) put it, the term "might be rendered most effectively as 'grassroots control.'" Contingent upon the right strategy and historical moment, it provides a recipe for transformation. In Lefebvre's words (2009a [1966]: 150), "It shows the practical way to change life, which remains the watchword, the goal, and the meaning of a revolution."

# BIBLIOGRAPHY

Agyeman, Julian. 2013. *Just Sustainabilities: Policy, Planning, and Practice.* London: Zed Books.

Agyeman, Julian & Jennifer Sien Erickson. 2012. "Culture, Recognition and the Negotiation of Difference: Some Thoughts on Cultural Competency in Planning Education." *Journal of Planning Education and Research*, 32(3): 358–66.

Alexander, Christopher. 1979. *The Timeless Way of Building.* Oxford: Oxford University Press.

Alexander, Christopher, Sara Ishikawa, & Murray Silverstein. 1977. *A Pattern Language: Towns, Buildings, Construction.* Oxford: Oxford University Press.

Alexander, Christopher, Hajo Neis, Artemis Anninou, & Ingrid King. 1987. *A New Theory of Urban Design.* Oxford: Oxford University Press.

Alkon, Alison H. & Christie G. McCullen. 2010. "Whiteness and Farmers Markets: Performances, Perpetuations . . . Contestations?" *Antipode*, 43(4): 937–59.

Altvater, Elmar. 2009. "Postneoliberalism or Postcapitalism." *Development Dialogue* 51(1): 73–88.

Alvelos, Heitor. 2004. "The Desert Imagination in the City of Signs: Cultural Implications of Sponsored Transgression and Branded Graffiti." In *Cultural Criminology Unleashed*, edited by J. Ferrell et al., 181–91. London: Glass House Press.

American Public Transportation Association. 2016. *Public Transportation Ridership Report: Fourth Quarter 2015.* Washington, DC: American Public Transportation Association. Accessed 26 January 2017 at http://www.apta.com/resources/statistics/Pages/RidershipArchives.aspx.

Anderson, Elijah. 1990. *Streetwise: Race, Class, and Change in an Urban Community.* Chicago: University of Chicago Press.

Anderson, Elijah. 1999. *Code of the Streets.* New York: Alfred A. Knopf.

Angela, Alberto. 2009. *A Day in the Life of Ancient Rome*, translated by G. Conti. New York: Europa Editions.

Ankrom, Richard. 2009. "Freeway Signs: The Installation of Guide Signs on the 110 Pasadena Freeway." *Ankrom.org* website. Accessed 28 October 2015 at http://ankrom.org/freeway_signs.html.

Arefi, Mahyar & Conrad Kickert, eds. Forthcoming. *The Palgrave Handbook of Bottom-Up Urbanism.* New York: Palgrave.

Argan, Giulio C. 1969. *The Renaissance City.* New York: George Braziller.

Armstrong, Gail. 1977. "Females under the Law: Protected but Unequal." *Crime & Delinquency*, 23: 109–20.

Artz, Mathew. 2013. "Oakland Hopes Latham Square Plaza Brings Uptown Vibe to City Center." *San Jose Mercury News*, 2 August. Accessed 27 March 2014 at http://www.mercurynews.com/top-stories/ci_23784803/ section-telegraph-become-oakland-pedestrian-plaza.

Asch, Steven, Barbara Leake, & Lillian Gelberg. 1994. "Does Fear of Immigration Authorities Deter Tuberculosis Patients from Seeking Care?" *Western Journal of Medicine*, 161(4): 373–76.

Astor, Maggie. 2017. "Protestors in Durham Topple a Confederate Monument." *New York Times* website, 14 August. Accessed 14 August 2017 at https://www. nytimes.com/2017/08/14/us/protesters-in-durham-topple-a-confederate-monument.html.

Babbie, Earl. 2001. *The Practice of Social Research*, 9th ed. Belmont, CA: Wadsworth Thomson.

Bacon, Edmund N. 1967. *Design of Cities*. London: Penguin.

Baiocchi, Gianpaolo & Ernesto Ganuza. 2015. "Becoming a Best Practice: Neoliberalism and the Curious Case of Participatory Budgeting." In *Democratizing Inequalities*, edited by C. W. Lee, M. McQuarrie, & E. T. Walker, 187–203. New York: New York University Press.

Baiocchi, Gianpaolo & Ernesto Ganuza. 2017. *Popular Democracy: The Paradox of Participation*. Redwood City, CA: Stanford University Press.

Barak, Gregg, Paul Leighton, & Jeanne Flavin. 2006. *Class, Race, Gender, and Crime: The Social Realities of Justice in America*, 2nd ed. Lanham, MD: Rowman & Littlefield.

Bartholome, Lynn & Philip Snyder. 2004. "Is It Philosophy or Pornography? Graffiti at the Dinosaur Bar-B-Que." *Journal of American Culture*, 27(1): 86–98.

Becker, Howard S. 1974. "Photography and Sociology." *Studies in the Anthropology of Visual Communication*, 1: 3–26.

Becker, Howard S. 1998. "Visual Sociology, Documentary Photography and Photojournalism: It's (almost) All a Matter of Context." In *Image-based Research*, edited by J. Prosser, 84–96. London: Falmer Press.

Berger, Joseph, Bernard B. Cohen, & Morris Zelditch Jr. 1972. "Status Characteristics and Social Interaction." *American Sociological Review*, 37(3): 241–55.

Bienenstock, Elisa Jayne & Alison J. Bianchi. 2004. "Activating Performance Expectations and Status Differences through Gift Exchange." *Social Psychology Quarterly*, 67(3): 310–18.

Blau, Peter M. 1977. *Inequality and Heterogeneity: A Primitive Theory of Social Structure*. New York: Free Press.

Bloom, Brett & Ava Bromberg, eds. 2004. *Belltown Paradise/Making Their Own Plans*. Chicago: White Walls.

Bonds, Michael. 2004. *Race, Politics, and Community Development Funding: The Discolor of Money*. Binghamton, NY: Haworth Social Work Practice Press.

Bourriaud, Nicolas. 2002 (1998). *Relational Aesthetics*, translated by S. Pleasance & F. Woods. Paris: Le presses du reel.

Brash, Julian. 2011. *Bloomberg's New York: Class and Governance in the Luxury City*. Athens, GA: University of Georgia Press.

Breines, Wini. 1986. "The 1950s: Gender and Some Social Science." *Sociological Inquiry*, 56(1): 69–92.

Brenner, Neil. 2004. *New State Spaces: Urban Governance and the Rescaling of Statehood*. Oxford: Oxford University Press.

Brenner, Neil & Stuart Elden. 2009. "Introduction. State, Space World: Levebvre and the Survival of Capitalism." In *State, Space, World: Selected Essays,* edited by N. Brenner & S. Elden, 1–48. Minneapolis: University of Minnesota Press.

Brenner, Neil, Jamie Peck, & Nik Theodore. 2010. "After Neoliberalization?" *Globalizations,* 7(3): 327–45.

Brenner, Neil & Nik Theodore, eds. 2002. *Spaces of Neoliberalism: Urban Restructuring in Western Europe and North America.* Oxford: Blackwell.

Broidy, Lisa & Robert Agnew. 1997. "Gender and Crime: A General Strain Theory Perspective." *Journal of Research in Crime and Delinquency,* 34(3): 275–305.

Brown, Barbara B. & Douglas D. Perkins. 1992. "Disruptions in Place Attachment." *Human Behavior and Environment,* 12: 279–304.

Brown-Saracino, Japonica. 2009. A Neighborhood that Never Changes: Gentrification, Social Preservation, and the Search for Authenticity. Chicago: University of Chicago Press.

Bruno, Stephanie. 2016. "With Goats, Bees and Veggies, Once Blighted Central City Plot Now a Land of Milk and Honey." *New Orleans Advocate* website, 26 February. Accessed 26 February 2016 at http://www.theneworleansadvocate.com/opinion/14967392-148/with-goats-bees-and-veggies-once-blighted-central-city-plot-now-a-land-of-milk-and-honey.

Brunson, Rodik K. 2007. "'Police Don't Like Black People': African-American Young Men's Accumulated Police Experiences." *Criminology & Public Policy,* 6: 71–102.

Burke, Peter. 1975. "Some Reflections on the Preindustrial City." *Urban History Yearbook,* 13–21.

Burnham, Scott. 2012. *Urban Guide for Alternative Use: The City as Source Material* website. Accessed 21 June 2012 at http://www.altuseguide.com/.

Burrows, Edwin G. & Mike Wallace. 1999. *Gotham: A History of New York City to 1898.* Oxford: Oxford University Press.

Burt, Ronald S. 2005. *Brokerage and Closure: An Introduction to Social Capital.* Oxford: Oxford University Press.

Buttimer, Anne. 1971. "Sociology and Planning." *Town Planning Review,* 42(2): 145–80.

Buzawa, Eve S. & Gerald T. Hotaling. 2006. "The Impact of Relationship Status, Gender, and Minor Status in the Police Response to Domestic Assaults." *Victims & Offenders,* 1(4): 323–60.

Calder, Rich. 2008. "Hasid Street Fight." *New York Post* website, 28 December. Accessed 20 January 2016 at http://nypost.com/2008/12/28/hasid-street-fight/.

Caldwell, Glenda A. & Marcus Foth. 2014. "DIY Media Architecture: Open and Participatory Approaches to Community Engagement." *MAB 14—Proceedings of the 2nd Media Architecture Biennale Conference: World Cities:* 1–10.

Calthorpe, Peter. 1993. *The Next American Metropolis: Ecology, Community, and the American Dream.* New York: Princeton Architectural Press.

Castells, Manuel. 1977 (1972). *The Urban Question,* translated by A. Sheridan. Cambridge, MA: MIT Press.

Castells, Manuel. 1996. *The Rise of the Network Society.* Oxford: Blackwell.

Castells, Manuel. 1998. *End of Millennium.* Oxford: Blackwell.

Catungal, John Paul, Deborah Leslie, & Yvonne Hii. 2009. "Geographies of Displacement in the Creative City: The Case of Liberty Village, Toronto." *Urban Studies,* 46(5&6): 1095–114.

Cavill, Sue & Muhammad Sohail. 2003. "Accountability in the Provision of Urban Services." *Municipal Engineer*, 156(ME4): 235–44.

CBS2 Chicago. 2011. "Crews Need Police Escort to Shut Off Fire Hydrants." *CBS Chicago* website, 22 July. Accessed 18 May 2014 at http://chicago.cbslocal.com/2011/07/22/crews-need-police-escort-to-shut-off-fire-hydrants/.

Center for Constitutional Rights. 2009. *Racial Disparity in NYPD Stops-and-Frisks: The Center for Constitutional Rights Preliminary Report on UF-250 Data Obtained for 2005 through June 2008*. New York: Center for Constitutional Rights. Accessed 9 April 2014 at http://ccrjustice.org/files/Report-CCR-NYPD-Stop-and-Frisk.pdf.

Cerdà, Ildefons. 1867. *Teoría general de la urbanización y aplicación de sus principios y doctrinas a la reforma y ensanche de Barcelona*. Madrid: Imprenta Española.

Chalfant, Henry & James Prigoff. 1987. *Spraycan Art*. New York: Thames and Hudson.

Chavkin, Sasha. 2011. "Women Ride in Back on Sex-Segregated Brooklyn Bus Line. *New York World* website, 18 October. Accessed 20 January 2016 at http://www.thenewyorkworld.com/2011/10/18/women-ride-in-back-on-sex-segregated-brooklyn-bus-line/.

Checker, Melissa. 2011. "Wiped Out by the 'Greenwave': Environmental Gentrification and the Paradoxical Politics of Urban Sustainability." *City & Society*, 23(2): 210–20.

Chesney-Lind, Meda. 1986. "Women and Crime: The Female Offender." *Signs*, 12(1): 78–96.

Chesney-Lind, Meda & Lisa Pasko. 2013. *The Female Offender: Girls, Women and Crime*. Thousand Oaks, CA: Sage.

Christoforidis, Alexander. 1994. "New Alternatives to the Suburb: Neo-Traditional Development." *Journal of Planning Literature*, 8(4): 429–40.

Cho, Crystall. 2013. "Parklet Boosts Local Business Sales." *KOMU 8 News* website, 3 October. Accessed 27 March 2014 at http://www.komu.com/news/parklet-boosts-local-business-sales/.

City of Oakland. 2013. "Latham Square Pilot Project." City of Oakland Agenda Report from Vitaly B. Troyan, Director, City of Oakland Public Works Agency. Accessed 31 March 2017 at https://oakland.legistar.com/LegislationDetail.aspx?ID=1343358&GUID=E3713552-A781-4700-9CAA-6BD5709ADC9F.

City Project. 2014. *The City Project* website. Accessed 22 June 2014 at http://www.cityprojectca.org/.

Ciudad de México. 2010. *Carta de la Ciudad de México por el Derecho a la Ciudad (Mexico City Charter for the Right to the City)*. Accessed 9 January 2017 at http://www.hic-al.org/documento.cfm?id_documento=1505.

Clark, Amy Sara. 2013. "Bike Corral Critics Petition to Get Parking Spot Back: Longtime Residents Call Bike Racks Part of a Gentrification Trend That Feels 'More Like a Takeover Than a Partnership.'" *Prospect Heights Patch* website. Accessed 12 January 2017 at http://patch.com/new-york/prospectheights/bike-corral-critics-petition-to-get-parking-spot-back.

Clark, Terry Nichols & Vincent Hoffmann-Martinot, eds. 1998. *The New Political Culture*. Boulder: Westview.

Cobb, Carrie L., Mary C. King, & Leopoldo Rodriguez. 2009. "Betwixt and Between: The Spectrum of Formality Revealed in the Labor Market Experiences of Mexican Migrant Workers in the United States." *Review of Radical Political Economics*, 41(3): 365–71.

Colomb, Claire. 2007. "Unpacking New Labour's 'Urban Renaissance' Agenda: Towards a Socially Sustainable Reurbanization of British Cities." *Planning Practice and Research*, 22(1): 1–27.

Condry, Rachel. 2006. "Stigmatised Women: Relatives of Serious Offenders and the Broader Impact of Gender and Crime." In *Gender and Justice: New Concepts and Approaches*, edited by F. Heidensohn, 96–120. Cullompton, UK: Willan.

Cook, Philip W. 1997. *Abused Men: The Hidden Side of Domestic Violence*. Westport, CT: Praeger.

Cooley, Charles Horton. 1909. *Social Organization: A Study of the Larger Mind*. New York: Charles Scribner's Sons.

Correal, Anne. 2009. "April Showers Bring Seed-Sewing Volunteers." *New York Times*, New York ed., 12 April, A27.

Correal, Anne. 2015. "Now Arriving in No Man's Land." *New York Times*, New York ed., 6 Dec., MB1-9.

Correia, Mark E. 2010. "Determinants of Attitudes Toward Police of Latino Immigrants and Non-Immigrants." *Journal of Criminal Justice*, 38(1): 99–107.

Corsín Jimenez, Alberto. 2014. "The Right to Infrastructure: A Prototype for Open-Source Urbanism." *Environment and Planning D: Society and Space*, 32: 342–62.

Currid, Elizabeth. 2007. *The Warhol Economy: How Fashion, Art, and Music Drive New York City*. Princeton, NJ: Princeton University Press.

Davidoff, Paul. 1965. "Advocacy and Pluralism in Planning." *Journal of the American Institute of Planners*, 31(4): 331–38.

Davidson, Mariko Mura. 2013. *Tactical Urbanism, Public Policy Reform, and 'Innovation Spotting' by Government: From Park(ing) Day to San Francisco's Parklet Program*. Master's thesis, Massachusetts Institute of Technology, Department of Urban Studies and Planning.

Davis, Mike. 1990. *City of Quartz: Excavating the Future in Los Angeles*, photographs by Robert Morrow. London: Verso.

Davis, Mike. 2001. *Magical Urbanism: Latinos Reinvent the U.S. City*. London: Verso.

Davey, Monica. 2013. "A Private Boom amid Detroit's Public Blight." *New York Times*, New York ed., 5 March, A1.

Deener, Andrew. 2012. *Venice: A Contested Bohemia in Los Angeles*. Chicago: University of Chicago Press.

Deslandes, Ann. 2013. "Exemplary Amateurism: Thoughts on DIY Urbanism." *Cultural Studies Review* 19(1): 216–27.

Deuze, Mark. 2006. "Participation, Remediation, Bricolage: Considering Principal Components of a Digital Culture." *The Information Society: An International Journal*, 22(2): 63–75.

Deuze, Mark. 2008. "The Professional Identity of Journalists in the Context of Convergence Culture." *Observatorio*, 2(4): 103–17.

Dexter, Lewis A. 1970. *Elite and Specialized Interviewing*. Evanston, IL: Northwestern University Press.

Donovan, Geoffrey H. & David T. Butry. 2010. "Trees in the City: Valuing Street Trees Portland, Oregon." *Landscape & Urban Planning*, 94: 77–83.

Donovan, Geoffrey H. & Jeffrey P. Prestemon. 2012. "The Effect of Trees on Crime in Portland, Oregon." *Environments and Behavior*, 44(1): 3–30.

Dottolo, Andrea L. & Abigail J. Stewart. 2008. "'Don't Ever Forget Now, You're a Black Man in America': Intersections of Race, Class and Gender in Encounters with the Police." *Sex Roles*, 59: 350–64.

Douglas, Gordon C. C. 2005. *The Art of Urban Warfare: The Global Urban Network of Street Art*. Global Media master's thesis, London School of Economics and Political Science.

Douglas, Gordon C. C. 2011. "DIY Urban Design, From Guerrilla Gardening to Yarn Bombing." *GOOD*, 12 April. Accessed 21 June 2012 at http://www.good.is/post/diy-urban-design-from-guerrilla-gardening-to-yarn-bombing/.

Douglas, Gordon C. C. 2012a. "Cultural Expectations and Urban Development: The Role of 'Cultural Sensitivity' and 'Cultural Sincerity' in Local Growth Politics." *Sociological Perspectives*, 55(1): 213–36.

Douglas, Gordon C. C. 2012b. "The Edge of the Island: Cultural Ideology and Neighborhood Identity at the Gentrification Frontier." *Urban Studies*, 49(16): 3579–94.

Douglas, Gordon C. C. 2014. "Do-It-Yourself Urban Design: The Social Practice of Informal 'Improvement' through Unauthorized Alteration." *City & Community*, 13(1): 5–25. (Published online 16 September 2013.)

Douglas, Gordon C. C. 2016. "The Formalities of Informal Improvement: Technical and Scholarly Knowledge at Work in Do-It-Yourself Urban Design." *City & Community*, 9(2): 117–34.

Duany, Andrés. 2014. "A Lean Means of Reinventing Our Communities." *Knight Blog: The Blog of the John S. and James L. Knight Foundation*, 19 February. Accessed 9 June 2014 at http://www.knightfoundation.org/blogs/knightblog/2014/2/19/lean-means-reinventing-communities/.

Duneier, Mitchell. 1999. *Sidewalk*. Photographs by Ovie Carter. New York: Farrar, Straus & Giroux.

Edwards, Ian. 2009. "Banksy's Graffiti: A Not-so-Simple Case of Criminal Damage?" *Journal of Criminal Law*, 73: 345–61.

Egan, Timothy. 1995. "Many Seek Security in Private Communities." *New York Times*, 3 September, A1–22.

Elet, Yvonne. 2002. "Seats of Power: The Outdoor Benches of Early Modern Florence." *Journal of the Society of Architectural Historians*, 61(4): 444–69.

Elliot, Delbert & Harwin Voss. 1974. *Delinquency and Dropout*. Lexington, MA: Lexington Books.

Epstein, Richard A. 2002. "The Allocation of the Commons: Parking on Public Roads." *Journal of Legal Studies*, 31(S2): S515–S544.

Erbacher, Eric C. 2012. "From Conflict Spaces to Contact Zones: The Contested Landscapes of Gentrification in the American Inner City." In *Contact Spaces of American Culture: Globalizing Local Phenomena*, edited by P. Eckhard, K. Rieser, & S. Schultermandl, 113–29. Vienna: Lit Verlag.

Fairbanks, Robert P. II & Richard Lloyd. 2011. "Critical Ethnography and the Neoliberal City: The US Example." *Ethnography*, 12(1): 3–11.

Fairey, Shepard. 1990. "Manifesto." *Obey* website. Accessed 14 August 2011 at http://obeygiant.com/about.

Farr, Jo-Ann H. & Carol Gordon. 1975. "A Partial Replication of Kinsey's Graffiti Study." *Journal of Sex Research*, 11(2): 158–63.

Fenton, Mark. 2012. "Community Design and Policies for Free-Range Children: Creating Environments that Support Routine Physical Activity." *Childhood Obesity*, 8(1): 44–51.

Ferrell, Jeff. 1995. "Urban Graffiti." *Youth and Society*, 27(1): 73–92.

Ferrell, Jeff. 2001. *Tearing Down the Streets: Adventures in Urban Anarchy*. New York: Palgrave.

Finn, Donovan. 2014. "DIY Urban Design: Implications for Cities." *Journal of Urbanism*, 7(4): 381–98. Published online 12 March.

Fishman, Robert, ed. 2000. *The American Planning Tradition*. Washington, DC: Woodrow Wilson Center.

Florida, Richard. 2002. *The Rise of the Creative Class: And How It's Transforming Work, Leisure, Community, and Everyday Life*. New York: Basic Books.

Florida, Richard. 2003. "The New American Dream." *Washington Monthly*, January/February, 31–37.

Florida, Richard. 2005. *Cities and the Creative Class*. New York: Routledge.

Florida, Richard. 2017. *The New Urban Crisis*. New York: Basic Books.

Foley, Donald. 1960. "British Town Planning: One Ideology or Three?" *British Journal of Sociology*, 11(3): 211–31.

Foschi, Martha. 2000. "Double Standards for Competence: Theory and Research." *Annual Review of Sociology*, 26: 21–42.

France, Julie. 2002. "Glass War." *Guardian*, 17 November.

Franklin, Anderson J. & Nancy Boyd-Franklin. 2000. "Invisibility Syndrome: A Clinical Model Towards Understanding the Effects of Racism Upon African American Males." *American Journal of Orthopsychiatry*, 70(1): 33–41.

Franklin, Anderson J., Nancy Boyd-Franklin & Sharonda Kelly. 2006. "Racism and Invisibility: Race-Related Stress, Emotional Abuse, and Pscyhological Trauma for People of Color." *American Journal of Drug and Alcohol Abuse*, 6: 9–30.

Fried, Marc. 2000. "Continuities and Discontinuities of Place." *Journal of Environmental Psychology*, 20(3): 193–205.

Friedman, Milton. 1962. *Capitalism and Freedom*. Chicago: University of Chicago Press.

Frug, Gerald. 1999. *City Making: Building Communities without Building Walls*. Princeton, NJ: Princeton University Press.

Furness, Zack. 2010. *One Less Car: Bicycling and the Politics of Automobility*. Philadelphia: Temple University Press.

Gabbidon, S. L. & G. E. Higgins. 2009. "The Role of Race/Ethnicity and Race Relations on Public Opinion Related to the Treatment of Blacks by the Police." *Police Quarterly*, 12: 102–15.

Gabbidon, S. L. & H. Taylor Greene. 2009. *Race and Crime*, 2nd ed. Thousand Oaks, CA: Sage.

Gaffikin, Frank & David C. Perry. 2012. "The Contemporary Urban Condition: Understanding the Globalizing City as Informal, Contested, and Anchored." *Urban Affairs Review*, 48(5): 701–30.

Galofaro, Claire & Juliet Linerman. 2017. "Immigrants Wait in Fear; Trump Takes Credit." *Associated Press*, 12 February. Accessed 19 February 2017 at http://hosted2.ap.org/APDEFAULT/3d281c11a96b4ad082fe88aa0db04305/Article_2017-02-12-US-Immigration-Raids/id-5727609edae347c58f17ab907f805a09.

Gans, Herbert J. 1961. "The Balanced Community: Homogeneity or Heterogeneity in Residential Areas." *Journal of the American Institute of Planners*, 27(3): 176–84.

Gans, Herbert J. 1968. "Planning for the Everyday Life and Problems of Suburban and New Town Residents." In *People and Plans,* edited by H. J. Gans, 183–201.

Gans, Lydia. 2011. "Who Has the Right to Remove Benches at Bus Stops? A Bus Stop Bench Story." *Berkeley Daily Planet*, 3 October. Accessed 2 January 2014 at http://www.berkeleydailyplanet.com/issue/2011-10-03/article/38508?headline=Who-has-the-Right-to-Remove-Benches-At-Bus-Stops-A-Bus-Stop-Bench-Story--By-Lydia-Gans.

Ganz, Nicholas. 2004. *Graffiti World: Street Art from Five Continents*. New York: Harry N. Abrams.

Garcetti, Eric. 2014. "Mayor's Message." *People St.* website. Accessed 3 March 2014 at http://peoplest.lacity.org/mayors-message/.

Gelsthorpe, Loraine. 1989. *Sexism and the Female Offender: An Organizational Analysis.* Aldershot, UK: Gower.

Ghaziani, Amin. 2014. *There Goes the Gayborhood?* Princeton, NJ: Princeton University Press.

Gibbons, Don & Manzer J. Griswold. 1957. "Sex Differences among Juvenile Court Referrals." *Sociology and Social Research,* 42: 106–10.

Gibbons, Steve. 2004. "The Costs of Urban Property Crime." *Economic Journal,* 114: 441–63.

Glaeser, Edward. 2011. *Triumph of the City: How Our Greatest Invention Makes Us Richer, Smarter, Greener, Healthier, and Happier.* London: Penguin.

Glass, Ruth. 1956. "The Evaluation of Planning: Some Sociological Considerations." *International Social Science Journal,* 11(3): 393–409.

Gleeson, Brendan. 2012. "Critical Commentary—The Urban Age: Paradox and Prospect." *Urban Studies,* 49(5): 931–43.

Gonick, Sophie. 2015. "Interrogating Madrid's 'Slum of Shame': Urban Expansion, Race, and Place-Based Activisms in the Cañada Real Galiana." *Antipode,* 47(5): 1224–42.

Good, Max & Julien de Benedictis. *Vigilante Vigilante: The Battle for Expression.* DVD. Directed by M. Good. USA: Open Ranch Productions, 2011. http://www.vigilantefilm.com/.

Goodman, Penelope J. 2007. *The Roman City and Its Periphery.* London: Routledge.

Goodman, Robert. 1971. *After the Planners.* New York: Touchstone.

Goodyear, Sara. 2010. "Taming the Mean Streets: A Talk with NYC Transportation Chief Janette Sadik-Khan." *Grist* website, 22 December. Accessed 30 January 2017 at http://grist.org/article/2010-12-21-taming-the-mean-streets-of-new-york-a-talk-with-nyc-dot/.

Goodyear, Sarah. 2011. "Bike Lane Backlash, Even in Portland." *Citylab,* 20 September. Accessed 29 May 2014 at http://www.citylab.com/commute/2011/09/portland-bike-lanes-open-racial-wounds/138/.

Gotham, Kevin Fox & Miriam Greenberg. 2014. *Crisis Cities: Disaster and Redevelopment in New York and New Orleans.* Oxford: Oxford University Press.

Gramsci, Antonio. 1971. *Selections from the Prison Notebooks,* translated by Q. Hoare & G. N. Smith. New York: International.

Granzow, Kara & Amber Dean. 2007. "Revanchism in the Canadian West: Gentrification and the Resettlement in a Prairie City." *TOPIA,* 18: 89–106.

Grazian, David. 2003. *Blue Chicago: The Search for Authenticity in Urban Blues Clubs.* Chicago: University of Chicago Press.

Greenberg, Miriam. 2008. *Branding New York: How a City in Crisis Was Sold to the World.* New York: Routledge.

Greif, Mark. 2010. "Preface." In *What Was the Hipster?,* edited by M. Greif, K. Ross, & D. Tortorici, vii–xvii. New York: n+1 Foundation.

Grossman, Andrew. 2010. "MTA to Lay Off 250 Subway-Station Agents." *Wall Street Journal* website, 8 May. Accessed 19 March 2013 at http://online.wsj.com/news/articles/SB10001424052748704858104575232852656303036.

Groves, Martha. 2014. "Agreement Reached in Malibu Beach Access Dispute." *Los Angeles Times* website, 18 December 2014. Accessed 8 January 2015 at http://www.latimes.com/local/lanow/la-me-In-paradise-cove-agreement-20141218-story.html.

Gustafson, Per. 2001. "Meanings of Place: Everyday Experience and Theoretical Conceptualizations." *Journal of Environmental Psychology*, 21(1): 5–16.

Hajnal, Zoltan & Jessica Trounstine. 2014. "Identifying and Understanding Perceived Inequities in Local Politics." *Political Research Quarterly*, 67(1): 56–70. (Originally published online 7 May 2013.)

Hammond, John. L. 2013. "The Significance of Space in Occupy Wall Street." *Interface*, 5(2): 499–524.

Hampton, Bruce & David Cole. 1988. *Soft Paths: How to Enjoy the Wilderness without Harming It*. Harrisburg, PA: Stackpole Books.

Hardt, Michael & Antonio Negri. 2000. *Empire*. Cambridge, MA: Harvard University Press.

Harris, Anthony. 1977. "Sex and Theories of Deviance." *American Sociological Review*, 42: 3–16.

Harris, David A. 1999. "Driving While Black: Racial Profiling on Our Nation's Highways: American Civil Liberties Union Special Report." *ACLU* website. Accessed 2 April 2014 at https://www.aclu.org/racial-justice/driving-while-black-racial-profiling-our-nations-highways.

Hartman, Chester. 1984. "The Right to Stay Put." In *Land Reform, American Style*, edited by C. Geisler & F. Popper, 302–18. Totawa, NJ: Rowman and Allanheld.

Harvey, David. 1976. *Social Justice and the City*. Baltimore, MD: Johns Hopkins University Press.

Harvey, David. 1982. *The Limits to Capital*. Oxford: Blackwell.

Harvey, David. 1997. "The New Urbanism and the Communitarian Trap." *Harvard Design Magazine*, Winter/Spring: 68–69.

Harvey, David. 2005. *A Brief History of Neoliberalism*. Oxford: Oxford University Press.

Harvey, David. 2006. *Spaces of Global Capitalism: A Theory of Uneven Geographical Development*. London: Verso.

Harvey, David. 2007. "Neoliberalism as Creative Destruction." *Annals of the American Academy of Political and Social Science*, 610: 22–44.

Harvey, David. 2008. "The Right to the City." *New Left Review*, 53: 23–40.

Hawthorne, Christopher. 2014. "Latino Urbanism Influences a Los Angeles in Flux." *Los Angeles Times* website, 6 December. Accessed 18 July 2017 at http://www.latimes.com/entertainment/arts/la-et-cm-latino-immigration-architecture-20141206-story.html.

Healey, Patrick. 1977. "The Sociology of Urban Transportation Planning: A Sociological Perspective." In *Urban Transport Economics,* edited by D. Hersher, 199–227. Cambridge: Cambridge University Press.

Heavy Trash. 2004. "Aqua Line." *Heavy Trash* website. Accessed 13 October, 2012 at http://heavytrash.blogspot.com/2005/04/aqua-line.html.

Heavy Trash. 2005. "Heavy Trash Installs Viewing Platforms at Los Angeles Gated Communities." *Heavy Trash* website. Accessed 24 March 2013 at http://heavytrash.blogspot.com/.

Henderson, Jason. 2011. "Level of Service: The Politics of Configuring Streets in San Francisco." *Journal of Transport Geography*, 19(6): 1138–44.

Heidensohn, Frances & Marisa Silvestri. 2012. "Gender and Crime." In *The Oxford Handbook of Criminology*, 5th ed., edited by M. Maguire, R. Morgan, & R. Reiner, 336–69. Oxford: Oxford University Press.

Higgins, Michelle. 2014. "No MetroCard Needed: Bikes Change Your Brooklyn Apartment Hunt." *New York Times*, New York ed., 25 May, E1.

Ho, Cathy Lang (Commissioner). 2012. *Spontaneous Interventions: Design Actions for the Common Good*, exhibition. United States Pavilion, 13th Venice International Biennale of Architecture, Venice, August–November.

Ho, Cathy Lang & Gordon Douglas, eds. 2012. *Spontaneous Interventions: Design Actions for the Common Good*. Washington, DC: Architect/Hanley Wood.

Hoffmann, Melody L. 2015. "Recruiting People Like You: Socioeconomic Sustainability in Minneapolis's Bicycle Infrastructure." In *(In)Complete Streets: Processes, Practices, and Possibilities*, edited by S. Zavestoski & J. Agyeman, 139–53. New York: Routledge.

Hoffmann, Melody L. 2016. *Bike Lanes Are White Lanes: Bicycle Advocacy and Urban Planning*. Lincoln: University of Nebraska Press.

Hoffmann, Melody L. & Adonia Lugo. 2014. "Who Is 'World Class'? Transportation Justice and Bicycle Policy." *Urbanites*, 4(1): 45–61.

Hooke, Roger LeB. 1994. "On the Efficacy of Humans as Geomorphic Agents." *GSA Today*, 4(9): 217, 224–25.

Hooke, Roger LeB. 2000. "On the History of Humans as Geomorphic Agents." *Geology*, 28(9): 843–46.

Horowitz, Ruth & Ann Pottieger. 1991. "Gender Bias in Juvenile Justice Handling of Seriously Crime-Involved Youth." *Journal of Research in Crime and Delinquency*, 28: 75–100.

Hou, Jeffrey, ed. 2010. *Insurgent Public Space: Guerrilla Urbanism and the Remaking of Contemporary Cities*. New York: Routledge.

Hou, Jeffrey & Isami Kinoshita. 2007. "Bridging Community Differences through Informal Processes: Reexamining Participatory Planning in Seattle and Matsudo." *Journal of Planning Education and Research*, 26(3): 301–13.

Hoyt, Lorlene. 2004. "Collecting Private Funds for Safer Public Spaces: An Empirical Examination of the Business Improvement District Concept." *Environment and Planning B: Planning and Design*, 31: 367–80.

Hoyt, Lorlene. 2005. "Planning through Compulsory Commercial Clubs: Business Improvement Districts." *Economic Affairs*, 25(4): 24–27.

Hunter, Albert. 1974. *Symbolic Communities: The Persistence and Change of Chicago's Local Communities*. Chicago: University of Chicago Press.

Huo, Yuen J. & Tom R. Tyler. 2000. *How Different Ethnic Groups React to Legal Authority*. San Francisco: Public Policy Institute of California.

Hussain, Sophia. 2013. "Latham Square Marks Oakland's Latest Foray into Pop-Up Public Space." *Oakland Local* website, 19 August. Accessed 5 May 2014 at http://oaklandlocal.com/2013/08/latham-square-marks-oaklands-latest-foray-into-pop-up-public-space/.

Hyra, Derek. 2008. *The New Urban Renewal: The Economic Transformation of Harlem and Bronzeville*. Chicago: University of Chicago Press.

Hyra, Derek. 2017. *Race, Class, and Politics in the Cappuccino City*. Chicago: University of Chicago Press.

Idov, Michael. 2010. "Clash of the Bearded Ones: Hipsters, Hasids, and the Williamsburg Street." *New York Magazine* website, 11 April. Accessed 14 May 2014 at http://nymag.com/realestate/neighborhoods/2010/65356/.

Innes, Judith E., Sarah Connick & David Booher. 2007. "Informality as a Planning Strategy: Collaborative Water Management in the CALFED Bay-Delta Program." *Journal of the American Planning Association*, 73(2): 195–210.

Iseki, Hiroyuki & Brian D. Taylor. 2010. "Style versus Service? An Analysis of User Perceptions of Transit Stops and Stations." *Journal of Public Transportation*, 13(3): 23–48.

Iseki, Hiroyuki, Michael Smart, Brian D. Taylor, & Allison Yoh. 2012. "Thinking Outside the Bus." *Access*, 40: 9–15.

Iveson, Kurt. 2013. "Cities within the City: Do-It-Yourself Urbanism and the Right to the City." *International Journal of Urban and Regional Research*, 37(3): 941–56.

Jacobs, Jane. 1961. *The Death and Life of Great American Cities*. New York: Random House.

JCDecaux. 2010. "Advertising in Los Angeles." *JCDecaux North American, Outdoor Advertising* website. Accessed 28 January 2013 at http://www.jcdecauxna.com/ street-furniture/los-angeles/advertising-los-angeles.

JCDecaux. 2013. "Street Furniture Advertising." *JCDecaux North America, Outdoor Advertising* website. Accessed 19 March 2013 at http://www.jcdecauxna.com/ street-furniture/street-furniture-advertising.

Johnson, Chip. 2014. "Buddha Seems to Bring Tranquility to Oakland Neighborhood." SFGate website, 15 September. Accessed 18 July 2017 at http://www.sfgate. com/bayarea/johnson/article/Buddha-seems-to-bring-tranquillity-to-Oakland-5757592.php.

Katz, Jack. 2008. *Seductions of Crime: Moral and Sensual Attractions in Doing Evil*. New York: Basic Books.

Katz, Peter. 1994. *The New Urbanism: Toward an Architecture of Community*. New York: McGraw-Hill Education.

Keating, W. Dennis & Norman Krumholz. 2000. "Neighborhood Planning." *Journal of Planning Education and Research*, 20(1): 111–14.

Keizer, Kees, Siegwart Lindenberg, & Linda Steg. 2008. "The Spreading of Disorder." *Science* 322(5908):1681–85.

Keller, Lisa. 2009. *Triumph of Order: Democracy and Public Space in New York and London*. New York: Columbia University Press.

Khan, Shamus R. 2011. *Privilege: The Making of an Adolescent Elite at St. Paul's School*. Princeton, NJ: Princeton University Press.

Kidder, Jeffrey. 2006. "'It's the Job that I Love': Bike Messengers and Edgework." *Sociological Forum*, 21(1): 31–54.

Kidder, Jeffrey. 2009. "Appropriating the City: Space, Theory, and Bike Messengers." *Theory and Society*, 38(3): 307–28.

Kidder, Jeffrey. 2011. *Urban Flow: Bike Messengers and the City*. Ithaca, NY: ILR Press.

Kidder, Jeffrey. 2012. "Parkour, the Affective Appropriation of Urban Space, and the Real/Virtual Dialectic." *City & Community*, 11(3): 229–53.

Kimmelman, Michael. 2010. "D.I.Y. Culture." *New York Times*, New York ed., 18 April, AR1, 19.

Kingfisher, Catherine & Jeff Maskovsky. 2008. "Introduction: The Limits of Neoliberalism." *Critique of Anthropology*, 28(2): 115–126.

Kinsey, Alfred C., Wardell B. Pomoroy, Clyde E. Martin, & Paul H. Gebhard. 1953. *Sexual Behavior in the Human Female*. Philadelphia: Saunders.

Klanten, Robert, Sven Ehmann, & Matthias Hubner, eds. 2010. *Urban Interventions: Personal Projects in Public Spaces*. Berlin: Gestalten.

Klayko, Brenden. 2012. "Talking Tactical Urbanism." *Architect's Newspaper* website, 18 June. Accessed 22 May 2014 at http://archpaper.com/news/articles. asp?id=6120.

Koeppel, Dan. 2009. "LA's Department of DIY is Back!" *Dan Koeppel's Blog* website, 18 September. Accessed May 15 2012 at www.bananabook.org/wordpress/archives/806.

Kremer, Peleg, Zoé A. Hamstead, & Timon McPhearson. 2013. "A Social-Ecological Assessment of Vacant Lots in New York City." *Landscape and Urban Planning*, 120: 218–33.

Krivý, Maroš. 2013. "Don't Plan! The Use of the Notion of 'Culture' in Transforming Obsolete Industrial Space." *International Journal of Urban and Regional Research*, 37(5): 1724–46.

Krohn, Marvin, James Curry, & Shirley Nelson-Kilger. 1983. "Is Chivalry Dead? An Analysis of Changes in Police Dispositions of Males and Females." *Criminology*, 21(3): 417–37.

Kuo, Frances E. & William C. Sullivan. 2001. "Environment and Crime in the Inner City: Does Vegetation Reduce Crime?" *Environment and Behavior*, 33(3): 343–67.

Kwan, Samantha. 2010. "Navigating Public Spaces: Gender, Race, and Body Privilege in Everyday Life." *Feminist Formations*, 22(2): 144–66.

Kwan, Samantha & Mary Nell Trautner. 2009. "Beauty Work: Individual and Institutional Rewards, the Reproduction of Gender, and Questions of Agency." *Sociology Compass*, 3(1): 49–71.

Kwon, Miwon. 2002. *One Place after Another: Site-Specific Art and Locational Identity*. Cambridge, MA: MIT Press.

LA Bureau of Street Services. 2013. "Los Angeles Coordinated Street Furniture Program." *City of Los Angeles Bureau of Street Services* website. Accessed 27 January 2017 at http://bss.lacity.org/Engineering/pdfs/background.pdf.

LA Dept. of Transportation. 2014. "About People St." *People St.* website. Accessed 3 March 2014 at http://peoplest.lacity.org/about/.

Lacy, Susan, ed. 1995. *Mapping the Terrain: New Genre Public Art*. Seattle: Bay Press.

Lambert-Beatty, Carrie. 2010. "Fill in the Blank: Culture Jamming and the Advertising of Agency." *New Directions for Youth Development*, 125: 99–112.

Lefebvre, Henri. 1968. *Le Droit à la ville*. Paris: Editions du Seuil.

Lefebvre, Henri. 1989 (1959). *La Somme et le reste*. Paris: Méridiens Klincksieck.

Lefebvre, Henri. 2008a (1947). *Critique of Everyday Life*, Vol. I: *Introduction*, 2nd ed., translated by J. Moore. London: Verso.

Lefebvre, Henri. 2008b (1961). *Critique of Everyday Life*, Vol. II: *Foundations for a Sociology of the Everyday*, translated by J. Moore. London: Verso.

Lefebvre, Henri. 2008c (1981). *Critique of Everyday Life*, Vol. III: *From Modernity to Modernism*, translated by G. Elliot. London: Verso.

Lefebvre, Henri. 2009a (1966). "Theoretical Problems of *Autogestion*." Translated by G. Moore, N. Brenner, & S. Elden. In *State, Space, World: Selected Essays*, edited by N. Brenner & S. Elden, 138–152. Minneapolis: University of Minnesota Press.

Lefebvre, Henri. 2009b (1979). "Space: Social Product and Use Value." Translated by J. W. Freiberg. In *State, Space, World: Selected Essays*, edited by N. Brenner & S. Elden, 185–195. Minneapolis: University of Minnesota Press.

Leland, John. 2004. *Hip: The History*. New York: Harper Collins.

Lepeska, David. 2012. "When We're All Urban Planners: Making a Virtual Village to Create a Better City." *Next City—Forefront* website, 27 September. Accessed 1 November 2012 at http://nextcity.org/forefront/view/when-were-all-urban-planners.

Lerner, Jonathan. 2012. "Street Makeovers Put New Spin on the Block." *Pacific Standard* website, 16 January. Accessed 21 June 2012 at http://www.psmag.com/environment/street-makeovers-put-new-spin-on-the-block-38926/.

Levy, John M. 2011. *Contemporary Urban Planning*, 9th ed. Boston: Longman.

Lewis, Seth C. 2012. "The Tension Between Professional Control and Open Participation: Journalism and Its Boundaries." *Information, Communication, and Society*, 15(6): 836–66.

Lin, C. J. 2012. "'No Stopping' Sign Placed in Front of Studio City Red Curb that Someone Keeps Painting Gray." *Los Angeles Daily News* website, 25 April. Accessed 27 January 2014 at http://www.dailynews.com/20120426/no-stopping-sign-placed-in-front-of-studio-city-red-curb-that-someone-keeps-painting-gray.

Lindell, Ilda. 2010. "Between Exit and Voice: Informality and the Spaces of Popular Agency." *African Studies Quarterly*, 11(2 & 3): 1–11.

Linthicum, Kate. 2011. "The Bus Bench Doesn't Sit Here Anymore." *Los Angeles Times* website, 12 August. Accessed 24 April 2014 at http://articles.latimes.com/2011/aug/12/local/la-me-bus-benches-20110812.

Lloyd, Richard. 2006. *Neo-Bohemia: Art & Commerce in the Postindustrial City*. New York: Routledge.

Lloyd, Richard & Terry Nichols Clark. 2001. "The City as an Entertainment Machine." *Critical Perspectives on Urban Redevelopment*, 6: 357–78.

Loftus-Farren, Zoe. 2011. "Tent Cities: An Interim Solution to Homelessness and Affordable Housing Shortages in the United States." *California Law Review*, 99(4): 1037–81.

Logan, John & Harvey Molotch. 2007 (1987). *Urban Fortunes: The Political Economy of Place*, 20th Anniversary ed. Berkeley: University of California Press.

Logan, John R. & Mark Schneider. 1981. "The Stratification of Metropolitan Suburbs, 1960–1970." *American Sociological Review*, 46(2): 175–86.

Loukaitou-Sideris, Anastasia. 1993. "Privatization of Public Open Space: The Los Angeles Experience." *Town Planning Review*, 64(2): 139–67.

Loukaitou-Sideris, Anastasia & Trinib Banerjee. 1993. "The Negotiated Plaza: Design and Development of Corporate Open Space in Downtown Los Angeles and San Francisco." *Journal of Planning Education and Research*, 13(1): 11–12.

Low, Setha, Dana Taplin, & Suzanne Scheld. 2005. *Rethinking Urban Parks: Public Space and Cultural Diversity*. Austin: University of Texas Press.

Low, Setha. 2006. "How Private Interests Take Over Public Space: Zoning, Taxes, and Incorporation in Gated Communities." In *The Politics of Public Space*, edited by S. Low & N. Smith, 81–104. New York: Routledge.

Lubitow, Amy & Thaddeus R. Miller. 2013. "Contesting Sustainability: Bikes, Race, and Politics in Portlandia." *Environmental Justice*, 6(4): 121–25.

Lugo, Adonia. 2010. "From Observer to Ethnographer: Flânerie on a Bicycle." Paper presented at Urbanity on the Move: Planning, Mobility, and Displacement workshop, University of California, Irvine, 21 May.

Lugo, Adonia. 2012a. "Planning for Diverse Use/ers: Ethnographic Research on Bikes, Bodies, and Public Space in L.A." *Kroeber Anthropological Society*, 101(1): 49–65.

Lugo, Adonia. 2012b. "Bicycling and Ethnographic Access." *Savage Minds: Notes and Queries in Anthropology* blog, 1 November. Accessed 17 June 2014 at http://savageminds.org/2012/11/01/bicycling-and-ethnographic-access/.

Lugo, Adonia. 2013. "CicLAvia and Human Infrastructure in Los Angeles: Ethnographic Experiments in Equitable Bike Planning." *Journal of Transport Geography*, 30: 202–7.

Lundman, Richard J. & Robert L. Kaufman. 2003. "Driving While Black: Effects of Race, Ethnicity, and Gender on Citizen Self-Reports of Traffic Stops and Police Actions." *Criminology*, 41(1): 195–220.

Lydon, Mike. 2011. *Tactical Urbanism Handbook*, vol. 1. Published online 23 March. Accessed 22 June 2012 at http://www.scribd.com/khawarzad/d/51354266-Tactical-Urbanism-Volume-1.

Lydon, Mike. 2012. *Tactical Urbanism: Short-Term Action, Long-Term Change*, vol. 2. Published online 2 March. Accessed 1 March 2014 at http://issuu.com/streetplanscollaborative/docs/tactical_urbanism_vol_2_final.

Lydon, Mike & Anthony Garcia. 2015. *Tactical Urbanism: Short-Term Action for Long-Term Change*. Washington, DC: Island.

Main, Bill & Gail Greet Hannah. 2009. *Site Furnishings: A Complete Guide to the Planning, Selection and Use of Landscape Furniture and Amenities*. Hoboken, NJ: John Wiley.

Manco, Tristan. 2004. *Street Logos*. New York: Thames & Hudson.

Marcuse, Peter. 2014. "Reading the Right to the City." *City*, 18(1): 4–9.

Markusen, Ann & Anne Gadwa. 2010. *Creative Placemaking*. White paper for the Mayors' Institute on City Design. Washington: National Endowment for the Arts.

Marshall, Catherine. 1984. "Elites, Bureaucrats, Ostriches, and Pussycats: Managing Research in Policy Settings." *Anthropology and Education Quarterly*, 15(3): 235–51.

Martens, China. 2010. "Hampden's Bus Benches, Removed Because of Loiterers, Missed by Riders." *Baltimore Brew* website, 3 March. Accessed 2 January 2014 at http://www.baltimorebrew.com/2012/03/03/hampdens-bus-benches-removed-because-of-loiterers-missed-by-riders/.

Massey, Jonathan & Brett Snyder. 2012. "Occupying Wall Street: Places and Spaces of Political Action." *Places*, September 2012. Accessed 20 October 2016 at https://placesjournal.org/article/occupying-wall-street-places-and-spaces-of-political-action/.

Maus, Jonathan. 2011. "Meeting on Williams Project Turns into Discussion of Race, Gentrification." *Bike Portland* website, 21 July. Accessed 18 July 2017 at https://bikeportland.org/2011/07/21/racism-rears-its-head-on-williams-project-56633.

McCarny, Laura. 2014. "Latham Square Outcomes Show Flaws in Oakland City Planning." *Oakland Local* website, 8 January. Accessed 8 February 2017 at http://oaklandlocal.com/2014/01/latham-square-outcomes-show-flaws-in-oakland-city-planning/.

McCarty, Meghan & Aaron Mendelson. 2016. "Hundreds of LA Bus Shelters Go Unbuilt, Millions in Promised Revenue Evaporate under City Contract." *KPCC / SCPR.org* website, 2 May. Accessed 26 January 2017 at https://www.scpr.org/news/2016/05/02/60085/hundreds-of-la-bus-shelters-go-unbuilt-millions-in/.

McCullen, Grace. 2008. *Why Are All the White Kids Sitting Together at the Farmers Market?: Whiteness in the Davis Farmers Market and Alternative Agrifood Movements*. Master's thesis, University of California at Davis.

McFarlane, Colin. 2012. "Rethinking Informality: Politics, Crisis, and the City." *Planning Theory & Practice*, 13(1): 89–108.

McIntosh, Peggy. 1989. "White Privilege: Unpacking the Invisible Knapsack." *Peace and Freedom*, July/August: 9–10.

Mehaffy, Michael W. 2008. "Generative Methods in Urban Design: A Progress Assessment." *Journal of Urbanism: International Research on Placemaking and Urban Sustainability*, 1(1): 57–75.

Mehta, Vikas. 2007. "Lively Streets: Determining Environmental Characteristics to Support Social Behavior." *Journal of Planning Education and Research*, 27(2): 165–87.

Menjivar, Cecilia & Cynthia Bejarano. 2004. "Latino Immigrants' Perceptions of Crime and Police Authorities in the United States: A Case Study from the Phoenix Metropolitan Area." *Ethnic and Racial Studies*, 27: 120–48.

Merrifield, Andy. 2006. *Henri Lefebvre: A Critical Introduction*. New York: Routledge.

Michelson, Michelle R. 2003. "The Corrosive Effect of Acculturation: How Mexican Americans Lose Political Trust." *Social Science Quarterly*, 84: 918–33.

Michelson, Michelle R. 2007. "All Roads Lead to Rust: How Acculturation Erodes Latino Immigrant Trust in Government." *Aztlán: A Journal of Chicano Studies*, 32: 21–46.

Mirowski, Philip. 2013. Never Let a Serious Crisis Go to Waste: How Neoliberalism Survived the Financial Meltdown. London and New York: Verso.

Mitter, Siddhartha. 2009. "Bed-Stuy Meadow." *WNYC News*, WNYC, New York, 13 April. Accessed 13 March 2014 at http://www.wnyc.org/story/74769-bed-stuy-meadow/.

Mollenkopf, John H. 1983. *The Contested City*. Princeton, NJ: Princeton University Press.

Molotch, Harvey. 1976. "The City as a Growth Machine: Toward a Political Economy of Place." *American Sociological Review*, 82(2): 309–32.

Molotch, Harvey. 2012. *Against Security: How We Go Wrong at Airports, Subways, and Other Sites of Ambiguous Danger*. Princeton, NJ: Princeton University Press.

Molotch, Harvey & Noah McClain. 2003. "Dealing with Urban Terror: Heritages of Control, Varieties of Intervention, Strategies of Research." *International Journal of Urban and Regional Research*, 27(3): 679–98.

Monahan, Thomas. 1970. "Police Dispositions of Juvenile Offenders." *Phylon*, 31: 91–107.

Montgomery, Charles. 2013. *Happy City: Transforming Our Lives through Urban Design*. New York: Farrar, Straus and Giroux.

Moore, Mandy & Leanne Prain. 2009. *Yarn Bombing: The Art of Crochet and Knit Graffiti*. Vancouver, BC: Arsenal Pulp Press.

Moran, Joe. 2005. *Reading the Everyday*. New York: Taylor & Francis.

Morand, David A. 1995. "The Role of Behavioral Formality and Informality in the Enactment of Bureaucratic versus Organic Organizations." *Academy of Management Review*, 20(4): 831–72.

Moss, Jeremiah. 2016. "Controlling Astor Place." *Jeremiah's Vanishing New York* blog, 12 October. Accessed 30 January 2017 at http://vanishingnewyork.blogspot.com/2016/10/controlling-astor-place.html.

Mukhija, Vinit & Anastasia Loukaitou-Sideris, eds. 2014. *The Informal American City: Beyond Taco Trucks and Day Labor*. Cambridge, MA: MIT Press.

Namako, Tom. 2010. "MTA Approves Massive Service Cuts." *New York Post* website, 24 March. Accessed 19 March 2013 at http://nypost.com/2010/03/24/mta-approves-massive-service-cuts/.

Nettler, Jonathan. 2012. "Top Planning Trends of 2011–2012," *Planetizen* website, 27 February. Accessed 9 March 2015 at http://www.planetizen.com/node/54838.

Nevius, C. W. 2015. "Guerrilla War against Cyclists in Woodside Is Wrong Tack." *San Francisco Chronicle* website, 14 October. Accessed 13 February 2016 at http://www.sfchronicle.com/bayarea/nevius/article/Guerrilla-war-against-cyclists-in-Woodside-is-6571397.php.

New York Civil Liberties Union. 2013. *Stop and Frisk 2012—NYCLU Briefing*. New York: New York Civil Liberties Union. Accessed 9 April 2014 at http://www.nyclu.org/files/releases/2012_Report_NYCLU.pdf.

Newman, Peter. 1998. "From Symbolic Gesture to the Mainstream: Next Steps in Local Urban Sustainability." *Local Environment: International Journal of Justice and Sustainability*, 3(3): 299–311.

Nicholas, David. 1997. *The Growth of the Medieval City: From Late Antiquity to the Early Fourteenth Century*. London & New York: Longman.

Nicol, Jake. 2014. "Latham Square Set to Re-Open Two-Way Traffic." *Oakland North* website, 16 January. Accessed 8 February 2014 at http://oaklandnorth.net/2014/01/16/latham-square-set-to-reopen-two-way-traffic/.

Norton, Peter D. 2008. *Fighting Traffic: The Dawn of the Motor Age in the American City*. Cambridge, MA: MIT Press.

Nossiter, Adam. 2013. "In Nigeria's Largest City, Homeless Are Paying the Price of Progress." *New York Times*, late ed., 2 March, A4–A6.

NYC Dept. of Environmental Protection. 2013. "Department of Environmental Protection Issues Safety Alert on Opening Fire Hydrants," press release, *NYC Dept. of Environmental Protection* website, 8 July. Accessed 3 April 2014 at http://www.nyc.gov/html/dep/html/press_releases/13-075pr.shtml#.Uz00avldV8E+.

NYC Department of City Planning. 2013. *MapPLUTO* dataset. Accessed 15 May 2014 at http://www.nyc.gov/html/dcp/html/bytes/applbyte.shtml#pluto.

NYC Dept. of Transportation. 2014. "Public Plazas." *NYC Dept. of Transportation* website. Accessed 27 March 2014 at http://www.nyc.gov/html/dot/html/pedestrians/public-plazas.shtml.

NYC Parks. 2014. "Hattie Carthan Garden." *NYC Parks* website. Accessed 20 May 2014 at http://www.nycgovparks.org/about/history/historical-signs/listings?id=11891.

Ocejo, Richard. 2011. "The Early Gentrifier: Weaving a Nostalgia Narrative on the Lower East Side." *City and Community*, 10(3): 285–310.

Orlov, Steve. 2012. "City Controller Says L.A. Lost 23.1M on Bus Stop Ads." *Los Angeles Daily News* website, 12 January. Accessed 27 January at http://www.dailynews.com/breakingnews/ci_19732563.

Ostrander, Susan. 1984. *Women of the Upper Class*. Philadelphia: Temple University Press.

Ostrander, Susan A. 1993. "Surely You're Not in This Just to Be Helpful. Access, Rapport, and Interviews in Three Studies of Elites." *Journal of Contemporary Ethnography*, 22(1): 7–27.

Pagano, Celeste B. 2013. "DIY Urbanism: Property and Process in Grassroots City Building." *Marquette Law Review*, 97(2): 335–89

Page, Helan & R. Brooke Thomas. 1994. "White Public Space and the Construction of White Privilege in U.S. Health Care: Fresh Concepts and a New Model of Analysis." *Medical Anthropology Quarterly*, 8(1): 109–16.

Pallares-Barbera, Montserrat, Anna Badia, & Jordi Duch. 2011. "Cerdà and Barcelona: The Need for a New City and Service Provision." *Urbani izziv*, 22(2): 122–36.

Parkin, Stephen & Ross Coomber. 2009. "Value in the Visual: On Public Injecting, Visual Methods and Their Potential for Informing Policy (and Change)." *Methodological Innovations Online*, 4(2): 21–36.

Partizaning. 2012. *Partizaning: Participatory Urban Planning* website. Accessed 21 June 2012 at http://eng.partizaning.org/.

Patillo, Mary. 2007. *Black on the Block: The Politics of Race and Class in the City*. Chicago: University of Chicago Press.

Patillo-McCoy, Mary. 1999. *Black Picket Fences: Privilege and Peril among the Black Middle Class*. Chicago: University of Chicago Press.

Peck, Jamie. 2005. "Struggling with the Creative Class." *International Journal of Urban and Regional Research*, 29(4): 740–70.

Peck, Jamie. 2010. "Zombie Neoliberalism and the Ambidextrous State." *Theoretical Criminology*, 14(1):104–10.

Pells, Richard H. 1989. *The Liberal Mind in a Conservative Age: American Intellectuals in the 1940s and 1950s*. Middletown, CT: Wesleyan University Press.

Perl, Larry. 2010. "Loitering a 'Royal' Pain on the Avenue in Hampden." *Baltimore Messenger* website, 25 March. Accessed 2 January 2014 at http://archives.explorebaltimorecounty.com/news/105268/loitering-royal-pain-hampden/.

Petroski, Henry. 1995. *Engineers of Dreams: Great Bridge Builders and the Spanning of America*. New York: Alfred A. Knopf.

Phillips, Susan A. 1999. *Wallbangin': Graffiti and Gangs in L.A.* Chicago: University of Chicago Press.

Pickerill, Jenny & Paul Chatterton. 2006. "Notes towards Autonomous Geographies: Creation, Resistance and Self-Management as Survival Tactics." *Progress in Human Geography,* 30(6): 730–46.

Pink, Sarah. 2004. "Applied Visual Anthropology Social Intervention, Visual Methodologies, and Anthropology Theory." *Visual Anthropology Review*, 20(1): 3–16.

Pojani, Dorina. 2008. "Santa Monica's Third Street Promenade: The Failure and Resurgence of a Downtown Pedestrian Mall." *Urban Design International*, 13: 141–55.

Portney, Kent E. & Jeffrey M. Berry. 1997. "Mobilizing Minority Communities: Social Capital and Participation in Urban Neighborhoods." *American Behavioral Scientist*, 40(5): 632–44.

Pristin, Terry. 2010. "In Times Square, at Least, Retailing Is Booming." *New York Times*, New York ed., 27 October, B6.

Prosser, Jon, ed. 1998. *Image-Based Research: A Handbook for Qualitative Researchers*. London: Routledge/Falmer.

Pulver, Alexandra. 2009. *Pop-Up Lunch: Taking It to the Streets*. Master of Industrial Design thesis, Pratt Institute School of Industrial Design.

Purcell, Mark. 2002. "Excavating Lefebvre: The Right to the City and Its Urban Politics of the Inhabitant." *GeoJournal*, 58: 99–108.

Purcell, Mark. 2008. *Recapturing Democracy: Neoliberalization and the Struggle for Alternative Urban Futures*. Florence, KY: Routledge.

Quarles, Philip. 2012. "Jane Jacobs Defends Urbanism in 1960s New York City Planning." *WNYC* website, 24 October. Accessed 8 May 2014 at www.wnyc.org/story/192689-jane-jacobs/.

Rahn, Janice. 2002. *Painting without Permission: Hip-Hop Graffiti Subculture*. Westport, CT: Bergin and Garvey.

Randall, David K. 2007. "Maybe Only God Can Make a Tree, but Only People Can Put a Price on It." *New York Times* website, 18 April. Accessed 18 May 2013 at http://www.nytimes.com/2007/04/18/nyregion/18trees.html.

Real Deal. 2009. "Manhattan Retail Rents Fall 11 Percent." *Real Deal* website, 7 May.
Accessed 30 January 2017 at https://therealdeal.com/2009/05/07/times-square-retail-rents-soar-while-flatiron-falls/.

Reiss, Aaron. 2014. "New York's Shadow Transit." *New Yorker* website. Accessed 27
January, 2017 at http://projects.newyorker.com/story/nyc-dollar-vans/.

Rex, John. 1968. "Economic Growth and Decline and Their Consequences for the
Sociology of Planning." *Town and Country Planning Association Summer School
Proceedings* (Town Planning Institute): 28–33.

Reynolds, Richard. 2008. *On Guerrilla Gardening: A Handbook for Gardening without
Boundaries*. New York: Bloomsbury.

Riano, Quilian. 2014. "Which Public?" *ARPA Journal*, 1 (online). Accessed 6 January
2017 at http://www.arpajournal.net/which-public/.

Ridgeway, Cecilia. 1991. "The Social Construction of Status Value: Gender and Other
Nominal Characteristics." *Social Forces*, 70(2): 367–86.

Ridgeway, Cecilia. 2001. "Gender, Status, and Leadership." *Journal of Social Issues*,
57: 637–55.

Right to the City Alliance. 2017. *righttothecity.org* website. Accessed January 9 2017 at
http://righttothecity.org/.

Riis, Jacob. 1890. *How the Other Half Lives: Studies among the Tenements of New York*.
New York: Charles Scribner's Sons.

Rios, Michael. 2010. "Claiming Latino Space: Cultural Insurgency in the Public
Realm." In *Insurgent Public Space: Guerrilla Urbanism and the Remaking of
Contemporary Cities*, edited by Jeffrey Hou. New York: Routledge.

Rius Ulldemolins, Joaquim. 2014. "Culture and Authenticity in Urban Regeneration
Processes: Place Branding in Central Barcelona." *Urban Studies*, OnlineFirst
version published 7 January 2014. Accessed 29 May 2014 at http://usj.
sagepub.com/content/early/2014/01/06/0042098013515762.

Rockefeller Foundation. 2013. "Constrained Opportunities in Slum Economies."
Decision Intelligence Document, Search Cycle 2, November 2013.
New York: Rockefeller Foundation. Accessed 11 November 2016 at https://
www.rockefellerfoundation.org/report/constrained-opportunities-in-slum-
economies/.

Rojas, James T., 1991. *The Enacted Environment: The Creation of 'Place' by Mexicans and
Mexican Americans in East Los Angeles*. Master's thesis, Massachusetts Institute
of Technology, Department of Architecture.

Rojas, James. 2010. "Latino Urbanism in Los Angeles: A Model for Urban
Improvisation and Reinvention." In *Insurgent Public Space: Guerrilla
Urbanism and the Remaking of Contemporary Cities*, edited by Jeffrey Hou.
New York: Routledge.

Rose, Cedric. 2016. "These Covington 'Parklets' Are Way Cute. Also, 'Parklets' Are
a Thing Now." *Cincinnati Magazine*, July 2016. Photographs by Alexandra
Taylor. Accessed 13 February 2017 at http://www.cincinnatimagazine.com/
citywiseblog/covington-parklets/.

Rosenberg, Shmarya. 2011. "Illegally Posted Signs Tell Women to Step Aside to Make
Way for Hasidic Men." *Failed Messiah* website, 4 October. Accessed 14 May 2014
at http://failedmessiah.typepad.com/failed_messiahcom/2011/10/illegally-
posted-signs-tell-women-to-step-aside-to-make-way-for-men-345.html.

Rosenthal, Lawrence. 2001. "Gang Loitering and Race." *Journal of Criminal Law and
Criminology*, 91(1): 99–160.

Roy, Ananya & Nezar AlSayyad, eds. 2004. *Urban Informality: Transnational Perspectives from the Middle East, Latin America, and South Asia*. Lanham, MD: Lexington Books.

Rupp, Leila J. & Verta Taylor. 2003. *Drag Queens at the 801 Cabaret*. Chicago: University of Chicago Press.

Ryzick, Melena. 2007. "Where the Crafts Babes and D.I.Y. Dudes Are." *New York Times* online, 14 June. Accessed 16 August 2012 at http://www.nytimes.com/2007/06/24/fashion/24renegade.html.

Saalman, Howard. 1968. *Medieval Cities*. New York: George Braziller.

Sadik-Khan, Janette & Seth Solomonow. 2016. *Street Fight: Handbook for an Urban Revolution*. New York: Viking.

Sæter, Oddrun, Venke Aure, & Kristin Bergaust. 2012. "Artists and Gentrification in Specific Urban Contexts. A Case Study from Williamsburg, New York." *International Journal of the Arts in Society*, 6(6): 67–82.

Sakash, Tom. 2012. "New Dining Space Will Enhance E Street Downtown." *Davis Enterprise*, 10 October, A1. Accessed 27 March 2014 at http://www.davisenterprise.com/local-news/city/new-dining-space-will-enhance-e-street-downtown/.

Sampson, Robert. 2012. *Great American City: Chicago and the Enduring Neighborhood Effect*. Chicago: University of Chicago Press.

Sampson, Robert & W. Byron Groves. 1989. "Community Structures and Crime: Testing Social Disorganization Theory." *American Journal of Sociology*, 94: 774–802.

Sampson, Robert J. & Stephen W. Raudenbush. 1999. "Systematic Social Observation of Public Spaces: A New Look at Disorder in Urban Neighborhoods." *American Journal of Sociology*, 105(3): 603–51.

Sander, Heather, Stephen Polasky, & Robert G. Haight. 2008. "The Value of Urban Tree Cover: A Hedonic Property Price Model in Ramsey and Dakota Counties, Minnesota, USA." *Ecological Economics*, 69: 1646–56.

Santia, Marc. 2017. "ICE Raids Spark Fear, Rumors in NYC's Immigrant Communities." *NBC 4 New York* website. 14 February. Accessed 19 February, 2017 at http://www.nbcnewyork.com/news/local/ICE-Raids-Spark-Fear-Rumors-Immigrant-Neighborhoods-New-York-City-413769443.html.

Sawhney, Nita, Christo de Klerk, & Shriya Malhotra. 2015. "Civic Engagement through DIY Urbanism and Collective Networked Action." *Planning Practice & Research*, 30(3): 337–54.

Schilt, Kristen. 2010. *Just One of the Guys: Transgender Men and the Persistence of Gender Equality*. Chicago: University of Chicago Press.

Schindler, Sarah. 2014. "Unpermitted Urban Agriculture: Transgressive Actions, Changing Norms, and the Local Food Movement." *Wisconsin Law Review*, 2014(2): 369–96.

Schmelzkopf, Karen. 1995. "Urban Community Gardens as Contested Space." *Geographical Review*, 85(3): 364–381.

Schmidt, Jessica. 2010. "Revisiting Pedestrian Malls." Institute of Transportation Engineers 2010 Technical Conference, Compendium of Technical Papers. Accessed 30 April 2010 at http://nacto.org/docs/usdg/revisiting_pedestrian_malls_scmidt.pdf.

Schroeder, David A., Louis A. Penner, John F. Dovidio, & Jane A. Piliavin. 1995. *The Psychology of Helping and Altruism*. New York: McGraw-Hill.

Schumaker, Paul D. & Russell W. Getter. 1977. "Responsiveness Bias in 51 American Communities." *American Journal of Political Science*, 21(2): 247–81.

Scott, James C. 1985. *Weapons of the Weak: Everyday Forms of Peasant Resistance*. New Haven, CT: Yale University Press.

Seno, Ethel, Carlo McCormick, Marc Schiller, & Sarah Schiller, eds. 2010. *Trespass: A History of Uncomissioned Urban Art*. Los Angeles: Taschen.

SF Planning Department. 2013. *San Francisco Parklet Manual*, ver. 1.0, February. San Francisco: City of San Francisco.

Shane, Graham (sic). 1979. "Il Ritorno della Strada Urbana: Nascita e Decadenza dal Rinascimento a Oggi / The Revival of the Street: Birth and Decline from the Renaissance to Today." *Lotus*, 24: 103–14.

Shane, D. Grahame. 2013. "Urban Patch Dynamics and Resilience: Three London Urban Design Ecologies." In *Resilience in Ecology and Urban Design*, edited by S. T. A. Pickett, M. L. Cadenasso, B. McGrath, 131–61.

Shankaran, Janani. 2013. "Turning Parking into Parklets." *Regional Plan Association* website, 30 September. Accessed 25 November 2013 at http://www.rpa.org/spotlight/turning-parking-into-parklets.

Sharp, Joanne, Venda Pollock, & Ronan Paddison. 2005. "Just Art for a Just City: Public Art and Social Inclusion in Urban Regeneration." *Urban Studies*, 42(5–6): 1001–23.

Shear, Michael D. & Jonathan Weisman. 2013. "Washington Fails to Reach a Deal to Head Off Cuts." *New York Times*, late ed. 2 March, A1–A10.

Shepard, Benjamin. 2014. "DIY Urbanism as an Environmental Justice Strategy: The Case Study of Time's Up! 1987–2012." *Theory in Action* 7(2): 42–73.

Short, Aaron. 2011. "Walk This Way! Yiddish Sign Orders Women to Move Over." *Brooklyn Paper* website, 7 October. Accessed 20 January 2016 at http://www.brooklynpaper.com/stories/34/41/dtg_hasidicsidewalks_2011_10_14_bk.html.

Silber, Judy. 2014. "How a Buddhist Shrine Transformed a Neighborhood in Oakland." PRI (Public Radio International) website, 19 November. Accessed 18 July 2017 at https://www.pri.org/stories/2014-11-19/how-buddhist-shrine-transformed-neighborhood-oakland.

Silbey, Susan S. 2010. "J. Locke, op cit.: Invocations of Law on Snowy Streets." *Journal of Comparative Law*, 5(2): 66–91.

Simpson, Charles. 2015. *An Overview of Tactical Urbanism in Los Angles*. Bachelor of arts thesis, Department of Urban and Environmental Policy, Occidental College.

Slater, Cliff. 1997. "General Motors and the Demise of Streetcars." *Transportation Quarterly*, 51(3): 45–66.

Small, Mario L. 2004. *Villa Victoria: The Transformation of Social Capital in a Boston Barrio*. Chicago: University of Chicago Press.

Small, Mario L. 2008. "Four Reasons to Abandon the Idea of the 'Ghetto.'" *City & Community*, 7(4): 389–96.

Small, Mario L. 2009a. "How Many Cases Do I Need? On Science and the Logic of Case Selection in Field Research." *Ethnography*, 10(1): 5–38.

Small, Mario L. 2009b. *Unanticipated Gains: Origins of Network Inequality in Everyday Life*. Oxford: Oxford University Press.

Smith, Michael. 2007. "Form and Meaning in the Earliest Cities: A New Approach to Ancient Planning." *Journal of Planning History*, 6(1): 3–47.

Smith, Neil. 1996. *The New Urban Frontier: Gentrification and the Revanchist City*. New York: Routledge.

Smith, Neil. 2008 (1984). *Uneven Development*, 3rd ed. Athens: University of Georgia Press.

Snell, Bradford. 1974. "Statement of Bradford C. Snell before the United States Senate Subcommittee on Antitrust and Monopoly." *Hearings on the Ground Transportation Industries in Connections with S1167*, S.C.R.T.D. Library archives. Accessed 29 April 2014 at http://libraryarchives.metro.net/DPGTL/testimony/1974_statement_bradford_c_snell_s1167.pdf.

Snyder, Gregory J. 2009. *Graffiti Lives: Beyond the Tag in New York's Urban Underground*. New York: New York University Press.

Sorkin, Michael, ed. 1992. *Variations on a Theme Park: The New American City and the End of Public Space*. New York: Hill and Wang.

Squatting Europe Kollective. 2013. *Squatting in Europe: Radical Spaces, Urban Struggles*. Wivenhoe, NY: Minor Compositions/Autonomedia.

St. John, Graham. 2004. "Counter-Tribes, Global Protest, and Carnivals of Reclamation." *Peace Review*, 16(4): 421–28.

Stamen Design. 2015. "The City from the Valley." *Stamen.com* website, 15 December. Accessed 27 January, 2017 at https://hi.stamen.com/the-city-from-the-valley-57e835ee3dc6#.c5hjs1qvt.

Steel, Emily & Andrew Edgecliffe-Johnson. 2013. "CBS Shake-up to Create Outdoor Ads REIT." *Financial Times* website, 17 January. Accessed 19 May 2017 at https://www.ft.com/content/080c3a42-6035-11e2-b657-00144feab49a.

Steffensmeier, Darrell & Emilie Allan. 1996. "Gender and Crime: Toward a Gendered Theory of Female Offending." *Annual Review of Sociology*, 22: 459–87.

Stein, Perry. 2015. "Why Are Bike Lanes Such Potent Symbols of Gentrification?" *Washington Post* website, 12 November. Accessed 13 November 2015 at https://www.washingtonpost.com/news/local/wp/2015/11/12/why-are-bike-lanes-such-heated-symbols-of-gentrification/.

Stephens, Craig. 2009. "Richard Ankrom's Freeway Art: Caltrans Buys into the Prank." *LA Weekly* website, 30 December. Accessed 18 September 2013 at http://www.laweekly.com/2009-12-31/la-life/richard-ankrom-s-freeway-art-caltrans-buys-into-the-prank/.

Stern, Steven. 2010. "Brooklyn: The Brand." *New York Times*, New York ed., 15 December, D5.

Stiglitz, Joseph. E. 2008. "The End of Neoliberalism?" *Project Syndicate Commentary*, July. Accessed 14 December 2010 at http://www.project-syndicate.org/commentary/stiglitz101/English.

Straus, Murray A. 1999. "The Controversy over Domestic Violence by Women: A Methodological, Theoretical, and Sociology of Science Analysis." In *Violence in Intimate Relationships*, edited by X. Arriaga & S. Oskamp, 17–44. Thousand Oaks, CA: Sage.

Sulaiman, Sahra. 2012. "Desperately Seeking Shade: How South L.A. Bus Riders Weather the Elements." *Streetsblog Los Angeles* website, 12 July. Accessed 29 January 2013 at http://la.streetsblog.org/2012/07/12/desperately-seeking-shade-how-south-l-a-bus-riders-weather-the-elements/.

Sutcliffe, Anthony, ed. 1980. *The Rise of Modern Urban Planning*. London: Mansell.

Sutcliffe, Anthony. 1981. *Towards the Planned City: Germany, Britain, the United States and France 1780–1914*. Oxford: Basil Blackwell.

Suttles, Gerald D. 1990. *The Man-Made City*. Chicago: University of Chicago Press.

Swaroop, Sapna & Jeffrey D. Morenoff. 2006. "Building Community: The Neighborhood Context of Social Organization." *Social Forces*, 84(3): 1665–95.

Tadeo, Lisa. 2010. "Janette Sadik-Khan: Urban Reengineer." *Esquire* website, 22 November. Accessed 30 January 2017 at http://www.esquire.com/entertainment/interviews/a8980/janette-sadik-khan-1210/.

Talen, Emily. 2015. "Do-It-Yourself Urbanism: A History." *Journal of Planning History* 14(2): 135–48.

Taşan-Kok, Tuna. 2012. "Introduction: Contradictions of Neoliberal Urban Planning." In *Contradictions of Neoliberal Planning,* edited by T. Taşan-Kok & G. Baeten. Dordrecht, Germany: Springer Science+Business Media B.V.

Taub, Richard P. 1988. *Community Capitalism: The South Shore Bank's Strategy for Neighborhood Revitalization.* Cambridge, MA: Harvard Business School Press.

Taub, Richard P., D. Garth Taylor, & Jan D. Dunham. 1984. *Paths of Neighborhood Change: Race and Crime in Urban America.* Chicago: University of Chicago Press.

Taylor, Nigel. 1998. *Urban Planning Theory since 1945.* London: Sage.

Tavernise, Sabrina. 2011. "A Population Changes, Uneasily." *New York Times,* New York ed., 18 July, A9.

Teilman, Katherin & Pierre Landry. 1981. "Gender Bias in Juvenile Justice Handling of Seriously Crime-Involved Youth." *Journal of Research in Crime and Delinquency,* 18: 47–80.

Tepper, Rachel. 2012. "'Parklet' Dining: Restaurants Embrace Growing Trend." *Huffington Post,* 24 August. Accessed 27 March 2014 at http://www.huffingtonpost.com/2012/08/24/parklets_n_1828325.html.

Thompson, Nato & Gregory Sholette, eds. 2004. *The Interventionists: Users' Manual for the Creative Disruption of Everyday Life.* Boston and North Adams, Mass.: MIT Press and MASS MoCA.

Thomson, Irene Taviss. 1992. "Individualism and Conformity in the 1950s vs. the 1980s." *Sociological Forum,* 7(3): 497–516.

Tilly, Charles. 1978. *From Mobilization to Revolution.* Reading, MA: Addison-Wesley.

Tippapart, Tilda. 2012. "Creating the Post-Hipster City: In Conversation with Aurash Khawarzad." *Huffington Post* website, 23 May. Accessed 1 November 2012 at http://www.huffingtonpost.com/tida-tippapart/new-york-art-hipsters-brooklyn-_b_1537126.html.

Tissot, Sylvie. 2015. *Good Neighbors: Gentrifying Diversity in Boston's South End.* London: Verso.

de Tocqueville, Alexis. 1956 (1835/1840). *Democracy in America,* edited by Richard D. Heffner. New York: American Library.

Tonkiss, Fran. 2013. *Cities by Design: The Social Life of Urban Form.* Cambridge, UK: Polity.

UN Habitat. 2004. *Carta Mundial por el Derecho a la Ciudad (World Charter for the Right to the City).* Accessed January 9 2017 at http://www.onuhabitat.org/index.php?option=com_docman&task=doc_download&gid=50&Itemid=3.

Vasquez, Leonardo. 2009. "Principles of Culturally Competent Planning and Placemaking." *Placemakers Advisor* blog, 11 November. Accessed 26 May 2014 at http://placemakerhub.blogspot.com/2009/11/principles-of-culturally-competent.html.

Veloz, Jimena. 2011. "WikiCity—How Citizens Improve Their Cities." *This Big City* website, 8 June. Accessed 21 June 2012 at http://thisbigcity.net/wikicity-citizens-improve-cities/.

Venkatesh, Sudhir A. 2009. *Off the Books: The Underground Economy of the Urban Poor.* Cambridge, MA: Harvard University Press.

Vergara, Camilo José. 2016. *Detroit is No Dry Bones: The Eternal City of the Industrial Age.* Ann Arbor, MI: University of Michigan Press.

Visconti, Luca M., John F. Sherry Jr., Stefania Borghini, & Laurel Anderson. 2010. "Street Art, Sweet Art? Reclaiming the 'Public' in Public Space." *Journal of Consumer Research,* 37(3): 511–29.

Visher, Christy. 1983. "Gender, Police Arrest Decisions, and Notions of Chivalry." *Criminology,* 21(1): 5–28.

Vivoni, Francisco. 2009. "Spots of Spatial Desire: Skateparks, Skateplazas, and Urban Politics." *Journal of Sport and Social Issues,* 33(2): 130–49.

Von Hassell, Malve. 2002. *The Struggle for Eden: Community Gardens in New York City.* Santa Barbara, CA: Praeger.

Wacquant, Loïc. 2001. "Deadly Symbiosis: When Ghetto and Prison Meet and Mesh." *Punishment and Society,* 3(1): 95–133.

Walker, Alissa. 2014. "Why People Keep Trying to Erase the Hollywood Sign from Google Maps." *Gizmodo,* 21 November 2014. Accessed 22 November 2014 at http://gizmodo.com/ why-people-keep-trying-to-erase-the-hollywood-sign-from-1658084644.

Walker, Edward T., Michael McQuarrie, & Caroline W. Lee. 2015. "Rising Participation and Declining Democracy." In *Democratizing Inequalities: Dilemmas of the New Public Participation,* edited by C. W. Lee, M. McQuarrie, & E. T. Walker, 3–26. New York: New York University Press.

Wallerstein, Immanuel. 2008. "2008: The Demise of Neoliberal Globalization." Commentary no. 226, *Immanuel Wallerstein* personal website, 1 February. Retrieved 14 December 2010 at http://www.iwallerstein.com/2008-the-demise-of-neoliberal-globalization/.

Walljasper, Jay. 2013. "Do Bike Lanes Promote Gentrification?" *Huffington Post,* 5 November. Accessed 29 May 2014 at http://www.huffingtonpost.com/jay-walljasper/do-bike-lanes-promote-gen_b_4178505.html.

Warner, Kee & Harvey Molotch. 1995. "Power to Build: How Development Persists Despite Local Controls." *Urban Affairs Review,* 30(3): 378–406.

Weber, Max. 1978 (1922). *Economy and Society,* edited by G. Roth & C. Wittich, translated by E. Fischoff, H. Gerth, A. M. Henderson, F. Kolegar, C. W. Mills, T. Parsons, M. Rheinstein, G. Roth, E. Shils, & C. Wittich. Berkeley: University of California Press.

Weisman, Alan. 2005. "Earth without People." *Discover Magazine* website, 6 February. Retrieved 3 November 2014 at http://discovermagazine.com/2005/feb/ earth-without-people.

Weiss, Robert S. 1994. *Learning from Strangers: The Art and Method of Qualitative Interview Studies.* New York: Free Press.

Weitzer, Ronald & Steven A. Tuch. 1999. "Race, Class, and Perceptions of Discrimination by the Police." *Crime & Delinquency,* 45(4): 494–507.

Weitzer, Ronald & Steven A. Tuch. 2002. "Perceptions of Racial Profiling: Race, Class, and Personal Experience." *Criminology,* 40(2): 435–56.

Wells, Gail. 2010. "Calculating the Green in Green: What's an Urban Tree Worth?" *PNWRS Science Findings,* 126: 1–5.

WFSB. 2011. "Handicapped Parking Sign Removed." *WFSB TV Eyewitness News* webpage, 14 July. Accessed 29 April 2014 at http://www.wfsb.com/story/ 15083291/handicap-parking-signs-stolen-to-snag-space.

Whitzman, Carolyn, Crystal Legacy, Caroline Andrew, Fran Klodawsky, Margaret Shaw, & Kalpana Viswanath, eds. 2012. *Building Inclusive Cities: Women's Safety and the Right to the City.* New York: Routledge.

Whyte, William H. 1956. *The Organization Man.* New York: Simon & Schuster.

Whyte, William H. 1980. *The Social Life of Small Urban Spaces*. New York: Project for Public Spaces.

Wildman, Stephanie M. 1996. *Privilege Revealed: How Invisible Preference Undermines America*. New York: New York University Press.

Wilson, James Q. & George Kelling. 1982. "The Police and Neighborhood Safety: Broken Windows." *Atlantic Monthly*, 127: 29–38.

Wilson, Peter L. & Bill Weinberg, eds. 1999. *Avant Gardening: Ecological Struggle in the City and the World*. Brooklyn: Autonomedia.

Wilson, William J. 1987. *The Truly Disadvantaged: The Inner City, the Underclass, and Public Policy*. Chicago: University of Chicago Press.

Wolf, Kathleen L. 2004. "Trees and Business District Preferences: A Case Study of Athens, Georgia, US." *International Society of Arboriculture*, 30(6): 336–46.

Yee, Vivian. 2017. "Migrants Hide, Fearing Capture on 'Any Corner.'" *New York Times*, New York ed., A1.

Yen, Irene H. & Lynda A. Anderson. 2012. "Built Environments and Mobility of Older Adults: Important Policy and Practice Efforts." *Journal of the American Geriatrics Society*, 60(5): 951–56.

Yin, Robert K. 2002. *Case Study Research: Design and Methods*, 3rd ed. Thousand Oaks, CA: Sage.

Young, Victoria. 2014. "DIY Design Kits Transform LA Streets into Urban Arts Spaces." *PSFK* website. Accessed 1 February 2014 at http://www.psfk.com/ 2014/01/diy-street-design-kit-la.html#!CeTSb.

Zimmerman, Jeffrey. 2008. "From Brew Town to Cool Town: Neoliberalism and the Creative City Development Strategy in Milwaukee." *Cities*, 25(4): 230–42.

Zukin, Sharon. 2010. *Naked City: The Death and Life of Authentic Urban Places*. Oxford: Oxford University Press.

Zukin, Sharon & Laura Braslow. 2011. "The Life Cycle of New York's Creative Districts: Reflections on the Unanticipated Consequences of Unplanned Cultural Zones." *City, Culture and Society*, 2(3): 131–40.

# INDEX

Printed in the USA/Agawam, MA
October 22, 2019

740911.015